S0-BRG-468

The Imperial Austrian Councillors are thrown out of the window of the castle of the Hradschin, at Prague, by the enraged Bohemian Deputies, thus precipitating the Thirty Years' War

Painting by Vacslav Brezik.

The Imperial Austrian Councillors are thrown out of the window of the castle of the Hradschin, at Prague, by the enraged Bohemian Deputies, thus precipitating the Thirty Years' War

Painting by Vaclav Brozik.

THE GREAT EVENTS

BY

FAMOUS HISTORIANS

A COMPREHENSIVE AND READABLE ACCOUNT OF THE WORLD'S HISTORY, EMPHASIZING THE MORE IMPORTANT EVENTS, AND PRESENTING THESE AS COMPLETE NARRATIVES IN THE MASTER-WORDS OF THE MOST EMINENT HISTORIANS

NON-SECTARIAN NON-PARTISAN NON-SECTIONAL

ON THE PLAN EVOLVED FROM A CONSENSUS OF OPINIONS GATHERED FROM THE MOST DISTINGUISHED SCHOLARS OF AMERICA AND EUROPE, INCLUDING BRIEF INTRODUCTIONS BY SPECIALISTS TO CONNECT AND EXPLAIN THE CELEBRATED NARRATIVES, ARRANGED CHRONOLOGICALLY, WITH THOROUGH INDICES, BIBLIOGRAPHIES, CHRONOLOGIES, AND COURSES OF READING

EDITOR-IN-CHIEF

ROSSITER JOHNSON, LL.D.

ASSOCIATE EDITORS

CHARLES F. HORNE, Ph.D.
JOHN RUDD, LL.D.

With a staff of specialists

VOLUME XI

The National Alumni

CONTENTS

VOLUME XI

LIST OF ILLUSTRATIONS

VOLUME XI

AN OUTLINE NARRATIVE

TRACING BRIEFLY THE CAUSES, CONNECTIONS, AND CONSEQUENCES OF

THE GREAT EVENTS

(ERA OF POLITICAL-RELIGIOUS WARS)

CHARLES F. HORNE

GAZING across the broader field of universal history, one comes more and more to overlook the merely temporary, constantly shifting border lines of states, and to see Western Europe as a whole, to watch its nations as a single people guided by similar developments of the mind, impelled by similar stirrings of the heart, taking part in but a single story, the marvellous tale of man's advance.

This sense of an all-enfolding unity, an ever-advancing common destiny, sinks weakest perhaps in the period we now approach. The nations seem sharply separated in their careers. In the preceding age the power of Spain and the fanaticism of its monarch, Philip II, had made the reëstablishment of Catholicism the dominant question throughout Europe. But in 1609 Philip III of Spain abandoned his father's attempt to conquer Holland and again enforce a universal religion. In 1610 Henry IV of France, who had brought peace and amity out of the savage religious wars within his own realm, fell under an assassin's knife. These two events may be accepted as marking a turn in the current of the world, a change in the thoughts of men. The next half-century saw wars indeed, bloody and bitter wars, but they were no longer primarily religious. The strife was more than half political, and men of opposite faiths found themselves at times allied upon the battle-field. The feeling of religious brotherhood grew weaker, that of political allegiance stronger.

GROWTH OF NATIONAL SPIRIT

The triumph of Holland had much to do with this. During almost a generation the Catholics of the Southern Netherlands had been united with the Protestants of the Northern Provinces in desperate war against the tyranny of Spain; and though only Holland finally achieved independence, her people could scarce forget their long brotherhood with the Catholic South. And now Holland was a republic, her people were self-governing! Looking with prophetic vision into the future, we may assert that this was only the first step toward a broader union of all the nations when every man shall be self-governing, and hence all shall be equal and united and progressive. But for its own time at least the freedom of Holland was a sharp influence toward division among the people of Europe, toward the establishment of differences, the growth of national as opposed to universal brotherhood.

There was, to be sure, an earlier republic in Europe, Switzerland. But the Swiss maintained themselves by their isolation, their remoteness from other nations and from one another in their bleak mountain valleys. The Dutch, on the contrary, inhabited a flat sea-coast; they were traders; their very existence depended on intercourse with other lands. Hence they had to be ever alert in defence of their hard-won freedom. The spirit of nationality, of patriotism grew strong within them. At one time they had been members of the German empire; at another, subjects of France, of Burgundy, of Spain. Now they were Hollanders, a distinct nation by themselves, and an example to all others of what a united land of men might do.

France also had learned a stronger sense of nationality from her hero-king, Henry IV. Always, through all his religious wars, he had insisted that he was king of all Frenchmen, both Catholic and Protestant, and would be a father to them all. He withdrew his Protestant army from besieging Paris when the surrender of the city seemed certain, abandoned his triumph "lest Frenchmen starve." Englishmen, too, in the age of Elizabeth, had learned to regard themselves not only as different from but as far superior to men of other races. Spain both by her victories and by her sufferings had opened a gap between her people and others. Only Germany, through her very importance and vague imperial predominance over the surrounding lands, failed to find within herself that necessity for union which made other kingdoms strong.

By this internal division Germany was now plunged into the awful tragedy of the Thirty Years' War, a partly political, partly religious contest in which all the nations of Europe by degrees took some part. Thus the war forms to a certain extent a centre around which the movements of the age are grouped. England also had her great religious strife, her Puritan revolution, which collapsed in 1660. Yet on the whole the age is political even more than religious, and the ablest statesman of the day, Richelieu, the most successful guardian France has ever known, reaped for his own land all the benefits of the world-wide turmoil. France, which had so often seemed on the point of assuming the foremost place in Europe and had been so often checked, now advanced definitely to the front. The Bourbons, descendants of Henry IV, took the rank of the decaying Hapsburg family as the chief rulers of Europe. Historians often call this the age of Richelieu.

DECAY OF THE HAPSBURG POWER

Spain and Austria, the two great Hapsburg states, both decayed in power. Italy, the Hapsburg dependent, lost the last vestiges of her ancient intellectual supremacy. Everywhere the South of Europe gave place to the North.

The blight of the Inquisition was upon Spain. The Moors were banished, the Jews were banished; and it had been the industry of these two races which had largely supported the pride and laziness of the hidalgos. In Italy, too, the Inquisition held sway. Galileo with his telescope revealed facts which proved the theories of Copernicus, and made impossible the ancient idea that our earth was the centre of the universe.[1] All Europe rang with his discoveries; but the Church refused to understand, forbade him to teach doctrines which it declared heretical. For a time the astronomer's mouth was closed,

[1] See *Galileo Overthrows Ancient Philosophy*, page 14.

but not so the minds of those who had listened to him. In England, where thought was free, Harvey founded medical science by his proof of the circulation of the blood;[1] the Lord Chancellor Bacon wrote his celebrated *Novum Organum*, pointing out to modern investigators the methods they must follow. In Germany Comenius revitalized the dead world of education.[2] In France Descartes created within his own mind a revolution scarce less important than that of Luther. He freed philosophy from its thraldom to religion. He bade the mind of man to stand by itself, lone in the midst of an unmeasured universe, and discover of what one thing it could feel assured by its own unbiassed thought. His famous first conclusion, "I think, therefore I exist," stands as the corner-stone of modern philosophy.[3]

Meanwhile Galileo, roused by the encouragement of scientific friends, began a second time with infinite wit and sarcasm to expound and defend his doctrines. The Church took him more sternly in hand. He was imprisoned by the Inquisition and emerged from its dark chambers a broken and silent man. Philosophy, terrified, fled from Italy, not to return until over two centuries of the world's advance had prepared for her a less barbaric greeting.[4]

Southern Italy was ruled by viceroys from Spain, but so feeble had the Hapsburg grip become that Masaniello, a fisherman of Naples, was able to rouse his city against its tyrants, and for over a year Spain was unable to reëstablish her authority. When she did, it was only by the treachery of the peasant leaders who had succeeded the murdered Masaniello.[5]

The internal decay of Spain and the lassitude of her two feeble sovereigns, Philip III (1598–1621) and Philip IV (1621–1665), prevented her from rendering any material assistance to Austria, where the other branch of the Hapsburgs, descendants of Charles V's brother Ferdinand, were reduced to struggle for their very existence. Ferdinand and his immediate successor as

[1] See *Harvey Discovers the Circulation of the Blood*, page 50.
[2] See *Educational Reform of Comenius*, page 192.
[3] See *Birth of Modern Scientific Methods: Bacon and Descartes*. page 116.
[4] See *Recantation of Galileo*, page 184.
[5] See *Masaniello's Revolt at Naples*, page 253.

Emperor of Germany had kept the religious peace carefully, and Germany had prospered. But then came new emperors who repudiated their methods—Ferdinand had been deemed by the Church little better than a Protestant. In 1608 the Protestant princes, becoming suspicious, formed a league for mutual defence. The Catholics under Maximilian of Bavaria formed an answering league in 1609. They almost came to open war that year over a disputed succession in one of the smaller duchies, the Protestants appealing to Holland for help and the Catholics to Spain. Fortunately the terrible example of the civil wars they had seen in France, held them back for a time. But always there were arising new grounds for quarrel.

THE THIRTY YEARS' WAR

In 1618 the actual war began. A new leader, Ferdinand II, young and intensely Catholic, had risen to guide the Hapsburg fortunes in Austria, had successfully forced that land to resume the old religion, and now aimed to do the same in Bohemia. The Bohemians, famed fanatics of the unforgotten Hussite wars, broke into open rebellion, threw Ferdinand's ministers through a window, and so roused the war that ruined Germany.[1]

Ferdinand became Emperor of Germany the next year (1619), and called the Catholic league to his aid in Bohemia. The rebels elected as king one of the German electors, a son-in-law of the King of England, and head of the Protestant league. Slowly, unwillingly, the various German states, and the surrounding countries also, found themselves dragged into the struggle. At first Emperor Ferdinand was successful, Bohemia was completely subdued and made Catholic, as Austria had been. A great general and shrewd contriver, Wallenstein, rose to the Emperor's aid and laid Germany prostrate at his feet. For a moment the Hapsburgs seemed as all-powerful as in the proudest days of Charles V. But his own coreligionists turned against Ferdinand. The princes of the Catholic league grew frightened; he was indeed crushing Protestantism, but he was trampling on their rights as well. They fell away from his alliance. Richelieu, also dreading the Hapsburg aggrandizement, brought

[1] See *The "Defenestration" at Prague: The Thirty Years' War*, page 62.

France to take part in the war. Sweden's hero-king Gustavus Adolphus invaded Germany to defend the Protestant faith. He won splendid victories, but at last fell in his supreme battle at Luetzen, from which Wallenstein's troops fled defeated (1632).[1]

The war had now lasted fourteen years. The Emperor could raise no more armies. His one able general, Wallenstein, was slain as a traitor. Germany was exhausted. Yet because no one power would consent to the others' proposed terms of peace, the war dragged on and on, in such feeble fashion as it could. Its misery fell almost wholly upon the unhappy peasantry. The armies of both sides lived upon the country; what they could not devour they destroyed, lest it be of use to the enemy. Germany became a desert, and its people starved amid their desolated homes. The troops, brutalized by long familiarity with suffering, tortured their captives to extort money or sometimes, it would seem, for the mere pleasure of the sport.

The Emperor Ferdinand died in the midst of the hideous ruin he had wrought. The Swedes, who had long abandoned the high principles of Gustavus, demanded territory as the price of peace. So did France. At last in 1648 the Peace of Westphalia was arranged. By it France became the foremost state of Europe; Sweden became one of the great powers; England, engrossed in her own civil war, could pull no chestnuts from the fire; but the German empire fell practically to pieces. Switzerland and Holland were formally declared outside of it. Each little prince got what increase of power he wanted, and the authority of the empire disappeared. The Hapsburgs still retained their title as its heads, but their real authority was confined entirely to their personal domains, Austria, Bohemia, and such part of Hungary as they could hold against the Turks.[2]

Historians tell us that in those terrible thirty years the population of Germany had dwindled from thirty million to only twelve million; nearly two-thirds of its common people had perished, mostly of starvation. The stored-up wealth of ages had been destroyed. The very character of the race had changed,

[1] See *Triumph and Death of Gustavus Adolphus at Luetzen*, page 174.

[2] See *Peace of Westphalia*, page 285.

broken from its old hardihood to temporary feebleness and fawning. The land had been set back an entire century, perhaps two, in its advance toward civilization. That is what war means. That is glory!

RULE OF RICHELIEU

Meanwhile France, profiting by the feebleness of her neighbors, had made great strides. At first the death of Henry IV had threatened her with the old anarchy. Louis XIII, Henry's son, was but a child; the Queen-mother, who became regent, was an Italian, Marie de' Medici, and devoted to the Spanish interests. The Huguenots feared renewed persecution. The nobles of the court grasped after renewed power.

In such turmoil was the land that it seemed necessary to summon the "States-General," the assembly of all the notables of France, the last one to be called until that eventful year of 1789. The States-General talked and dissolved, having done nothing but reveal that there was one capable man among its members, a young bishop who was to be a cardinal, Richelieu. His plans for reform and pacification were not adopted, but he drew the attention of the Queen Regent and became her chief adviser, later the chief adviser of the King.

Richelieu did four things for France. He broke the power of the Huguenots, who had become a political party, and a very troublesome one, a state within a state, independent and defiant, with their impenetrable capital at La Rochelle. After one of the most remarkable sieges of history Richelieu captured La Rochelle, crushed the resistance of the Huguenots by repeated defeats elsewhere, and then — granted them complete religious freedom! [1]

It is one of the epochs of the world, the beginning of toleration not through force, but through free-will. A Catholic and a cardinal, having complete power to force these Protestants to his will, bids them worship as they choose, asking only that they become patriotic Frenchmen.

Next Richelieu humbled the great nobles of France, hanging them when they disobeyed his laws. Next by his part in the Thirty Years' War he won territory from both Germany and

[1] See *Siege of La Rochelle: Richelieu Rules France*, page 129.

Spain. He was by no means the first Catholic ruler thus to seek Protestant allies; Francis I and Henry II had both done so in France; in Germany Charles V had sent a Lutheran army against the Pope. But it was Richelieu's successful adherence to this plan that positively and finally relegated religion to a minor place in statecraft, and made nationality, political supremacy, what some have called "vainglory," the foremost impulse.

Last, not least, in Richelieu's brilliant career, is to be noted that he revived literature in France. He created the "French Academy," the "forty immortals" in whose successors Paris still takes pride to-day. The French drama was born. Corneille wrote *The Cid*, and the Cardinal himself took his pen and attempted to produce a better tragedy. Comedy, too, arose. Molière began the marvellous career which a little later was to make him the undying idol of the stage in France.[1]

Nor did Richelieu's death (1642) turn his country from the triumphant course toward which he had led the way. His King died with him, and his power passed to another cardinal, Mazarin, ruling for another baby-king, who was to be Louis XIV. Mazarin found himself confronting an almost similar situation to that which had followed the death of Henry IV. There was a child upon the throne; an incapable queen-mother as regent, foreign, and friendly to the Spaniards; the nobles grasped after power; Paris grumbled under taxation. Mazarin had even to face a feeble, frivolous civil war against himself, the Fronde.[2] But he soon established his supremacy, secured for France in 1648 all she had earned out of the war with Germany, and then ruled with firm hand, bringing wealth and peace and prosperity to the state until his death in 1661. Richelieu and Mazarin made possible that most spectacular period of all French history which immediately followed under Louis XIV.

THE PURITAN REVOLUTION

Turn now to England, to see why she had held so apart from the continental struggles of the period. James I, her Scotch king of 1603, had indeed interfered a bit in the Thirty Years'

[1] See *Molière Creates Modern Comedy*, page 347.
[2] See *War of the Fronde*, page 285.

War, seeking to aid his unlucky son-in-law, the King of Bohemia. But James had soon found difficulties enough at home. The Elizabethan age had made Englishmen feel very highly their individual importance. Each man, through the entire social scale down even to the peasantry, had felt a personal interest, a personal pride in the repulse of the Spaniards and the upholding of the Queen. She tyrannized over them as a woman; they defended her as men. But when this foreigner, this Scotch king, came to rule them, they saw no need to yield him such exact obedience. Freedom of thought had brought with it new political ideas, and men talked much of the authority of Parliament and their right to tax themselves. James, on the contrary, had a large conception of the "divine right" of kings, not to be restricted by any law whatever, and a still larger opinion of his own personal ability and unfailing wisdom. Gradually there grew up a distinct opposition between King and Parliament, centring always on that one question—who should lay the taxes, that is, who provide the income of the King? The English revolution, like the American one to follow, gave to principles far more noble in themselves the air of a mere money dispute.

James, dying in 1625, left a very pretty quarrel to his son. Charles I, more able and kingly than his father, but equally obstinate, equally devoted to the Stuart doctrine of a king's divinity, finally endeavored to rule without summoning any of these arguing parliaments. To accomplish this he had to gather money by other methods, declared illegal by his people. Always appealing to the law, they grew more and more bitter as Charles turned it against them, putting in office judges who would do his will, reëstablishing the ancient Court of Star-Chamber, with its power to torture witnesses.

Moreover, there was growing up in England a type of more extreme Protestantism. The English Church had retained many of the forms of Rome, including its hierarchal system of priests and bishops. These were dear to the hearts of the Stuart kings, whose Protestantism had never been very radical. The Scotch Church, on the other hand, had swung far from Rome indeed, and many Protestants everywhere refused to have any priestly interpreter intervene between them and their own consciences, their own beliefs. In England these men came to be called Puritans. They were deeply earnest; religion was ever in their thoughts; they had protested even against the wickedness of the theatre in Shakespeare's time; and now as they watched the light frivolity of the court they became imbittered. They called Charles the "man of sin." Round these stern fanatics began to centre the general opposition to the King.

At length the Scotch Protestants broke into open revolt, and the King found he must have help, must summon a parliament at last. That was the beginning of the end. The Englishmen who gathered at his call were in no pleasant mood. They at once took steps to secure other parliaments to follow immediately on their own. All Charles' encroachments on the law were overturned; his courts, Star-Chamber and others, were abolished; his chief minister was declared a traitor and beheaded.[1] The King, helpless, infuriated, raised the standard of civil war (1642).

The strife was thus in its inception political; but it soon became religious as well. Since the King was the head of the English Church, most of its members rallied round him. The Puritans in Parliament secured the calling of a convention to settle the various religious questions before the nation. This "Westminster Assembly" established the Presbyterian Church.[2]

The less extreme members of the opposition to the King grew doubtful; they saw whither the Puritans would lead them. The war became one of stern religious fanaticism against gallant reckless Cavalier loyalty—of the middle classes against the aristocracy and their servitors. Cromwell rose as the type and model of the Puritans. Under his lead they defeated the Cavaliers and executed their King. Charles perished on the scaffold, and England, following Holland's lead, was declared a republic. This was in 1649, the year after the Peace of Westphalia.[3]

Cromwell remained practically the ruler of England. He defeated the Scotch, and compelled them to submit to England's sway. He went over to Ireland and stamped out revolt there,

[1] See *Abolition of the Star-Chamber: Popular Revolt against Charles I*, page 215.

[2] See *Presbyterianism Established: Meeting of the Westminster Assembly*, page 238.

[3] See *Civil War in England: Execution of Charles I*, page 311.

terrorized the land as no Englishman had ever done before, establishing English colonists, Protestants, over a considerable portion of its soil.[1] Secure of power at home, the mighty leader began next to take a part in European affairs, raising England to higher consideration than she had held even in Elizabeth's time. Yet toward the end he must have realized that he had failed in his life's dream, that England was unfitted to be the united religious republic he had hoped to make her. Even before his death the land was broken into endless factions, the majority dissatisfied with the strictness of Puritan rule, a small minority eager to go much further with its severity. Cromwell found himself compelled to dissolve his parliaments as autocratically as ever Charles had done; and when he died, when his iron hand dropped from the helm, no man knew what was to follow. No one wanted war. Each little wrangling party looked a different way for peace and security. At length the majority agreed to call back their Stuart kings. Charles II, son of the Charles I they had beheaded, was voluntarily replaced upon the English throne. Religion had once more proved inefficient as the central principle of government.[2]

ACQUISITION OF COLONIAL POSSESSIONS

Equally important for the future, though not for their own day, were the movements toward colonization in this period. Even while their war with Spain was in progress the Dutch merchants had begun to look for trading-stations in the distant seas. Following the Portuguese, they sailed around Africa, and wrenched from their feeble predecessors most of the Indian trade. They took possession of the Eastern isles, Java and Sumatra. In the very year of the truce, 1609, they turned their attention westward and sent Henry Hudson to explore the American coast.[3] Claiming possession of the river he had found, they built settlements at Albany and New York.[4]

England was their chief rival on the seas. Her ships followed theirs to India and fought with them, refusing to be dispossessed

[1] See *Cromwell's Campaign in Ireland*, page 335.
[2] See *Cromwell's Rule in England: The Restoration*, page 357.
[3] See *Henry Hudson Explores the Hudson River*, page 1.
[4] See *Dutch Settlement of New York*, page 44.

like the Portuguese.[1] The English colonists at Jamestown had preceded the Dutch in defiance of Spain and the denial of her claims upon America. England and Holland quarrelled for the carrying trade of the world. They became the two foremost naval powers, and in Cromwell's time fought a fierce and vigorous naval war. The two Protestant champions of Europe wasting their strength one against the other for commercial causes! Clearly indeed do we approach an age when religion becomes of little international prominence.

France also had the colonizing fever. Henry IV had sent an expedition to Quebec. Richelieu authorized one which settled Montreal, destined to be the chief metropolis of Canada.[2]

These early settlements had been movements authorized by their governments, encouraged by the parent state for its own purposes; but now there began a civilization very different in character. Some of the English Puritans finding the oppressive hand of King James I fall heavy upon them, extracted from his ministers a half-unwilling permission to settle on his American lands. So came the famous voyage of the Mayflower and the building of Plymouth on the Massachusetts coast.[3] King James had been a foster-father to the Virginia colony, he had drawn up a set of laws for it with his own hand, and when these failed he had granted it a local assembly of its own, the beginning of representative government in America.[4] Virginia was prospering. Slavery was introduced there in 1619 and, much to the royal patron's disgust, the cultivation of tobacco as well.[5] Soon the new colony was supplying the world with tobacco.

But the nest of Puritans farther north could expect no such favor from James. As the hand of oppression grew ever heavier at home, the Puritans, not yet dreaming of escape by rebellion, looked more and more thoughtfully to the land beyond the sea. They planned to expatriate themselves almost in a body. A

[1] See *Beginning of British Power in India*, page 30.
[2] See *Founding of Montreal*, page 232.
[3] See *English Pilgrims Settle at Plymouth*, page 93.
[4] See *First American Legislature*, page 76.
[5] See *Introduction of Negroes into Virginia: Spread of Slavery and the Cultivation of Tobacco*, page 81.

great preliminary fleet carrying over a thousand souls left England in 1630 and settled Boston.[1]

During the next ten years twenty thousand Puritans came to Massachusetts. This was colonization on a scale hitherto unconceived. A new and powerful commonwealth burst suddenly into being where the primeval wilderness had so lately been. And it was a commonwealth rebellious from the start. When the civil war broke out in England against Charles, large numbers of the Massachusetts men hurried back to take grim part in it. In America the rule of England became little more than a name. Other colonies were formed both north and south, and they stood by themselves with no mother-country to uphold them. They grew strong through wrestling with the wilderness. Connecticut was settled from Massachusetts, and its pioneers, seeing no arm of authority long enough to reach them, drew up a code of laws of their own, the first written constitution prepared by a free people for their own government.[2] A few years later we find the New England colonies uniting in a union for defence against the Indians—and, if necessary, against King Charles' tyranny as well.[3] Maryland was settled by English Catholics who had found themselves as oppressed as the Puritans at home, and there the assembly of burghers proclaimed religious toleration to all who joined them.[4] Surely the New World had something to teach the Old! Only Europe's brightest and bravest and best had ventured to cross the seas for the freedom they desired. It was with good material indeed, and after sore experience of European blunders, that the land beyond the ocean began its remarkable career.

[1] See *Great Puritan Exodus to New England: Founding of Boston*, page 153.

[2] See *First Written Free Constitution in the World*, page 205.

[3] See *Earliest Union among American Colonies*, page 205.

[4] See *Religious Toleration Proclaimed in Maryland*, page 303.

[FOR THE NEXT SECTION OF THIS GENERAL SURVEY SEE VOLUME XII]

HENRY HUDSON EXPLORES THE HUDSON RIVER

A.D. 1609

HENRY R. CLEVELAND

Although Henry Hudson was not the first discoverer of the waters to which his name was given, he was a bold sailor whose achievements justly gave him rank with the foremost navigators and explorers of his time. He was well versed in scientific navigation. His first recorded voyage was made in the service of the Muscovy or Russia Company of England in 1607. His object was to find a passage across the north pole to the Spice Islands (Moluccas), in the Malay Archipelago. Though failing in this purpose, he reached a higher latitude than had before been attained by any navigator.

His next venture (1608), for the same company, was for "finding a passage to the East Indies by the northeast," but he failed to pass in that direction beyond Nova Zembla, and returned to England. These two failures discouraged the Muscovy Company, but did not daunt Henry Hudson. Again he determined to sail the northern seas, and the story of his third great voyage and its results is here given to the reader.

HUDSON, whose mind was completely bent upon making the discovery which he had undertaken, now sought employment from the Dutch East India Company. The fame of his adventures had already reached Holland, and he had received from the Dutch the appellations of the bold Englishman, the expert pilot, the famous navigator. The company were generally in favor of accepting the offer of his services, though the scheme was strongly opposed by Balthazar Moucheron, one of their number, who had some acquaintance with the arctic seas. They accordingly gave him the command of a small vessel, named the Half Moon, with a crew of twenty men, Dutch and English, among whom was Robert Juet, who had accompanied him as mate on his second voyage. The journal of the present voyage, which is published in *Purchas' Pilgrims*, was written by Juet.

He sailed from Amsterdam March 25, 1609, and doubled the

North Cape in about a month. His object was to pass through the Vaygats, or perhaps to the north of Nova Zembla, and thus reach China by the northeast passage. But after contending for more than a fortnight with head winds, continual fogs, and ice, and finding it impossible to reach even the coast of Nova Zembla, he determined to abandon this plan, and endeavor to discover a passage by the northwest. He accordingly directed his course westerly, doubled the North Cape again, and in a few days saw a part of the western coast of Norway, in the latitude of 68°. From this point he sailed for the Faroe Islands, where he arrived about the end of May.

Having replenished his water-casks at one of these islands he again hoisted sail, and steered southwest, in the hope of making Buss Island, which had been discovered by Sir Martin Frobisher, in 1578, as he wished to ascertain if it was correctly laid down on the chart. As he did not succeed in finding it, he continued this course for nearly a month, having much severe weather and a succession of gales, in one of which the foremast was carried away. Having arrived at the 45th degree of latitude, he judged it best to shape his course westward, with the intention of making Newfoundland. While proceeding in this direction he one day saw a vessel standing to the eastward, and wishing to speak her he put the ship about and gave chase; but finding as night came on that he could not overtake her he resumed the westerly course again.

On July 2d he had soundings on the Grand Bank of Newfoundland, and saw a whole fleet of Frenchmen fishing there. Being on soundings for several days he determined to try his luck at fishing; and the weather falling calm he set the whole crew at work to so much purpose that, in the course of the morning, they took between one and two hundred very large cod. After two or three days of calm the wind sprang up again, and he continued his course westward till the 12th, when he first had sight of the coast of North America. The fog was so thick, however, that he did not venture nearer the coast for several days; but at length, the weather clearing up, he ran into a bay at the mouth of a large river, in the latitude of 44°. This was Penobscot Bay, on the coast of Maine.

He already had some notion of the kind of inhabitants he

was to find here, for a few days before he had been visited by six savages, who came on board in a very friendly manner and ate and drank with him. He found that from their intercourse with the French traders they had learned a few words of their language. Soon after coming to anchor he was visited by several of the natives, who appeared very harmless and inoffensive; and in the afternoon two boats full of them came to the ship, bringing beaver-skins and other fine furs, which they wished to exchange for articles of dress. They offered no violence whatever, though we find in Juet's journal constant expressions of distrust, apparently without foundation.

They remained in this bay long enough to cut and rig a new foremast, and being now ready for sea the men were sent on shore upon an expedition that disgraced the whole company. What Hudson's sentiments or motives with regard to this transaction were we can only conjecture from a general knowledge of his character, as we have no account of it from himself. But it seems highly probable that, if he did not project it, he at least gave his consent to its perpetration. The account is in the words of Juet, as follows: "In the morning we manned our scute with four muskets and six men, and took one of their shallops and brought it aboard. Then we manned our boat and scute with twelve men and muskets, and two stone pieces, or murderers, and drave the salvages from their houses, and took the spoil of them, as they would have done of us." After this exploit they returned to the ship and set sail immediately. It does not appear from the journal that the natives had ever offered them any harm or given any provocation for so wanton an act. The writer only asserts that they would have done it if they could. No plea is more commonly used to justify tyranny and cruelty than the supposed bad intentions of the oppressed.

He now continued southward along the coast of America. It appears that Hudson had been informed by his friend, Captain John Smith, that there was a passage to the western Pacific Ocean south of Virginia, and that, when he had proved the impossibility of going by the northeast, he had offered his crew the choice either to explore this passage spoken of by Captain John Smith or to seek the northwest passage by going through Davis Strait. Many of the men had been in the East

India service, and in the habit of sailing in tropical climates, and were consequently very unwilling to endure the severities of a high northern latitude. It was therefore voted that they should go in search of the passage to the south of Virginia.

In a few days they saw land extending north, and terminating in a remarkable headland, which he recognized to be Cape Cod. Wishing to double the headland, he sent some of the men in the boat to sound along the shore, before venturing nearer with the ship. The water was five fathoms deep within bowshot of the shore, and, landing, they found, as the journal informs us, "goodly grapes and rose-trees," which they brought on board with them. He then weighed anchor and advanced as far as the northern extremity of the headland. Here he heard the voice of someone calling to them, and, thinking it possible some unfortunate European might have been left there, he immediately despatched some of the men to the shore. They found only a few savages; but, as these appeared very friendly, they brought one of them on board, where they gave him refreshments and also a present of three or four glass buttons, with which he seemed greatly delighted. The savages were observed to have green tobacco and pipes, the bowls of which were made of clay and the stems of red copper.

The wind not being favorable for passing west of this headland into the bay, Hudson determined to explore the coast farther south, and the next day he saw the southern point of Cape Cod, which had been discovered and named by Bartholomew Gosnold in the year 1602. He passed in sight of Nantucket and Martha's Vineyard, and continued a southerly course till the middle of August, when he arrived at the entrance of Chesapeake Bay. "This," says the writer of the journal, "is the entrance into the King's river, in Virginia, where our Englishmen are." The colony, under the command of Newport, consisting of one hundred five persons, among whom were Smith, Gosnold, Wingfield, and Ratcliffe, had arrived here a little more than two years before, and if Hudson could have landed he would have enjoyed the satisfaction of seeing and conversing with his own countrymen, and in his own language, in the midst of the forests of the New World. But the wind was blowing a gale from the northeast, and, probably dreading a shore with which he was unacquainted, he made no attempt to find them.

He continued to ply to the south for several days, till he reached the latitude of 35° 41′, when he again changed his course to the north. It is highly probable that if the journal of the voyage had been kept by Hudson himself we should have been informed of his reasons for changing the southerly course at this point. The cause, however, is not difficult to conjecture. He had gone far enough to ascertain that the information given him by Captain Smith with respect to a passage into the Pacific south of Virginia was incorrect, and he probably did not think it worth while to spend more time in so hopeless a search. He therefore retraced his steps, and on August 28th discovered Delaware Bay, where he examined the currents, soundings, and the appearance of the shores, without attempting to land. From this anchorage he coasted northward, the shore appearing low, like sunken ground, dotted with islands, till September 2d, when he saw the highlands of Navesink, which, the journalist remarks, "is a very good land to fall with and a pleasant land to see."

The entrance into the southern waters of New York is thus described in the journal: "At three of the clock in the afternoon we came to three great rivers. So we stood along to the northernmost, thinking to have gone into it, but we found it to have a very shoal bar before it, for we had but ten foot water. Then we cast about to the southward and found two fathoms, three fathoms, and three and a quarter, till we came to the southern side of them; then we had five and six fathoms, and anchored. So we sent in our boat to sound, and they found no less water than four, five, six, and seven fathoms, and returned in an hour and a half. So we weighed and went in and rode in five fathoms, oozy ground, and saw many salmons, and mullets, and rays very great." The next morning having ascertained by sending in the boat that there was a very good harbor before him, he ran in and anchored at two cables' length from the shore. This was within Sandy Hook Bay.

He was very soon visited by the natives, who came on board his vessel, and seemed to be greatly rejoiced at his arrival among them. They brought green tobacco, which they desired to exchange for knives and beads, and Hudson observed that they had copper pipes and ornaments of copper. They also appeared to have plenty of maize, from which they made good bread. Their dress was of deerskins, well cured, and hanging loosely about them. There is a tradition that some of his men, being sent out to fish, landed on Coney Island. They found the soil sandy, but supporting a vast number of plum-trees loaded with fruit, and grapevines growing round them.

The next day, the men, being sent in the boat to explore the bay still farther, landed, probably on the Jersey shore, where they were very kindly received by the savages, who gave them plenty of tobacco. They found the land covered with large oaks. Several of the natives also came on board, dressed in mantles of feathers and fine furs. Among the presents they brought were dried currants, which were found extremely palatable.

Soon afterward five of the men were sent in the boat to examine the north side of the bay and sound the river, which was perceived at the distance of four leagues. They passed through the Narrows, sounding all along, and saw "a narrow river to the westward, between two islands," supposed to be Staten Island and Bergen Neck. They described the land as covered with trees, grass, and flowers, and filled with delightful fragrance. On their return to the ship they were assaulted by two canoes; one contained twelve and the other fourteen savages. It was nearly dark, and the rain which was falling had extinguished their match, so that they could only trust to their oars for escape. One of the men, John Colman, who had accompanied Hudson on his first voyage, was killed by an arrow shot into his throat, and two more were wounded. The darkness probably saved them from the savages, but at the same time it prevented their finding the vessel, so that they did not return till the next day, when they appeared, bringing the body of their comrade. Hudson ordered him to be carried on shore and buried, and named the place, in memory of the event, Colman's Point.

He now expected an attack from the natives, and accordingly hoisted in the boat and erected a sort of bulwark along the sides of the vessel, for the better defence. But these precautions were needless. Several of the natives came on board, but in a friendly manner, wishing to exchange tobacco and Indian corn for the trifles which the sailors could spare them. They did not appear to know anything of the affray which had taken place. But the day after two large canoes came off to the vessel, the one filled with armed men, the other under the pretence of trading. Hudson, however, would only allow two of the savages to come on board, keeping the rest at a distance. The two who came on board were detained, and Hudson dressed them up in red coats; the remainder returned to the shore. Presently another canoe, with two men in it, came to the vessel. Hudson also detained one of these, probably wishing to keep him as a hostage, but he very soon jumped overboard and swam to the shore. On the 11th Hudson sailed through the Narrows and anchored in New York Bay.

He prepared to explore the magnificent river which came rolling its waters into the sea from unknown regions. Whither he would be conducted in tracing its course he could form no conjecture. A hope may be supposed to have entered his mind that the long-desired passage to the Indies was now at length discovered; that here was to be the end of his toils; that here, in this mild climate, and amid these pleasant scenes, was to be found that object which he had sought in vain through the snows and ice of the Arctic zone. With a glad heart, then, he weighed anchor on September 12th, and commenced his memorable voyage up that majestic stream which now bears his name.

The wind only allowed him to advance a few miles the first two days of the voyage, but the time which he was obliged to spend at anchor was fully occupied in trading with the natives, who came off from the shore in great numbers, bringing oysters and vegetables. He observed that they had copper pipes, and earthen vessels to cook their meat in. They seemed very harmless and well disposed, but the crew were unwilling to trust these appearances, and would not allow any of them to come on board. The next day, a fine breeze springing up from the southeast, he was able to make great progress, so that he anchored at night nearly forty miles from the place of starting in the morning. He observes that "here the land grew very high and mountainous," so that he had undoubtedly anchored in the midst of the fine scenery of the Highlands.

When he awoke in the morning he found heavy mist overhanging the river and its shores and concealing the summits of the mountains. But it was dispelled by the sun in a short time, and taking advantage of a fair wind he weighed anchor and continued the voyage. A little circumstance occurred this morning which was destined to be afterward painfully remembered. The two savages, whom he held as hostages, made their escape through the portholes of the vessel and swam to the shore, and as soon as the ship was under sail they took pains to express their indignation at the treatment they had received, by uttering loud and angry cries. Toward night he came to other mountains, which, he says, "lie from the river's side," and anchored, it is supposed, near the present site of Catskill Landing. "There," says the journal, "we found very loving people and very old men, where we were well used. Our boat went to fish and caught great store of very good fish."

The next morning, September 16th, the men were sent again to catch fish, but were not so successful as they had been the day before, in consequence of the savages having been there in their canoes all night. A large number of the natives came off to the ship, bringing Indian corn, pumpkins, and tobacco. The day was consumed in trading with the natives and in filling the casks with fresh water, so that they did not weigh anchor till toward night. After sailing about five miles, finding the water shoal, they came to anchor, probably near the spot where the city of Hudson now stands. The weather was hot, and Hudson determined to set his men at work in the cool of the morning. He accordingly, on the 17th, weighed anchor at dawn and ran up the river about fifteen miles, when, finding shoals and small islands, he thought it best to anchor again. Toward night the vessel, having drifted near the shore, grounded in shoal water, but was easily drawn off by carrying out the small anchor. She was aground again in a short time in the channel, but, the tide rising, she floated off.

The two days following he advanced only about five miles, being much occupied by his intercourse with the natives. Being in the neighborhood of the present town of Castleton, he went on shore, where he was very kindly received by an old savage, "the governor of the country," who took him to his house, and gave him the best cheer he could. At his anchorage also, five miles above this place, the natives came flocking on board, bringing a great variety of articles, such as grapes, pumpkins, beaver and otter skins, which they exchanged for beads, knives, and hatchets or whatever trifles the sailors could spare them. The next day was occupied in exploring the river, four men being sent in the boat, under the command of the mate, for that purpose. They ascended several miles and found the channel narrow and in some places only two fathoms deep, but after that seven or eight fathoms. In the afternoon they returned to the ship. Hudson resolved to pursue the examination of the channel on the following morning, but was interrupted by the number of natives who came on board. Finding that he was not likely to gain any progress this day, he sent the carpenter ashore to prepare a new foreyard, and in the mean time prepared to make an extraordinary experiment on board.

From the whole tenor of the journal it is evident that great distrust was entertained by Hudson and his men toward the natives. He now determined to ascertain, by intoxicating some of the chiefs, and thus throwing them off their guard, whether they were plotting any treachery. He accordingly invited several of them into the cabin and gave them plenty of brandy to drink. One of these men had his wife with him, who, the journal informs us, "sate so modestly as any one of our countrywomen would do in a strange place"; but the men had less delicacy, and were soon quite merry with the brandy. One of them, who had been on board from the first arrival of the ship, was completely intoxicated, and fell sound asleep, to the great astonishment of his companions, who probably feared that he had been poisoned, for they all took to their canoes and made for the shore, leaving their unlucky comrade on board. Their anxiety for his welfare, however, soon induced them to return, and they brought a quantity of beads, which they gave him, perhaps to enable him to purchase his freedom from the spell that had been laid upon him.

The poor savage slept quietly all night, and when his friends came to visit him the next morning they found him quite well. This restored their confidence, so that they came to the ship again in crowds, in the afternoon, bringing various presents for Hudson. Their visit, which was one of unusual ceremony, is thus described in the journal: "So, at three of the clock in the afternoon, they came aboard and brought tobacco and more beads and gave them to our master, and made an oration, and showed him all the country round about. Then they sent one of their company on land, who presently returned and brought a great platter full of venison, dressed by themselves, and they caused him to eat with them. Then they made him reverence, and departed, all save the old man that lay aboard."

At night the mate returned in the boat, having been sent again to explore the river. He reported that he had ascended eight or nine leagues, and found but seven feet of water and irregular soundings.

It was evidently useless to attempt to ascend the river any farther with the ship, and Hudson therefore determined to return. We may well imagine that he was satisfied already with the result of the voyage, even supposing him to have been disappointed in not finding here a passage to the Indies. He had explored a great and navigable river to the distance of nearly a hundred forty miles; he had found the country along the banks extremely fertile, the climate delightful, and the scenery displaying every variety of beauty and grandeur; and he knew that he had opened the way for his patrons to possessions which might prove of inestimable value.

It is supposed that the highest place which the Half Moon reached in the river was the neighborhood of the present site of Albany, and that the boats being sent out to explore ascended as high as Waterford, and probably some distance beyond. The voyage down the river was not more expeditious than it had been in ascending; the prevalent winds were southerly, and for several days the ship could advance but very slowly. The time, however, passed agreeably in making excursions on the shore, where they found "good ground for corn and other garden herbs, with a great store of goodly oaks and walnut-trees, and chestnut-trees, ewe-trees and trees of sweetwood in great abundance, and great store of slate for houses, and other good stones"; or in receiving visits from the natives, who came on the ship in numbers. While Hudson was at anchor near the spot where the city bearing his name now stands, two canoes came from the place where the scene of the intoxication had occurred, and in one of them was the old man who had been the sufferer under the strange experiment. He brought another old man with him, who presented Hudson with a string of beads, and "showed all the country there about, as though it were at his command." Hudson entertained them at dinner, with four of their women, and in the afternoon dismissed them with presents.

He continued the voyage down the river, taking advantage of wind and tide as he could, and employing the time when at anchor in fishing or in trading with the natives, who came to the ship nearly every day, till on October 1st he anchored near Stony Point.

The vessel was no sooner perceived from the shore to be stationary than a party of the native mountaineers came off in their canoes to visit it, and were filled with wonder at everything it contained. While the attention of the crew was taken up with their visitors upon deck, one of the savages managed to run his canoe under the stern and, climbing up the rudder, found his way into the cabin by the window, where, having seized a pillow and a few articles of wearing-apparel, he made off with them in the canoe. The mate detected him as he fled, fired at and killed him. Upon this, all the other savages departed with the utmost precipitation, some taking to their canoes and others plunging into the water. The boat was manned, and sent after the stolen goods, which were easily recovered; but as the men were returning to the vessel, one of the savages, who were in the water, seized hold of the keel of the boat, with the intention, as was supposed, of upsetting it. The cook took a sword and lopped his hand off, and the poor wretch immediately sank. They then weighed anchor and advanced about five miles.

The next day Hudson descended about seven leagues and anchored. Here he was visited in a canoe by one of the two savages who had escaped from the ship as he was going up. But fearing treachery, he would not allow him or his companions to come on board. Two canoes filled with armed warriors then came under the stern and commenced an attack with arrows. The men fired at them with their muskets and killed three of them. More than a hundred savages now came down upon the nearest point of land to shoot at the vessel. One of the cannon was brought to bear upon these warriors, and at the first discharge two of them were killed and the rest fled to the woods.

The savages were not yet discouraged. They had doubtless been instigated to make this attack by the two who escaped near West Point, and who had probably incited their countrymen by the story of their imprisonment, as well as by representing to them the value of the spoil, if they could capture the vessel, and the small number of men who guarded it. Nine or ten of the boldest warriors now threw themselves into a canoe and put off toward the ship, but a shot from the cannon made a hole in the canoe and killed one of the men. This was followed by a discharge of musketry, which destroyed three or four more. This put an end to the battle, and in the evening, having descended about five miles, Hudson anchored in a part of the river out of the reach of his enemies, probably near Hoboken.

Hudson had now explored the bay of New York and the noble stream which pours into it from the north. For his employers he had secured a possession which would beyond measure reward them for the expense they had incurred in fitting out the expedition. For himself he had gained a name that was destined to live in the gratitude of a great nation through unnumbered generations. Happy in the result of his labors and in the brilliant promise they afforded, he spread his sails again for the Old World on October 4th, and in a little more than a month arrived safely at Dartmouth, in England.

The journal kept by Juet ends abruptly at this place. The question therefore immediately arises whether Hudson pursued his voyage to Holland, or whether he remained in England and sent the vessel home. Several Dutch authors assert that Hudson was not allowed, after reaching England, to pursue his voyage to Amsterdam; and this seems highly probable when we remember the well-known jealousy with which the maritime enterprises of the Dutch were regarded by King James.

Whether Hudson went to Holland himself or not, it seems clear from various circumstances that he secured to the Dutch Company all the benefits of his discoveries, by sending to them his papers and charts. It is worthy of note that the earliest histories of this voyage, with the exception of Juet's journal, were published by Dutch authors. Moreover, Hudson's own journal, or some portion of it at least, was in Holland, and was used by De Laet previously to the publication of Juet's journal in *Purchas' Pilgrims.* But the most substantial proof that the Dutch enjoyed the benefit of his discoveries earlier than any other nation, is the fact that the very next year they were trading in Hudson River, which it is not probable would have happened if they had not had possession of Hudson's charts and journal.

GALILEO OVERTHROWS ANCIENT PHILOSOPHY

THE TELESCOPE AND ITS DISCOVERIES

A.D. 1610

SIR OLIVER LODGE

When the Copernican system of astronomy was published to the world (1543) it had to encounter, as all capital theories and discoveries in science have done, the criticism, and, for some time, the opposition, of men holding other views. After Copernicus, the next great name in modern science is that of Tycho Brahe (1546–1601), who rejected the theory of Copernicus in favor of a modified form of the Ptolemaic system. This was still taught in the schools when two mighty contemporaries, geniuses of science, rose to overthrow it forever.

These men were Galileo Galilei—commonly known as Galileo—and Kepler, both astronomers, though Galileo's scientific work covered also a much wider field. He is regarded to-day as marking a distinct epoch in the progress of the world, and the following account of his work by the eminent scientist, Sir Oliver Lodge, expresses no more than a just appreciation of his great services to mankind.

GALILEO exercised a vast influence on the development of human thought. A man of great and wide culture, a so-called universal genius, it is as an experimental philosopher that he takes the first rank. In this capacity he must be placed alongside of Archimedes, and it is pretty certain that between the two there was no man of magnitude equal to either in experimental philosophy. It is perhaps too bold a speculation, but I venture to doubt whether in succeeding generations we find his equal in the domain of purely experimental science until we come to Faraday. Faraday was no doubt his superior, but I know of no other of whom the like can unhesitatingly be said. In mathematical and deductive science, of course, it is quite otherwise. Kepler, for instance, and many men before and since, have far excelled Galileo in mathematical skill and power, though at the same time his achievements in this department are by no means to be despised.

Born at Pisa on the very day that Michelangelo lay dying in Rome, he inherited from his father a noble name, cultivated tastes, a keen love of truth, and an impoverished patrimony. Vincenzo de Galilei, a descendant of the important Bonajuti family, was himself a mathematician and a musician, and in a book of his still extant he declares himself in favor of free and open inquiry into scientific matters, unrestrained by the weight of authority and tradition. In all probability the son imbibed these precepts: certainly he acted on them.

Vincenzo, having himself experienced the unremunerative character of scientific work, had a horror of his son's taking to it, especially as in his boyhood he was always constructing ingenious mechanical toys and exhibiting other marks of precocity. So the son was destined for business—to be, in fact, a cloth-dealer. But he was to receive a good education first, and was sent to an excellent convent school.

Here he made rapid progress, and soon excelled in all branches of classics and literature. He delighted in poetry, and in later years wrote several essays on Dante, Tasso, and Ariosto, besides composing some tolerable poems himself. He played skilfully on several musical instruments, especially on the lute, of which indeed he became a master, and on which he solaced himself when quite an old man. Besides this, he seems to have had some skill as an artist, which was useful afterward in illustrating his discoveries, and to have had a fine sensibility as an art critic, for we find several eminent painters of that day acknowledging the value of the opinion of the young Galileo.

Perceiving all this display of ability, the father wisely came to the conclusion that the selling of woollen stuffs would hardly satisfy his aspirations for long, and that it was worth a sacrifice to send him to the university. So to the university of his native town he went, with the avowed object of studying medicine, that career seeming the most likely to be profitable. Old Vincenzo's horror of mathematics or science as a means of obtaining a livelihood is justified by the fact that while the university professor of medicine received two thousand scudi a year, the professor of mathematics had only sixty; that is thirteen pounds a year, or seven and a half pence a day. So the son had been kept properly ignorant of such poverty-stricken subjects, and to study medicine he went.

But his natural bent showed itself even here. For praying one day in the cathedral, like a good Catholic as he was all his life, his attention was arrested by the great lamp which, after lighting it, the verger had left swinging to and fro. Galileo proceeded to time its swings by the only watch he possessed—viz., his own pulse. He noticed that the time of swing remained, as near as he could tell, the same, notwithstanding the fact that the swings were getting smaller and smaller.

By subsequent experiment he verified the law, and the isochronism of the pendulum was discovered. An immensely important practical discovery this, for upon it all modern clocks are based; and Huyghens soon applied it to the astronomical clock, which up to that time had been a crude and quite untrustworthy instrument.

The best clock which Tycho Brahe could get for his observatory was inferior to one that may now be purchased for a few shillings; and this change is owing to the discovery of the pendulum by Galileo. Not that he applied it to clocks; he was not thinking of astronomy, he was thinking of medicine, and wanted to count people's pulses. The pendulum served; and "pulsilogies," as they were called, were thus introduced to and used by medical practitioners.

The Tuscan court came to Pisa for the summer months—for it was then a seaside place—and among the suite was Ostillio Ricci, a distinguished mathematician and old friend of the Galileo family. The youth visited him, and one day, it is said, heard a lesson in Euclid being given by Ricci to the pages while he stood outside the door entranced. Anyhow, he implored Ricci to help him into some knowledge of mathematics, and the old man willingly consented. So he mastered Euclid, and passed on to Archimedes, for whom he acquired a great veneration.

His father soon heard of this obnoxious proclivity, and did what he could to divert him back to medicine again. But it was no use. Underneath his Galen and Hippocrates were secreted copies of Euclid and Archimedes, to be studied at every available opportunity. Old Vincenzo perceived the bent of genius to be too strong for him, and at last gave way. With prodigious rapidity the released philosopher now assimilated the elements of mathematics and physics, and at twenty-six we find him appointed for three years to the university chair of mathematics, and enjoying the paternally dreaded stipend of seven and a half pence a day.

Now it was that he pondered over the laws of falling bodies. He verified, by experiment, the fact that the velocity acquired by falling down any slope of given height was independent of the angle of slope. Also, that the height fallen through was proportional to the square of the time.

Another thing he found experimentally was that all bodies, heavy and light, fell at the same rate, striking the ground at the same time. Now this was clean contrary to what he had been taught. The physics of those days were a simple reproduction of statements in old books. Aristotle had asserted certain things to be true, and these were universally believed. No one thought of trying the thing to see if it really were so. The idea of making an experiment would have savored of impiety, because it seemed to tend toward scepticism, and cast a doubt on a reverend authority.

Young Galileo, with all the energy and imprudence of youth —what a blessing that youth has a little imprudence and disregard of consequences in pursuing a high ideal!—as soon as he perceived that his instructors were wrong on the subject of falling bodies, instantly informed them of the fact. Whether he expected them to be pleased or not is a question. Anyhow, they were not pleased, but were much annoyed by his impertinent arrogance.

It is, perhaps, difficult for us now to appreciate precisely their position. These doctrines of antiquity, which had come down hoary with age, and the discovery of which had reawakened learning and quickened intellectual life, were accepted less as a science or a philosophy than as a religion. Had they regarded Aristotle as a verbally inspired writer, they could not have received his statements with more unhesitating conviction. In any dispute as to a question of fact, such as the one before us concerning the laws of falling bodies, their method was not to make an experiment, but to turn over the pages of Aristotle; and he who could quote chapter and verse of this great writer was held to settle the question and raise it above the reach of controversy.

It is very necessary for us to realize this state of things clearly, because otherwise the attitude of the learned of those days toward every new discovery seems stupid and almost insane. They had a crystallized system of truth, perfect, symmetrical; it wanted no novelty, no additions; every addition or growth was an imperfection, an excrescence, a deformity. Progress was unnecessary and undesired. The Church had a rigid system of dogma which must be accepted in its entirety on pain of being treated as a heretic. Philosophers had a cast-iron system of truth to match—a system founded upon Aristotle—and so interwoven with the great theological dogmas that to question one was almost equivalent to casting doubt upon the other.

In such an atmosphere true science was impossible. The life-blood of science is growth, expansion, freedom, development. Before it could appear it must throw off these old shackles of centuries. It must burst its old skin, and emerge, worn with the struggle, weakly and unprotected, but free and able to grow and to expand. The conflict was inevitable, and it was severe. Is it over yet? I fear not quite, though so nearly as to disturb science hardly at all. Then it was different: it was terrible. Honor to the men who bore the first shock of the battle!

Now, Aristotle had said that bodies fell at rates depending on their weight. A five-pound weight would fall five times as quick as a one-pound weight; a fifty-pound weight fifty times as quick, and so on. Why he said so nobody knows. He cannot have tried. He was not above trying experiments, like his smaller disciples; but probably it never occurred to him to doubt the fact. It seems so natural that a heavy body should fall quicker than a light one; and perhaps he thought of a stone and a feather, and was satisfied.

Galileo, however, asserted that the weight did not matter a bit; that everything fell at the same rate—even a stone and a feather, but for the resistance of the air—and would reach the ground in the same time. And he was not content to be pooh-poohed and snubbed. He knew he was right, and he was determined to make everyone see the facts as he saw them. So one morning, before the assembled university, he ascended the famous leaning tower, taking with him a one-hundred-pound shot and a one-pound shot. He balanced them on the edge of the tower, and let them drop together. Together they fell, and together they struck the ground. The simultaneous clang of those two weights sounded the death-knell of the old system of philosophy, and heralded the birth of the new.

But was the change sudden? Were his opponents convinced? Not a jot. Though they had seen with their eyes and heard with their ears, the full light of heaven shining upon them, they went back muttering and discontented to their musty old volumes and their garrets, there to invent occult reasons for denying the validity of the observation, and for referring it to some unknown disturbing cause.

They saw that if they gave way on this one point they would be letting go their anchorage, and henceforward would be liable to drift along with the tide, not knowing whither. They dared not do this. No; they *must* cling to the old traditions; they could not cast away their rotting ropes and sail out on to the free ocean of God's truth in a spirit of fearless faith.

Yet they had received a shock: as by a breath of fresh salt breeze and a dash of spray in their faces, they had been awakened out of their comfortable lethargy. They felt the approach of a new era. Yes, it was a shock, and they hated the young Galileo for giving it them—hated him with the sullen hatred of men who fight for a lost and dying cause.

We need scarcely blame these men; at least we need not blame them overmuch. To say that they acted as they did is to say that they were human, were narrow-minded, and were the apostles of a lost cause. But *they* could not know this; *they* had no experience of the past to guide them; the conditions under which they found themselves were novel, and had to be met for the first time. Conduct which was excusable then would be unpardonable now, in the light of all this experience to guide us. Are there any now who practically repeat their error, and resist new truth? who cling to any old anchorage of dogma, and refuse to rise with the tide of advancing knowledge? There may be some even now.

Well, the unpopularity of Galileo smouldered for a time, until, by another noble imprudence, he managed to offend a semiroyal personage, Giovanni de' Medici, by giving his real opinion, when consulted, about a machine which De' Medici had invented for cleaning out the harbor of Leghorn. He said it was as useless as it in fact turned out to be. Through the influence of the mortified inventor he lost favor at court; and his enemies took advantage of the fact to render his chair untenable. He resigned before his three years were up, and retired to Florence.

His father at this time died, and the family were left in narrow circumstances. He had a brother and three sisters to provide for. He was offered a professorship at Padua for six years by the Senate of Venice, and willingly accepted it. Now began a very successful career. His introductory address was marked by brilliant eloquence, and his lectures soon acquired fame. He wrote for his pupils on the laws of motion, on fortifications, on sun-dials, on mechanics, and on the celestial globe: some of these papers are now lost, others have been printed during the present century.

Kepler sent him a copy of his new book, *Mysterium Cosmographicum*, and Galileo, in thanking him for it, writes him the following letter:

"I count myself happy, in the search after truth, to have so great an ally as yourself, and one who is so great a friend of the truth itself. It is really pitiful that there are so few who seek truth, and who do not pursue a perverse method of philosophizing. But this is not the place to mourn over the miseries of our times, but to congratulate you on your splendid discoveries in confirmation of truth. I shall read your book to the end, sure of finding much that is excellent in it. I shall do so with the more pleasure, because *I have been for many years an adherent of the Copernican system*, and it explains to me the causes of many of the appearances of nature which are quite unintelligible on the commonly accepted hypothesis. *I have collected many arguments for the purpose of refuting the latter;* but I do not venture to bring them to the light of publicity, for fear of sharing the fate of our master, Copernicus, who, although he has earned immortal fame with some, yet with very many (so great is the number of fools) has become an object of ridicule and scorn. I should certainly venture to publish my speculations if there were more people like you. But this not being the case, I refrain from such an undertaking."

Kepler urged him to publish his arguments in favor of the Copernican theory, but he hesitated for the present, knowing that his declaration would be received with ridicule and opposition, and thinking it wiser to get rather more firmly seated in his chair before encountering the storm of controversy. The six years passed away, and the Venetian Senate, anxious not to lose so bright an ornament, renewed his appointment for another six years at a largely increased salary.

Soon after this appeared a new star—the *stella nova* of 1604—not the one Tycho had seen—that was in 1572—but the same that Kepler was so much interested in. Galileo gave a course of three lectures upon it to a great audience. At the first the theatre was overcrowded, so he had to adjourn to a hall holding one thousand persons. At the next he had to lecture in the open air. He took occasion to rebuke his hearers for thronging to hear about an ephemeral novelty, while for the much more wonderful and important truths about the permanent stars and facts of nature they had but deaf ears.

But the main point he brought out concerning the new star was that it upset the received Aristotelian doctrine of the immutability of the heavens. According to that doctrine the heavens were unchangeable, perfect, subject neither to growth nor to decay. Here was a body, not a meteor but a real distant star, which had not been visible and which would shortly fade away again, but which meanwhile was brighter than Jupiter.

The staff of petrified professorial wisdom were annoyed at the appearance of the star, still more at Galileo's calling public attention to it; and controversy began at Padua. However, he accepted it, and now boldly threw down the gauntlet in favor of the Copernican theory, utterly repudiating the old Ptolemaic system, which up to that time he had taught in the schools according to established custom.

The earth no longer the only world to which all else in the firmament were obsequious attendants, but a mere insignificant speck among the host of heaven! Man no longer the centre and cynosure of creation, but, as it were, an insect crawling on the surface of this little speck! All this not set down in crabbed Latin in dry folios for a few learned monks, as in Copernicus' time, but promulgated and argued in rich Italian, illustrated by analogy, by experiment, and with cultured wit; taught not to a few scholars here and there in musty libraries, but proclaimed in the vernacular to the whole populace with all the energy and enthusiasm of a recent convert and a master of language! Had a bombshell been exploded among the fossilized professors it had been less disturbing.

But there was worse in store for them. A Dutch optician, Hans Lippershey by name, of Middleburg, had in his shop a curious toy, rigged up, it is said, by an apprentice, and made out of a couple of spectacle lenses, whereby, if one looked through it, the weather-cock of a neighboring church spire was seen nearer and upside down. The tale goes that the Marquis Spinola, happening to call at the shop, was struck with the toy and bought it. He showed it to Prince Maurice of Nassau, who thought of using it for military reconnoitring. All this is trivial. What is important is that some faint and inaccurate echo of this news found its way to Padua and into the ears of Galileo.

The seed fell on good soil. All that night he sat up and pondered. He knew about lenses and magnifying-glasses. He had read Kepler's theory of the eye, and had himself lectured on optics. Could he not hit on the device and make an instrument capable of bringing the heavenly bodies nearer? Who knew what marvels he might not so perceive! By morning he had some schemes ready to try, and one of them was successful. Singularly enough it was not the same plan as the Dutch optician's: it was another mode of achieving the same end. He took an old small organ-pipe, jammed a suitably chosen spectacle glass into either end, one convex, the other concave, and, behold! he had the half of a wretchedly bad opera-glass capable of magnifying three times. It was better than the Dutchman's, however: it did not invert.

Such a thing as Galileo made may now be bought at a toy-shop for I suppose half a crown, and yet what a potentiality lay in that "glazed optic tube," as Milton called it. Away he went with it to Venice and showed it to the Seigniory, to their great astonishment. "Many noblemen and senators," says Galileo, "though of advanced age, mounted to the top of one of the highest towers to watch the ships, which were visible through my glass two hours before they were seen entering the harbor, for it makes a thing fifty miles off as near and clear as if it were only five." Among the people, too, the instrument excited the greatest astonishment and interest, so that he was nearly mobbed. The Senate hinted to him that a present of the instrument would not be unacceptable, so Galileo took the hint and made another for them. They immediately doubled his salary at Padua, making it one thousand florins, and confirmed him in the enjoyment of it for life.

He now eagerly began the construction of a larger and better instrument. Grinding the lenses with his own hands with consummate skill, he succeeded in making a telescope magnifying thirty times. Thus equipped he was ready to begin a survey of the heavens. The first object he carefully examined was naturally the moon. He found there everything at first sight very like the earth, mountains and valleys, craters and plains, rocks, and apparently seas. You may imagine the hostility excited among the Aristotelian philosophers, especially, no doubt, those he had left behind at Pisa, on the ground of his spoiling the pure, smooth, crystalline, celestial face of the moon as they had thought it, and making it harsh and rugged, and like so vile and ignoble a body as the earth.

He went further, however, into heterodoxy than this: he not only made the moon like the earth, but he made the earth shine like the moon. The visibility of "the old moon in the new moon's arms" he explained by earth-shine. Leonardo had given the same explanation a century before. Now, one of the many stock arguments against Copernican theory of the earth being a planet like the rest was that the earth was dull and dark and did not shine. Galileo argued that it shone just as much as the moon does, and in fact rather more—especially if it be covered with clouds. One reason of the peculiar brilliancy of Venus is that she is a very cloudy planet.[1] Seen from the moon the earth would look exactly as the moon does to us, only a little brighter and sixteen times as big—four times the diameter.

[1] It is of course the "silver lining" of clouds that outside observers see.

Wherever Galileo turned his telescope new stars appeared. The Milky Way, which had so puzzled the ancients, was found to be composed of stars. Stars that appeared single to the eye were some of them found to be double; and at intervals were found hazy nebulous wisps, some of which seemed to be star clusters, while others seemed only a fleecy cloud.

Now we come to his most brilliant, at least his most sensational, discovery. Examining Jupiter minutely on January 7, 1610, he noticed three little stars near it, which he noted down as fixing its then position. On the following night Jupiter had moved to the other side of the three stars. This was natural enough, but was it moving the right way? On examination it appeared not. Was it possible the tables were wrong? The next evening was cloudy, and he had to curb his feverish impatience. On the 10th there were only two, and those on the other side. On the 11th two again, but one bigger than the other. On the 12th the three reappeared, and on the 13th there were four. No more appeared. Jupiter, then, had moons like the earth—four of them in fact!—and they revolved round him in periods which were soon determined.

The news of the discovery soon spread and excited the greatest interest and astonishment. Many of course refused to believe it. Some there were who, having been shown them, refused to believe their eyes, and asserted that although the telescope acted well enough for terrestrial objects, it was altogether false and illusory when applied to the heavens. Others took the safer ground of refusing to look through the glass. One of these who would not look at the satellites happened to die soon afterward. "I hope," says Galileo, "that he saw them on his way to heaven."

The way in which Kepler received the news is characteristic, though by adding four to the supposed number of planets it might have seemed to upset his notions about the five regular solids.

He says: "I was sitting idle at home thinking of you, most excellent Galileo, and your letters, when the news was brought me of the discovery of four planets by the help of the double eyeglass. Wachenfels stopped his carriage at my door to tell me, when such a fit of wonder seized me at a report which seemed so very absurd, and I was thrown into such agitation at seeing an old dispute between us decided in this way, that between his joy, my coloring, and the laughter of us both, confounded as we were by such a novelty, we were hardly capable, he of speaking, or I of listening.

"On our separating, I immediately fell to thinking how there could be any addition to the number of planets without overturning my *Mysterium Cosmographicon*, published thirteen years ago, according to which Euclid's five regular solids do not allow more than six planets round the sun. But I am so far from disbelieving the existence of the four circumjovial planets that I long for a telescope to anticipate you if possible in discovering two round Mars—as the proportion seems to me to require—six or eight round Saturn, and one each round Mercury and Venus."

As an illustration of the opposite school I will take the following extract from Francesco Sizzi, a Florentine astronomer, who argues against the discovery thus:

"There are seven windows in the head—two nostrils, two eyes, two ears, and a mouth; so in the heavens there are two favorable stars, two unpropitious, two luminaries, and Mercury alone undecided and indifferent. From which and many other similar phenomena of nature, such as the seven metals, etc., which it were tedious to enumerate, we gather that the number of planets is necessarily seven.

"Moreover, the satellites are invisible to the naked eye, and therefore can have no influence on the earth, and therefore would be useless, and therefore do not exist.

"Besides, the Jews and other ancient nations as well as modern Europeans have adopted the division of the week into seven days, and have named them from the seven planets: now if we increase the number of the planets this whole system falls to the ground."

To these arguments Galileo replied that whatever their force might be as a reason for believing beforehand that no more than seven planets would be discovered, they hardly seemed of sufficient weight to destroy the new ones when actually seen. Writing to Kepler at this time, Galileo ejaculates:

"Oh, my dear Kepler, how I wish that we could have one hearty laugh together! Here, at Padua, is the principal professor of philosophy whom I have repeatedly and urgently requested to look at the moon and planets through my glass, which he pertinaciously refuses to do. Why are you not here? What shouts of laughter we should have at this glorious folly! And to hear the professor of philosophy at Pisa laboring before the Grand Duke with logical arguments, as if with magical incantations, to charm the new planets out of the sky."

A young German *protégé* of Kepler, Martin Horkey, was travelling in Italy, and meeting Galileo at Bologna was favored with a view through his telescope. But supposing that Kepler must necessarily be jealous of such great discoveries, and thinking to please him, he writes: "I cannot tell what to think about these observations. They are stupendous, they are wonderful, but whether they are true or false I cannot tell." He concludes, "I will never concede his four new planets to that Italian from Padua, though I die for it." So he published a pamphlet asserting that reflected rays and optical illusions were the sole cause of the appearance, and that the only use of the imaginary planets was to gratify Galileo's thirst for gold and notoriety.

When after this performance he paid a visit to his old instructor Kepler he got a reception which astonished him. However, he pleaded so hard to be forgiven that Kepler restored him to partial favor, on this condition, that he was to look again at the satellites, and this time to see them and own that they were there.

By degrees the enemies of Galileo were compelled to confess to the truth of the discovery, and the next step was to outdo him. Scheiner counted five, Rheiter nine, and others went as high as twelve. Some of these were imaginary, some were fixed stars, and four satellites only are known to this day.[1]

Here, close to the summit of his greatness, we must leave him for a time. A few steps more and he will be on the brow of the hill; a short piece of table-land, and then the descent begins.

In dealing with these historic events will you allow me to repudiate once for all the slightest sectarian bias or meaning? I have nothing to do with Catholic or Protestant as such. I have nothing to do with the Church of Rome as such. I am dealing

[1] A fifth satellite of Jupiter has been recently discovered; and Kepler's guess at two moons for Mars has also been justified.

with the history of science. But historically at one period science and the Church came into conflict. It was not specially one church rather than another—it was the Church in general, the only one that then existed in those countries. Historically, I say, they came into conflict, and historically the Church was the conqueror. It got its way; and science, in the persons of Bruno, Galileo, and several others, was vanquished. Such being the facts, there is no help but to mention them in dealing with the history of science. Doubtless *now* the Church regards it as an unhappy victory, and gladly would ignore this painful struggle. This, however, is impossible. With their creed the churchmen of that day could act in no other way. They were bound to prosecute heresy, and they were bound to conquer in the struggle or be themselves shattered.

But let me insist on the fact that no one accuses the ecclesiastical courts of crime or evil motives. They attacked heresy after their manner, as the civil courts attacked witchcraft after *their* manner. Both erred grievously, but both acted with the best intentions.

We must remember, moreover, that his doctrines were scientifically heterodox, and the university professors of that day were probably quite as ready so condemn them as the Church was. To realize the position we must think of some subjects which *to-day* are scientifically heterodox, and of the customary attitude adopted toward them by persons of widely differing creeds.

If it be contended now, as it is, that the ecclesiastics treated Galileo well, I admit it freely: they treated him as well as they possibly could. They overcame him, and he recanted; but if he had not recanted, if he had persisted in his heresy, they would—well, they would still have treated his soul well, but they would have set fire to his body. Their mistake consisted not in cruelty, but in supposing themselves the arbiters of eternal truth; and by no amount of slurring and glossing over facts can they evade the responsibility assumed by them on account of this mistaken attitude.

We left Galileo standing at his telescope and beginning his survey of the heavens. We followed him indeed through a few of his first great discoveries—the discovery of the mountains and other variety of surface in the moon, of the nebulæ and a multitude of faint stars, and lastly of the four satellites of Jupiter.

This latter discovery made an immense sensation, and contributed its share to his removal from Padua, which quickly followed it. Before the end of the year 1610 Galileo had made another discovery—this time on Saturn. But to guard against the host of plagiarists and impostors he published it in the form of an anagram, which, at the request of the Emperor Rudolph—a request probably inspired by Kepler—he interpreted; it ran thus: The farthest planet is triple.

Very soon after he found that Venus was changing from a full-moon to a half-moon appearance. He announced this also by an anagram, and waited till it should become a crescent, which it did. This was a dreadful blow to the anti-Copernicans, for it removed the last lingering difficulty to the reception of the Copernican doctrine. Copernicus had predicted, indeed, a hundred years before, that, if ever our powers of sight were sufficiently enhanced, Venus and Mercury would be seen to have phases like the moon. And now Galileo with his telescope verifies the prediction to the letter.

Here was a triumph for the grand old monk, and a bitter morsel for his opponents.

Castelli writes, "This must now convince the most obstinate." But Galileo, with more experience, replies: "You almost make me laugh by saying that these clear observations are sufficient to convince the most obstinate; it seems you have yet to learn that long ago the observations were enough to convince those who are capable of reasoning and those who wish to learn the truth; but that to convince the obstinate and those who care for nothing beyond the vain applause of the senseless vulgar, not even the testimony of the stars would suffice, were they to descend on earth to speak for themselves. Let us, then, endeavor to procure some knowledge for ourselves, and rest contented with this sole satisfaction; but of advancing in popular opinion, or of gaining the assent of the book-philosophers, let us abandon both the hope and the desire."

What a year's work it had been! In twelve months observational astronomy had made such a bound as it has never made before or since.[1] Why did not others make any of these observations? Because no one could make telescopes like Galileo. He gathered pupils round him, however, and taught them how to work the lenses, so that gradually these instruments penetrated Europe, and astronomers everywhere verified his splendid discoveries.

[1] The next year Galileo discovered also the spots upon the sun and estimated roughly its time of rotation.

BEGINNING OF BRITISH POWER IN INDIA

A.D. 1612

BECKLES WILLSON

By chartering the original English East India Company, Queen Elizabeth took the first step toward establishing that empire in the Orient which has since become such an important appanage of the British crown. This oldest English company in India is also called the "Mother Company" and the "John Company." It began English trade with India, and its operations prepared the way for British government in that vast country.

After the Portuguese discovery of the passage round Africa, toward the end of the fifteenth century, other European nations for some time appeared to recognize Portugal's exclusive claim to the navigation of that route. In 1510 the Portuguese made a permanent settlement in India at Goa. But during this century the Dutch obtained a foothold in the country, and in 1580 Portugal was conquered by Spain.

Dutch enterprise and the Spanish absorption of Portugal's Indian establishments aroused the commercial spirit of England. In 1599 an English association was formed, with a large fund, "for trade to the East Indies." In December, 1600, Queen Elizabeth granted this association a charter, incorporating the "Adventurers" under the title of "the Governor and Company of Merchants of London trading into the East Indies." The company was allowed unlimited rights of purchasing lands, and a fifteen years' monopoly of trade. In 1609 the charter was renewed and made perpetual by James I; but at first the company appears to have done no very extensive business. The beginning of its more active career, in the midst of grave difficulties and conflicts, is well described by Willson, whose history thus covers an important period in the development of India and in the expansion of British power.

WHEN the East India Company had been in existence eleven years it possessed hardly more than the rudiments of factories in the Indies, while the Dutch boasted fully a dozen regularly established trading-settlements, from most of which they had ejected the Spaniards and Portuguese.

France, no longer restrained by Spain and the Pope, naturally looked jealously on these efforts of Englishmen and Dutchmen to exploit the East to their own advantage. In 1609 we learn that the subjects of Henry IV, "who had long aspired to make themselves strong by sea," took the opportunity of a treaty made between James I and the French King to "set on foot this invention, a society to trade into the East Indies," with a capital of four million crowns. Becher, the English ambassador at Paris, wrote in 1609 to Lord Salisbury that Dutch seamen were being "engaged at great pay and many of their ships bought." The States-General strongly remonstrated against this proceeding, and threatened to "board the French ships wherever they found them, and hang all Flemings found in them." This threat appears to have been effectual, and the project was abandoned. A little later, in 1614, the French again projected taking part in the East India trade, and accounts were current in London concerning ships and patents from King Louis, but this, too, ended lamely and nothing practical was effected for full half a century.

The company always had before it the danger of attack by Spanish or Portuguese, and its captains and agents were put perpetually on their guard. But it never seems to have occurred to the court of committees that there was any danger to be apprehended from the Dutch, so that they were all the more astonished and chagrined at the failure to establish trade with the Moluccas, where the natives were so friendly to the English and offered them every facility, but, owing to Dutch oppression, in vain.

In the first voyage James Lancaster had established factories at Achin and Bantam. In the second voyage Sir Henry Middleton was instructed to endeavor to found a factory on the island of Banda. He carried on some trade, but neither he nor his successor in the third voyage, Captain Keeling, was able to override the opposition of the Dutch and secure a foothold. In the instructions issued to the last-named he was requested to establish, if possible, a factory at Aden, from whence he was to proceed to the Gulf of Cambay, seeking a good harbor there "for the maintenance of a trade in those parts hereafter in safety from the danger of the Portuguese, or other enemies, endeavoring also to learn whether the King of Cambay or Surat, or any of his havens, be in subjection to the Portuguese—and what havens of his are not?—together with the dangers and depths of the water, there for passage, that by this certain notice and diligent inquiry —which we wish to be set down in writing for the company's better information—whereby we may hereafter attempt further trade there, or otherwise desist."

In no fighting mood, therefore, was the company—whatever their servants' views—but prudently inclined to keep out of the way of the once terrible and still dreaded Portuguese. In vain, as we have seen, did Captain Hawkins exert himself to obtain concessions from the Grand Mogul which would survive the displeasure of his European rivals, who had by their ships, arms, and intrigues completely terrified the governors and petty rajahs of the coast.

In 1611 Anthony Hippon, in the Globe, sailed for the Coromandel (or Madras) coast with the object of setting a factory, if possible, at Pulicat, and sharing in the port-to-port trade which the Dutch had lately built up there. The idea seems to have originated with a couple of Dutchmen, named Floris and Antheunis, formerly in the Dutch service, who were charged with the management of the business. So far as Pulicat was concerned, the scheme failed, but the captain of the Globe, resolved to land his factory somewhere, lit upon Pettapoli, farther up the coast, where he arrived on August 18, 1611. This was the company's first settlement in the Bay of Bengal. But although the reception from the local governor and the King of Golconda was friendly, yet the place proved to be a deadly swamp and the trade was small.

When the landing of certain factors and merchandise had thus taken place at Pettapoli, Captain Hippon set sail farther northward to the ancient port of Masulipatam, which, forming "a coveted roadstead on the open coast line of Madras," was destined to be the theatre of much truculent rivalry between the European traders on the Coromandel coast. Here, on the last day of August, Hippon and Floris landed, and a factory was set up. A cargo of calicoes was duly obtained, whereupon the Globe departed for Bantam and the Far East to seek spices and pepper in exchange. Such were the beginnings of English trade on the east of the Indian peninsula. Two years later the company's servants received from the Hindu King of Vitayanagar a firman to build a fort, written on a leaf of gold—a document which was preserved at Madras until its capture by the French in the next century.

Following hard upon their summary dismissal from Surat, Middleton, Hawkins, and the rest, disinclined for their masters' sake to come to close quarters with the Dutch in the Spice Islands, directed their views to the establishment of a factory at Dabul. In this likewise they failed. In despair at not procuring a cargo, they went in for piracy and fierce retaliation upon the Turkish authorities for their treatment of them in the Red Sea. A couple of vessels hailing from Cochin were captured, and some cloves, cinnamon, wax, bales of china silk, and rice were taken out of them and removed to the ship Trade's Increase.

In the midst of a lively blockade of the Red Sea ports they were joined by Captain John Saris, with four ships, belonging to the company's eighth voyage, who agreed to lend his forces for whatever the combined fleets undertook, if granted a third of the profits for the benefit of his particular set of subscribers. All this anomalous confusion between the various interests within the same body corporate could have but one issue. The rival commanders took to quarrelling over the disposition of the hundred thousand pieces-of-eight which Middleton hoped to squeeze out of the Governor of Mocha for outrages upon the English fleet. Strife ran high between them, and in the end Saris in the Clove and Towerson in the Hector sailed away from the Red Sea, leaving Middleton and Downton to settle matters on their own account.

Powerless to obtain compensation from the Governor of Mocha, Middleton proceeded to make unceremonious levy on all the shipping he could lay his hands upon. On August 16th the Trade's Increase set sail, in company with the Peppercorn, for Tiku, where two others of the company's ships were anchored. Middleton very soon discovered that the Trade's Increase was in a leaky condition; he had hardly got her out of Tiku when she ran aground—for the second time in her brief history. She was floated and brought opposite Pulo Panzang, in Bantam Bay, where the cargo was taken out and stored on shore. The ship, which King James had christened and in which Sir Henry Middleton took such pride, was careened on the beach for repairs. During the process a renegade Spaniard formed a plot to burn her to the water's edge, and one night carried it successfully into execution—a catastrophe which is said to have so affected the doughty old commander, Sir Henry Middleton, that he sickened and died at Bantam, May 24, 1613.

The many exploits of Middleton, the *doyen* of the company's servants in the East, well deserve to be read: the hardships he had suffered, the difficulties he had to contend with, the jealous cabals of which he had been the victim. Among the many insubordinates that prevailed, Captain Nicholas Downton, one of the ablest commanders in the service, was not to be persuaded, despite the plots and schemes occasionally undertaken for that purpose, to abandon the respect and loyalty he owed the old sea-dog. Once, when in the Red Sea, Middleton wrote sharply to Downton for an alleged fault; the latter was filled "with admiration and grief."

"Sir," he replied, "I can write nothing so plain, nor with that sincerity, but malicious men, when they list, may make injurious construction; but evil come to me if I meant ill to Sir Henry Middleton or any part of the business. God be judge between him and me, if ever I deserved the least evil thought from him. I desire that he were so much himself that he would neither be led nor carried by any injurious person to abuse an inseparable friend."

Wholly ignorant of the fate reserved for Middleton and the "mightie merchantman," the Trade's Increase, Downton resumed command of the Peppercorn and returned direct to England with a full cargo. Many times her timbers sprang aleak on the voyage—for she was but a jerry-built craft at best—but she finally got into the harbor of Waterford, September 13, 1613. Here the rudest of rude welcomes awaited Downton. He was visited by the sheriff and arrested on a warrant from the Earl of Ormond, charged with committing piracy. But, for the present, the plots of his and Middleton's enemies miscarried; their victim was released, and in a few weeks' time was back in the Thames. Downton's proved zeal and endurance won him the applause and favor of the merchant adventurers, and the command of the first voyage under the joint-stock system in the following year.

Meanwhile, each year the company had been sending out

a small fleet of ships to the East; it was now beginning also to receive communications from its agents and factors, who, as we have seen, were being slowly distributed at various points east of Aden. Irregular as the receipt of these advices was, and incomplete and belated in themselves, they yet were a useful guide to the company in equipping its new ventures.

"We are in great hope to get good and peaceful trade at Cambay and Surat," writes Anthony Marlowe to the company from Socotra, "where our ship, by God's grace, is to ride. Our cloth and lead, we hear, will sell well there; our iron not so well as at Aden; that indigo we shall have good store at reasonable rates; and also calicoes and musk, and at Dabul good pepper; so as I hope in God the Hector shall make her voyage at those places and establish a trade there, to the benefit of your worships and the good of our country."

For Captain Keeling, Marlowe has many words of praise. "His wisdom, language, and carriage are such as I fear we shall have great want of at Surat in the first settling of our trade." Of some of the other servants of the company Marlowe is not so enthusiastic, and he does not spare his opinion of their characters. In a subsequent letter we are brought right face to face with a very pretty quarrel between Hippon, the master of the Dragon, and his mate, William Tavernour, in which Hawkins tries to act as peacemaker, but is foiled by the bloodthirsty Matthew Mullinux, master of the Hector, who had himself a private grudge against the said Tavernour, or, as is written here, "a poniard in pickle for the space of six months."

"And not contented with this (he) afterward came up upon the deck and there before the boatswain and certain of us did most unchristianlike speak these words: that if he might but live to have the opportunity to kill the said Tavernour he would think it to be the happiest day that ever he saw in his life, an it were but with a knife."

There seems to have been a surfeit of these internecine brawls for some time to come, and, indeed, stories of dissensions among the servants of the company in the East are plentifully sprinkled throughout its history, both in this century and the next. Of hints for trade the company's agents are profuse in this growing correspondence.

"There is an excellent linen," writes one of them, "made at Cape Comorin, and may be brought hither from Cochin in great abundance if the Portugals would be quiet men. It is about two yards broad or better and very strong cloth, and is called *cachade Comoree.* It would certainly sell well in England for sheeting." Here we see the genesis of the calico trade.

The company is informed that "if Moorish girdles, Turks, and cloaks will yield any profit, I pray give advice. They are here in abundance and the great chief merchandise. There is also a market for cloth of all kinds of light and pleasing colors, pleasing to the eye, as Venice reds, stamels, some few scarlets for presents, and also to sell to great men, popinjay greens of the brightest dye, cinnamon colors, light dove colors, peach colors, silver colors, light yellows with others like, but no dark or sad colors, for here they are not vendible. Those of the last voyage are yet upon our hands and will not be sold for the monies that they cost in England." Thenceforward, it is to be supposed, the company bought no more of the "suitings of the Puritans," then growing to be the vogue at home.

"Of new drinking-glasses, trenchers for sweetmeats, but especially looking-glasses of all sorts and different prices—but not small baubles—some reasonable quantity would be sold to good profit, and I verily suppose that some fair large looking-glass would be highly accepted of this King, for he affects not the value in anything, but rarity in everything, insomuch that some pretty new-fangled toys would give him high content, though their value were small, for he wants no worldly wealth or riches, possessing an inestimable treasury, and is, it is thought, herein far exceeding the Great Turk."

Throughout all their reports and epistles the captains and factors appear above all anxious to establish themselves on the mainland, and express much indignation at the conduct of Macarab Khan, the Mogul's vizier, at his juggling with their hopes.

"If it please God we attain Surat," sighs one of the factors, "how comfortable it will be to those there, beneficial to the trade, and commodious to your worship." Jostled aside, tormented by the Dutch in the eastern archipelago and by the Turks in the Red Sea, what wonder that the company and its servants now longed to displace the Portuguese in India itself?

At home the company had despatched, in 1612, as its tenth expedition, three vessels. They comprised the stout old Dragon, commanded by Captain Thomas Best; the Solomon, alias the James, and the Hoseander. Was the new effort of Best and Kerridge, one of his supercargoes, to establish a factory at Surat to be more successful than that of Middleton in 1610?

While the Solomon was forthwith ordered elsewhere in search of trade, Best, with the other two vessels, reached Swally, near the mouth of the Surat River, early in the month of September, 1612. Here Kerridge, disembarking with several companions, was well received by the native merchants and inhabitants, although gaining the disapprobation of the Portuguese. He obtained permission to land some broadcloths, lead, iron, and quicksilver, procuring in exchange for these such Surat merchandise as the company had recommended him to acquire as suitable for the purchase of pepper and spices at Achin and Bantam.

In the midst of these agreeable transactions the Portuguese swept down upon the company's men, with four ships, mounting one hundred twenty-four guns, besides a large flotilla of small native galleys. As they advanced, thinking to cut him off and board him, Captain Best perceived, with the intuition of the trained mariner, the weakness of their formation. He called out to Captain Pettie, of the Hoseander, to follow him, and, singling out the two largest of the Portuguese vessels, prepared to dash straight for them, his gunners, half naked, standing ready and alert for the word of command which should begin the fray.

But to Best's confusion the Hoseander budged not a rod, being gripped fast by her anchors. In this predicament there was nothing for it. Best must close with the enemy single-handed. Placing his Red Dragon between the Portuguese admiral and vice-admiral, the company's commander gave orders to the gunners, and the battle commenced by the firing of a double broadside, which "well peppered" the enemy, who responded by splintering the Englishman's mainmast and sinking his long-boat.

"Having exchanged some forty great shot of each side," reports an eye-witness of the battle to the company, "the night being come they anchored in sight of each other, and the next morning our ships weighed again and began their fight again, which continued some three hours, in which time they drove three of their galleons on the sands. And so our ships came to anchor, and in the afternoon weighed anchor, in which time the flood being come the galleons, with the help of the frigates, were afloat again."

Yet there was to be more and fiercer fighting against even greater odds before the Portuguese had had their fill of the English off Swally. After an attempt on their part to set fire to the Hoseander by means of a fire-ship, which utterly failed, and cost the Portuguese a hundred lives, the company's ships sailed away on December 1st, thinking to draw the enemy after them. But not succeeding in this, Best anchored at Moha to await their pleasure. It was not until December 22d that the enemy bore up, having been strengthened by ships and men from Diu. The shores were lined with spectators to see Best gallantly front them with his two ships' colors flying.

This time it seemed as if Best and his men were doomed, yet to the astonishment, not merely of the natives and Portuguese, but of the company's servants themselves, they were victorious in this engagement. On the following day, at the close of another battle, the enemy, dazed and staggering from so much fighting and bloodshed, abruptly turned and fled, trailing their wrecked flotilla behind them. Nothing can convey a better idea of the overwhelming superiority of the company gunners and ordnance, as well as of the matchless audacity of their onslaught, than the fact of their having lost but three slain, while the Portuguese list of killed was upward of three hundred. Not only this, but Best's two ships were still in good condition.

On December 27th the Dragon and the Hoseander returned triumphantly to Surat, where a number of the company's factors and supercargoes were, as may be imagined, anxiously awaiting them. It was felt by most, on hearing the good news, that the promised firman of the Great Mogul would not be long delayed; but Best, worn out with fighting, was by no means so sanguine, and ordered Aldworth and the other factors to repair on board the fleet at once, with such merchandise as they had. But Aldworth, even after most of the others had given in to the "General's" views, insisted that Best's victory over the Portuguese had removed the opposition of the Mogul, who would surely despatch his firman. This was corroborated by Kerridge, who had gone to Agra to deliver a letter from King James to the Mogul. But Best had no relish for Aldworth's stubbornness, as he called it, and summoned a council "and so required the said Thomas Aldworth to come on board, which he again refused to do, for that he heard certainly the firman was coming."

Aldworth's confidence was rewarded, for just as Best was about to depart, Jehangir's decree, granting the company a factory at Surat and at three other places about the Gulf of Cambay, arrived bearing joy to the bosoms of the English traders.

At Agra, it appeared from Kerridge's account, he had been admitted to the monarch's chamber, where Jehangir "sat on his bed, newly risen from sleep." In his first letters Kerridge complains of a chilly reception and attributes it to his coming empty-handed. "No other treatment," he says, "is to be expected without continual gifts both to the King and others."

The character of Jehangir was described by Kerridge as "extremely proud and covetous," taking himself "to be the greatest monarch in the world," yet a "drunkard" and "given over to vice." The Mogul, however, was very fond of music, and revelled in Robert Trulley's cornet, though virginals were not esteemed, "perhaps because the player was not sufficiently expert," and "it is thought Lawes died with conceit at the King's indifference." Nevertheless, on the whole, Jehangir behaved civilly to the company's envoy, whose success in obtaining an audience was quickly followed up by Aldworth in sending William Edwards, who took with him from Surat "great presents," including portraits of King James and his Queen, and "one that will content the Mogul above all, the picture of Tamberlane, from whence he derives himself." At last, then, the coveted firman "for kind usage of the English, free trade, and so forth," was gained, Edwards remaining in Agra as "lieger" or ambassador, "which will be needful among this inconstant people."

By the terms of the firman a duty on imports of 3½ per cent. was to be exacted; but on the other hand no damages were to be claimed for Sir Henry Middleton's piratical exploits, and the company's factories were to be protected by law in event of any calamity overtaking its servants.

To Aldworth undoubtedly belongs the credit of having negotiated this concession, but it is doubtful if it would ever have received the imperial sanction had it not been for Best's victory. Even when he had the document in his hands the conqueror was diffident, and could hardly believe the good news. He was "doubtful whether it was the King's firman or not, and, being resolved, would not receive it until some of the chiefs of the city should bring it down unto him to Swally, which in fine they did. And the very day following the receipt of it, being the 4th, the galleons were again in sight, but came not near to proffer fight. Notwithstanding, the general resolved not to make any longer stay there, but took in such goods as were ready, and landed the rest of the cloth, quicksilver, and vermilion, all the elephants' teeth, and some twelve hundred bars of lead, carrying the rest along with him, as also all the pieces-of-eight and iron, and so, the 18th present, departed."

In such manner did the company gain at last a certain foothold in the Mogul empire. The factors stationed at the new post reported that Surat was the best situation in India to vend English goods, particularly broadcloths, kerseys, quicksilver, lead, and vermilion, to be exchanged for indigo, calicoes, cotton yarn, and drugs, and added a list of such goods as might annually be disposed of there. They requested the merchant adventurers in London to send them some four thousand pieces of broadcloth, sword-blades, knives, and looking-glasses. They hinted that toys and English bull-dogs should be sent as presents. But the new trade, they were careful to explain, could only be protected by stationing five or six ships in the river at Surat to defend the factory and its occupants against the Portuguese.

On his return home Best was summoned to Philport lane to give a detailed account of his exploits, and was considered by the court to have "deserved extraordinarily well." Yet his "great private trade," whereby he had enriched himself, caused some dissatisfaction, and the governor, Sir Thomas Smythe, while admitting that no one could be a fitter commander than Best, thought that "Captain Keeling was far before him for merchandise, and so should command at Surat." But this did not satisfy the victor of Swally. Unless he were allowed private trade he refused to make another voyage for the company, and finally insisted on an investigation into his conduct. The upshot was that the company was "content to remit all that is past and let these things die, which should not have been ripped up had he not called them in question himself."

The various inconveniences to the company from the separate classes of adventurers being enabled to fit out equipments on their own particular portions of stock, finally evoked a change in the constitution of the company. In 1612 it was resolved that in future the trade should be carried on by means of a joint stock only, and on the basis of this resolution the then prodigious sum of four hundred twenty-nine thousand pounds was subscribed. Although portions of this capital were applied to the fitting out of four voyages, the general instructions to the commanders were given in the name and by the authority of the governor, deputy governor, and committees of the Company of Merchants of London trading to the East Indies.

The whole commerce of the company was now a joint concern, and the embarrassing principle of trading on separate ventures came to an end. Experience had amply demonstrated that detached equipments exposed the whole trade to danger in the East, in their efforts to establish trade. The first twelve voyages were, therefore, regarded in the light of an experiment to establish a solid commerce between England and India.

Upon such terms the period known as the first joint stock was entered upon, which comprised four voyages between the years 1613 and 1616. The purchase, repair, and equipment of vessels during these four years amounted to two hundred seventy-two thousand five hundred forty-four pounds, which, with the stock and cargoes, made up the total sum raised among the members at the beginning of the period, viz., four hundred twenty-nine thousand pounds.

Under this new system Captain Downton was given command of the fleet, in the company's merchantmen, the New Year's Gift, thus named because it had been launched on January 1st—an armed ship of five hundred fifty tons—and three other vessels. Downton went equipped with legal as well as military implements. King James made him master of the lives of the crews, and empowered him to use martial law in cases of insubordination.

"We are not ignorant," said the monarch, in the royal commission which he vouchsafed to the company's commander, "of the emulation and envy which doth accompany the discovery of countries and trade, and of the quarrels and contentions which do many times fall out between the subjects of divers princes when they meet the one with the other in foreign and far remote countries in prosecuting the course of their discoveries." Consequently Captain Downton was warned not to stir up bad blood among the nations, but if he should be by the company's rivals unjustly provoked he was at liberty to retaliate, but not to keep to himself any spoils he might take, which were to be rendered account of, as by ancient usage, to the King.

Before Downton could reach his destination, the chief energies of the company's agents in India appear to have been bent upon forming a series of exchanges between the west coast and the factory at Bantam. The little band of servants at the new factory at Surat, headed by the redoubtable Aldworth, gave it as their opinion not only that sales of English goods could be effected at this port, but that they might be pushed to the inland markets and the adjoining seaports. Aldworth stated that in his journey to Ahmedabad he had passed through the cities of Baroche and Baroda, and had discovered that cotton, yarn and "baftees" could be bought cheaper from the manufacturers in that country than at Surat. At Ahmedabad he was able to buy indigo at a low rate, but in order to establish such a trade capital of from twelve to fifteen thousand pounds was required to be constantly in the hands of the factor. It was thought at Surat that it would be expedient to fix a resident at the Mogul's court at Agra to solicit the protection of that monarch and his ministers.

Downton arrived at Surat, October 15, 1614, to find the attitude of the Portuguese toward the English more than ever hostile. At the same time trouble impended between the Portuguese and the Nawab of Surat. In order to demolish all opposition at one blow, the former collected their total naval force at Goa for a descent upon both natives and new-comers at Surat. Their force consisted of six large galleons, several smaller vessels, and sixty native barges, or "frigates" as they were called, the whole carrying a hundred thirty-four guns and manned by twenty-six hundred Europeans and six thousand natives. To meet this fleet, Downton had but his four ships, and three or four Indian-built vessels called "galivats," manned altogether with less than six hundred men. The appearance of the Portuguese was the signal for fright and submission on the part of the Nawab; but his suit was contemptuously spurned by the Viceroy of Goa, who, on January 20th, advanced upon the company's little fleet. He did not attempt to force the northern entrance of Swally Hole, where the English lay, which would have necessitated an approach singly, but sent on a squadron of the native "frigates" to cross the shoal, surround and attack the Hope, the smallest of the English ships, and board her. But in this they were foiled after a severe conflict. Numbers of the boarders were slain and drowned, and their frigates burned to the water's edge. Again and again during the ensuing three weeks did the Portuguese make efforts to dislodge the English; but the dangerous fire-ships they launched were evaded by night and their onslaught repulsed by day, and so at length, with a loss of five hundred men, the Portuguese viceroy, on February 13th, withdrew.

His withdrawal marked a triumph for the company's men. Downton was received in state by the overjoyed Nawab, who presented him with his own sword, "the hilt of massive gold, and in lieu thereof," says Downton, "I returned him my suit, being sword, dagger, girdle, and hangers, by me much esteemed of, and which made a great deal better show, though of less value."

A week later Downton set out with his great fleet for Bantam. Just off the coast the enemy's fleet was again sighted approaching from the west. For three days the English were in momentary apprehension of an attack, but the Viceroy thought better of it, and on the 6th "bore up with the shore and gave over the hopes of their fortunes by further following of us."

DUTCH SETTLEMENT OF NEW YORK

A.D. 1614

DAVID T. VALENTINE

Greater fame ordinarily attaches to the discovery of some vast region of the earth than to the finding or exploring of a limited coast, district, or river-course. There are, however, some instances in which geographical conditions or historical developments magnify the seemingly lesser achievements. This has been the case with Henry Hudson's timely exploration of the river called after him.

The enterprising Dutch people, under whose auspices he accomplished this brilliant feat, had just emerged from their long contest with Spain. The return of peace to the Netherlands found many active spirits in readiness for fresh adventures, and Hudson's work opened for them a new and inviting field.

Increasing celebrity gathered about the name of Hudson from the very first settlements in the remarkable region which he made known to the world, and which was destined to become the seat of the world's second—perhaps of its greatest—metropolis, and the home of an imperial commonwealth. The simple beginnings of this mighty growth are as simply but quite adequately told in the following pages from the historian of New York city.

HAVING explored the river which bears his name, Hudson put to sea on October 4th, making directly for Europe, with news of his discovery of this fine river and its adjacent country, which he described as offering every inducement for settlers or traders that could be desired.

Besides the fertility or the soil, which was satisfactorily shown by the great abundance of grain and vegetables found in the possession of the Indians, a still more enticing prospect was held out to the view of the merchant, in the abundance of valuable furs observed in the country, which were to be had at a very little cost.

Hudson had, therefore, scarcely made publicly known the character of the country visited by him when several merchants of Amsterdam fitted out trading-vessels and despatched them to this river. Their returns were highly satisfactory, and arrangements were immediately made to establish a settled agency here to superintend the collection of the furs and the trade with the Indians while the ships should be on their long journey between the two hemispheres. The agents thus employed pitched their cabins on the south point of Manhattan Island, the head man being Hendrick Corstiaensen, who was still the chief of the settlement in 1614, at which period an English ship sailing along the coast from Virginia entered the harbor on a visit of observation. Finding Corstiaensen here, with his company of traders, the English captain summoned him to acknowledge the jurisdiction of Virginia over the country or else to depart. The former alternative was chosen by the trader, and he agreed to pay a small tribute to the Governor of Virginia in token of his right of dominion. The Dutch were thereupon left to prosecute their trade without further molestation.

The government of Holland did not, however, recognize the claims of England to jurisdiction over the whole American coast, and took measures to encourage the discovery and appropriation of additional territory, by a decree giving to discoverers of new countries the exclusive privilege of trading thither for four successive voyages, to the exclusion of all other persons. This enactment induced several merchants to fit out five small ships for coasting along the American shores in this vicinity. One of these vessels, commanded by Captain Block, soon after its arrival on the coast, was accidentally destroyed by fire. Block immediately began the construction of another, of thirty-eight-feet keel, forty-four and a half feet on deck, and eleven and a half feet beam, which was the first vessel launched in the waters of New York. She was called the Unrest, or Restless, and ploughed her keel through the waters of Hell Gate and the Sound, the pioneer of all other vessels except the bark canoes of the aboriginal inhabitants.

The several ships despatched on this exploring expedition having returned to Holland, from their journals and surveys a map of a large extent of country was made, over which the Dutch claimed jurisdiction, and to which they gave the name of "New Netherlands." The owners of these vessels, as the reward of their enterprise, were granted the promised monopoly of trade hither for four voyages, to be completed within three years, commencing on January 1, 1615.

These merchants seemed to have been composed in part of those who had established the first trading-post here, but having increased their number and capital, and enlarged their former designs of trade, formed themselves into a company under the name of the "United New Netherlands Company." Corstiaensen was continued the principal agent here, and they likewise established a post at the head of the river, on an island opposite the present site of Albany. Forts, of a rude description—being merely enclosures of high palisades—were erected at both places.

The privileges granted to the United New Netherlands Company being, however, limited in respect to time, their establishment on this island can hardly be considered as a permanent settlement; the cabins of the settlers were nearly of equal rudeness with those of their Indian neighbors; and but few of the luxuries of civilization found their way into their habitations. The great object of the settlement was, however, successfully carried on, and stores of furs were in readiness to freight the ships on their periodical visits from the fatherland. No interruption of the friendly intercourse carried on with the Indians took place, but, on the contrary, the whites were abundantly supplied by the natives with food and most other necessaries of life, without personal labor and at trifling cost.

The Indian tribes in the neighborhood of this trading-post were the Manhattans, occupying this island; the Pachamies, the Tankiteks, and the Wickqueskeeks, occupying the country on the east side of Hudson River south of the Highlands; the Hackingsacks and the Raritans on the west side of the river and the Jersey shore; the Canarsees, the Rockways, the Merrikokes, the Marsapeagues, the Mattinecocks, the Nissaquages, the Corchaugs, the Secataugs, and the Shinecocks on Long Island.

The trade of this colony of settlers was sufficiently profitable to render its permanency desirable to the United New Netherlands Company, as it is found that at the termination of their grant, in the year 1618, they endeavored to procure from the government in Holland an extension of their term, but did not succeed in obtaining more than a special license, expiring yearly, which they held for two or three subsequent years.

In the mean time a more extensive association had been formed among the merchants and capitalists in Holland, which in the year 1621, having matured its plans and projects, received a charter under the title of the West India Company. Their charter gave them the exclusive privilege of trade on the whole American coast, both of the northern and southern continents, so far as the jurisdiction of Holland extended.

This great company was invested with most of the functions of a distinct and separate government. It was allowed to appoint governors and other officers; to settle the forms of administering justice; to make Indian treaties and to enact laws.

Having completed arrangements for the organization of its government in New Netherlands, the West India Company despatched its pioneer vessel hither in the year 1623. This was the ship New Netherlands, a stanch vessel, which continued her voyages to this port as a regular packet for more than thirty years subsequently. On board the New Netherlands were thirty families to begin the colony. This colony being designed for a settlement at the head of the river, the vessel landed her passengers and freight near the present site of Albany, where a settlement was established. The return cargo of the New Netherlands was five hundred otter-skins, one thousand five hundred beavers, and other freight valued at about twelve thousand dollars.

It having been determined that the head-quarters of the company's establishment in New Netherlands should be fixed on Manhattan Island, preparations for a more extensive colony to be planted here were made, and in 1625 two ships cleared from Holland for this place. On board of these vessels were shipped one hundred three head of cattle, together with stallions, mares, hogs, and sheep in a proportionate number. Accompanying these were a considerable number of settlers, with their families, supplied with agricultural implements and seed for planting, household furniture, and the other necessaries for establishing the colony. Other ships followed with similar freight, and the number of emigrants amounted to about two hundred souls.

On the arrival of the ships in the harbor the cattle were landed in the first instance on the island now called Governor's Island, where they were left on pasturage until convenient arrangements could be made on the mainland to prevent their straying in the woods. The want of water, however, compelled their speedy transfer to Manhattan Island, where, being put on the fresh grass, they generally throve well, although about twenty died, in the course of the season, from eating some poisonous vegetable.

The settlers commenced their town by staking out a fort on the south point of the island, under the direction of one Kryn Frederick, an engineer sent along with them for that purpose; and a horse-mill having been erected, the second story of that building was so constructed as to afford accommodations for the congregation for religious purposes. The habitations of the settlers were of the simplest construction, little better, indeed, than those of their predecessors. A director-general had been sent to superintend the interests of the company in this country, in the person of Peter Minuit, who, in the year 1626, purchased Manhattan Island from the Indian proprietors for the sum of sixty guilders, or twenty-four dollars, by which the title to the whole island, containing about twenty-two thousand acres, became vested in the West India Company.

The success of the company proved itself, for a short period, by the rise in the value of its stock, which soon stood at a high premium in Holland. Various interests, however, were at work in the company to turn its advantages to individual account, and in 1628 an act was passed under the title of "Freedoms and Exemptions granted to all such as shall plant Colonies in New Netherlands." This edict gave, to such persons as should send over a colony of fifty souls above fifteen years old, the title of "patroons," and the privileges of selecting any land, except on the island of Manhattan, for a distance of eight miles on each side of any river, and so far inland as should be thought convenient; the company stipulating, however, that all the products of the plantations thus established should be first brought to the Manhattans, before being sent elsewhere, for trade. They also reserved to themselves the sole trade with the Indians for peltries in all places where they had an agency established.

With respect to such private persons as should emigrate at

their own expense, they were allowed as much land as they could properly improve, upon satisfying the Indians therefor.

These privileges gave an impetus to emigration, and assisted, in a great degree, in permanently establishing the settlement of the country. But from this era commenced the decay of the profits of the company, as with all its vigilance it could not restrain the inhabitants from surreptitiously engaging in the Indian trade, and drawing thence a profit which would otherwise have gone into the public treasury.

HARVEY DISCOVERS THE CIRCULATION OF THE BLOOD

A.D. 1616

THOMAS H. HUXLEY

Contemporary with Galileo, and ranking but little below him in influence upon the modern world, was William Harvey. Harvey's discovery of the circulation of the blood, combined with the truly scientific methods by which he reached, and afterward proved, his great result, has placed his name high on the roll of science. Not only does his work stand at the foundation of modern anatomy and medicine, but it has given him place in the ranks of great philosophers as well. Huxley, himself so long and justly renowned in modern science, rises to enthusiasm in the following account of his mighty predecessor.

Harvey was born at Folkestone, England, in 1578, and lived till 1657. He was educated as a physician, studying at Padua in Italy, and was early appointed a lecturer in the London College of Physicians. In his lectures, somewhere about the year 1616 or a little later, he began to explain his new doctrine to his students; but it was not until the publication of his book *Exercitatio Anatomica de Motu Cordis et Sanguinis*, in 1628, that the theory spread beyond his immediate circle.

Huxley's account will perhaps give a clearer idea of Harvey's relation to his predecessors and contemporaries, and of the value of his services to mankind, than would a far longer biography of the great physician, physiologist, and anatomist.

MANY opinions have been held respecting the exact nature and value of Harvey's contributions to the elucidation of the fundamental problem of the physiology of the higher animals; from those which deny him any merit at all—indeed, roundly charge him with the demerit of plagiarism—to those which enthrone him in a position of supreme honor among great discoverers in science. Nor has there been less controversy as to the method by which Harvey obtained the results which have made his name famous. I think it is desirable that no obscurity should hang around these questions; and I add my mite to the store of disquisitions on Harvey, in the hope that it may help to throw light upon several points about which darkness has accumulated, partly by accident and partly by design.

About the year B.C. 300 a great discovery, that of the valves of the heart, was made by Erasistratus. This anatomist found, around the opening by which the vena cava communicates with the right ventricle, three triangular membranous folds, disposed in such a manner as to allow any fluid contained in the vein to pass into the ventricle, but not back again. The opening of the vena arteriosa into the right ventricle is quite distinct from that of the vena cava; and Erasistratus observed that it is provided with three pouch-like, half-moon-shaped valves; the arrangement of which is such that a fluid can pass out of the ventricle into the vena arteriosa, but not back again. Three similar valves were found at the opening of the aorta into the left ventricle. The arteria venosa had a distinct opening into the same ventricle, and this was provided with triangular membranous valves, like those on the right side, but only two in number. Thus the ventricles had four openings, two for each; and there were altogether eleven valves, disposed in such a manner as to permit fluids to enter the ventricles from the vena cava and the arteria venosa respectively, and to pass out of the ventricles by the vena arteriosa and the aorta respectively, but not to go the other way.

It followed from this capital discovery that, if the contents of the heart are fluid, and if they move at all, they can only move in one way; namely, from the vena cava, through the ventricle, and toward the lungs, by the vena arteriosa, on the right side; and, from the lungs, by way of the arteria venosa, through the ventricle, and out by the aorta for distribution in the body, on the left side.

Erasistratus thus, in a manner, laid the foundations of the theory of the motion of the blood. But it was not given to him to get any further. What the contents of the heart were, and whether they moved or not, was a point which could be determined only by experiment. And, for want of sufficiently careful experimentation, Erasistratus strayed into a hopelessly misleading path. Observing that the arteries are usually empty of blood after death, he adopted the unlucky hypothesis that this is their normal condition, and that during life they are filled with air. And it will be observed that it is not improbable that Erasistratus' discovery of the valves of the heart and of their mechanical action strengthened him in this view. For, as the arteria venosa branches out in the lungs, what more likely than that its ultimate ramifications absorb the air which is inspired; and that this air, passing into the left ventricle, is then pumped all over the body through the aorta, in order to supply the vivifying principle which evidently resides in the air; or, it may be, of cooling the too great heat of the blood? How easy to explain the elastic bounding feel of a pulsating artery by the hypothesis that it is full of air! Had Erasistratus only been acquainted with the structure of insects, the analogy of their tracheal system would have been a tower of strength to him. There was no *prima-facie* absurdity in his hypothesis—and experiment was the sole means of demonstrating its truth or falsity.

More than four hundred years elapsed before the theory of the motion of the blood returned once more to the strait road which leads truthward; and it was brought back by the only possible method, that of experiment. A man of extraordinary genius, Claudius Galenus, of Pergamus, was trained to anatomical and physiological investigation in the great schools of Alexandria, and spent a long life in incessant research, teaching, and medical practice. More than one hundred fifty treatises from his pen, on philosophical, literary, scientific, and practical topics, are extant; and there is reason to believe that they constitute not more than a third of his works. No former anatomist had reached his excellence, while he may be regarded as the founder of experimental physiology. And it is precisely because he was a master of the experimental method that he was able to learn more about the motions of the heart and of the blood than any of his predecessors, and to leave to posterity a legacy of knowledge which was not substantially increased for more than thirteen hundred years.

The conceptions of the structures of the heart and vessels, of their actions, and of the motion of the blood in them, which Galen entertained, are not stated in a complete shape in any one of his numerous works. But a careful collation of the various passages in which these conceptions are expressed leaves no doubt upon my mind that Galen's views respecting the structure of the organs concerned were, for the most part, as accurate as the means of anatomical analysis at his command permitted; and that he had exact and consistent, though by no means equally just, notions of the actions of these organs and of the movements of the blood.

Starting from the fundamental facts established by Erasistratus respecting the structure of the heart and the working of its valves, Galen's great service was the proof, by the only evidence which could possess demonstrative value; namely, by that derived from experiments upon living animals, that the arteries are as much full of blood during life as the veins are, and that the left cavity of the heart, like the right, is also filled with blood.

Galen, moreover, correctly asserted—though the means of investigation at his disposition did not allow him to prove the fact—that the ramifications of the vena arteriosa in the substance of the lungs communicate with those of the arteria venosa, by direct, though invisible, passages, which he terms anastomoses; and that, by means of these communications, a certain portion of the blood of the right ventricle of the heart passes through the lungs into the left ventricle. In fact, Galen is quite clear as to the existence of a current of blood through the lungs, though not of such a current as we now know traverses them. For, while he believed that a part of the blood of the right ventricle passes through the lungs, and even, as I shall show, described at length the mechanical arrangements by which he supposes this passage to be effected, he considered that the greater part of the blood in the right ventricle passes directly, through certain pores in the septum, into the left ventricle. And this was where Galen got upon his wrong track, without which divergence a man of his scientific insight must infallibly have discovered the true character of the pulmonary current, and not improbably have been led to anticipate Harvey.

The best evidence of the state of knowledge respecting the motions of the heart and blood in Harvey's time is afforded by those works of his contemporaries which immediately preceded the publication of the *Exercitatio Anatomica*, in 1628. And none can be more fitly cited for this purpose than the *de Humani Corporis Fabrica*, Book X, of Adrian van den Spieghel, who, like Harvey, was a pupil of Fabricius of Aquapendente, and was of such distinguished ability and learning that he succeeded his master in the chair of anatomy of Padua.

Van den Spieghel, or Spigelius, as he called himself in accordance with the fashion of those days, died comparatively young, in 1625, and his work was edited by his friend Daniel Bucretius, whose preface is dated 1627. The accounts of the heart and vessels, and of the motion of the blood, which it contains, are full and clear; but, beyond matters of detail, they go beyond Galen in only two points; and with respect to one of these, Spigelius was in error.

The first point is the "pulmonary circulation," which is taught as Realdus Columbus taught it nearly eighty years before. The second point is, so far as I know, peculiar to Spigelius himself. He thinks that the pulsation of the arteries has an effect in promoting the motion of the blood contained in the veins which accompany them. Of the true course of the blood as a whole, Spigelius has no more suspicion than had any other physiologist of that age, except William Harvey; no rumor of whose lectures at the College of Physicians, commenced six years before Spieghel's death, was likely in those days of slow communication and in the absence of periodical publications to have reached Italy.

Now, let anyone familiar with the pages of Spigelius take up Harvey's treatise and mark the contrast.

The main object of the *Exercitatio* is to put forth and demonstrate by direct experimental and other accessory evidence a proposition which is far from being hinted at either by Spigelius or by any of his contemporaries or predecessors, and which is in diametrical contradiction to the views respecting the course of the blood in the veins which are expounded in their works.

From Galen to Spigelius, they one and all believed that the blood in the vena cava and its branches flows from the main trunk toward the smaller ramifications. There is a similar consensus in the doctrine that the greater part, if not the whole, of the blood thus distributed by the veins is derived from the liver; in which organ it is generated out of the materials brought from the alimentary canal by means of the vena portæ. And all Harvey's predecessors further agree in the belief that only a small fraction of the total mass of the venous blood is conveyed by the vena arteriosa to the lungs and passes by the arteria venosa to the left ventricle, thence to be distributed over the body by the arteries. Whether some portion of the refined and "pneumatic" arterial blood traversed the anastomotic channels, the existence of which was assumed, and so reached the systemic veins, or whether, on the contrary, some portion of the venous blood made its entrance by the same passages into the arteries, depended upon circumstances. Sometimes the current might set one way, sometimes the other.

In direct opposition to these universally received views Harvey asserts that the natural course of the blood in the veins is from the peripheral ramifications toward the main trunk; that the mass of the blood to be found in the veins at any moment was a short time before contained in the arteries, and has simply flowed out of the latter into the veins; and, finally, that the stream of blood which runs from the arteries into the veins is constant, continuous, and rapid.

According to the view of Harvey's predecessors, the veins may be compared to larger and smaller canals, fed by a spring which trickles into the chief canals, whence the water flows to the rest. The heart and lungs represent an engine set up in the principal canal to aerate some of the water and scatter it all over the garden. Whether any of this identical water came back to the engine or not would be a matter of chance, and it would certainly have no sensible effect on the motion of the water in the canals. In Harvey's conception of the matter, on the other hand, the garden is watered by channels so arranged as to form a circle, two points of which are occupied by propulsive engines. The water is kept moving in a continual round within its channels, as much entering the engines on one side as leaves them on the other; and the motion of the water is entirely due to the engines.

It is in conceiving the motion of the blood, as a whole, to be circular, and in ascribing that circular motion simply and solely to the contractions of the walls of the heart, that Harvey is so completely original. Before him, no one, that I can discover, had ever so much as dreamed that a given portion of blood, contained, for example, in the right ventricle of the heart, may, by the mere mechanical operation of the working of that organ, be made to return to the very place from which it started, after a long journey through the lungs and through the body generally. And it should be remembered that it is to this complete circuit of the blood alone that the term "circulation" can, in strictness, be applied. It is of the essence of a circular motion that that which moves returns to the place from whence it started. Hence the discovery of the course of the blood from the right ventricle, through the lungs, to the left ventricle was in no wise an anticipation of the discovery of the circulation of the blood. For the blood which traverses this part of its course no more describes a circle than the dweller in a street who goes out of his own house and enters his next-door neighbor's does so. Although there may be nothing but a party wall between him and the room he has just left, it constitutes an efficient *défense de circuler*. Thus, whatever they may have known of the so-called pulmonary circulation, to say that Servetus or Columbus or Cæsalpinus deserves any share of the credit which attaches to Harvey appears to me to be to mistake the question at issue.

It must further be borne in mind that the determination of the true course taken by the whole mass of the blood is only the most conspicuous of the discoveries of Harvey; and that his analysis of the mechanism by which the circulation is brought about is far in advance of anything which had previously been published. For the first time it is shown that the walls of the heart are active only during its systole or contraction, and that the dilatation of the heart, in the diastole, is purely passive. Whence it follows that the impulse by which the blood is propelled is a *vis à tergo*, and that the blood is not drawn into the heart by any such inhalent or suctorial action as not only the predecessors, but many of the successors, of Harvey imagined it to possess.

Harvey is no less original in his view of the cause of the arterial pulse. In contravention of Galen and of all other anatomists up to his own time, he affirms that the stretching of the arteries which gives rise to the pulse is not due to the active dilatation of their walls, but to their passive distention by the blood which is forced into them at each beat of the heart; reversing Galen's dictum, he says that they dilate as bags and not as bellows. This point of fundamental, practical as well as theoretical, importance is most admirably demonstrated, not only by experiment, but by pathological illustrations.

One of the weightiest arguments in Harvey's demonstration of the circulation is based upon the comparison of the quantity of blood driven out of the heart, at each beat, with the total quantity of blood in the body. This, so far as I know, is the first time that quantitative considerations are taken into account in the discussion of a physiological problem. But one of the most striking differences between ancient and modern physiological science, and one of the chief reasons of the rapid progress of physiology in the last half-century, lies in the introduction of exact quantitative determinations into physiological experimentation and observation. The moderns use means of accurate measurement which their forefathers neither possessed nor could conceive, inasmuch as they are products of mechanical skill of the last hundred years, and of the advance of branches of science which hardly existed, even in germ, in the seventeenth century.

Having attained to a knowledge of the circulation of the blood, and of the conditions on which its motion depends, Harvey had a ready deductive solution for problems which had puzzled the older physiologists. Thus the true significance of the valves in the veins became at once apparent. Of no importance while the blood is flowing in its normal course toward the heart, they at once oppose any accidental reversal of its current which may arise from the pressure of adjacent muscles or the like. And in like manner the swelling of the veins on the farther side of the ligature, which so much troubled Cæsalpinus, became at once intelligible as the natural result of the damming up of the returning current.

In addition to the great positive results which are contained in the treatise which Harvey modestly calls an *Exercise* and which is, in truth, not so long as many a pamphlet about some wholly insignificant affair, its pages are characterized by such precision and simplicity of statement, such force of reasoning, and such a clear comprehension of the methods of inquiry and of the logic of physical science, that it holds a unique rank among physiological monographs. Under this aspect, I think I may fairly say that it has rarely been equalled and never surpassed.

Such being the state of knowledge among his contemporaries, and such the immense progress effected by Harvey, it is not wonderful that the publication of the *Exercitatio* produced a profound sensation. And the best indirect evidence of the originality of its author, and of the revolutionary character of his views, is to be found in the multiplicity and the virulence of the attacks to which they were at once subjected.

Riolan, of Paris, had the greatest reputation of any anatomist of those days, and he followed the course which is usually adopted by the men of temporary notoriety toward those of enduring fame. According to Riolan, Harvey's theory of the circulation was not true; and besides that, it was not new; and, furthermore, he invented a mongrel doctrine of his own, composed of the old views with as much of Harvey's as it was safe to borrow, and tried therewith to fish credit for himself out of the business. In fact, in wading through these forgotten controversies, I felt myself quite at home. Substitute the name of Darwin for that of Harvey, and the truth that history repeats itself will come home to the dullest apprehension. It was said of the doctrine of the circulation of the blood that nobody over forty could be got to adopt it; and I think I remember a passage in the *Origin of Species* to the effect that its author expects to convert only young and flexible minds.

There is another curious point of resemblance in the fact that even those who gave Harvey their general approbation and support sometimes failed to apprehend the value of some of those parts of his doctrine which are, indeed, merely auxiliary to the theory of the circulation, but are only a little less important than it. Harvey's great friend and champion, Sir George Ent, is in this case; and I am sorry to be obliged to admit that Descartes falls under the same reprehension.

This great philosopher, mathematician, and physiologist, whose conception of the phenomena of life as the results of mechanism is now playing as great a part in physiological science as Harvey's own discovery, never fails to speak with admiration, as Harvey gratefully acknowledges, of the new theory of the circulation. And it is astonishing—I had almost said humiliating—to find that even he is unable to grasp Harvey's profoundly true view of the nature of the systole and the diastole, or to see the force of the quantitative argument. He adduces experimental evidence against the former position, and is even further from the truth than Galen was, in his ideas of the physical cause of the circulation.

Yet one more parallel with Darwin. In spite of all opposition, the doctrine of the circulation propounded by Harvey was, in its essential features, universally adopted within thirty years of the time of its publication. Harvey's friend, Thomas Hobbes, remarked that he was the only man, in his experience, who had the good-fortune to live long enough to see a new doctrine accepted by the world at large.

It is, I believe, a cherished belief of Englishmen that Francis Bacon, Viscount St. Albans and sometime lord chancellor of England, invented that "inductive philosophy" of which they speak with almost as much respect as they do of church and state; and that, if it had not been for this "Baconian induction," science would never have extricated itself from the miserable condition in which it was left by a set of hair-splitting folk known as the ancient Greek philosophers. To be accused of departing from the canons of the Baconian philosophy is almost as bad as to be charged with forgetting your aspirates; it is understood as a polite way of saying that you are an entirely absurd speculator.

Now the *Novum Organon* was published in 1620, while Harvey began to teach the doctrine of the circulation, in his public lectures, in 1619. Acquaintance with the Baconian induction, therefore, could not have had much to do with Harvey's investigations. The *Exercitatio*, however, was not published till 1628. Do we find in it any trace of the influence of the *Novum Organon?* Absolutely none. So far from indulging in the short-sighted and profoundly unscientific depreciation of the ancients in which Bacon indulges, Harvey invariably speaks of them with that respect which the faithful and intelligent study of the fragments of their labors that remain to us must inspire in everyone who is practically acquainted with the difficulties with which they had to contend, and which they so often mastered. And, as to method, Harvey's method is the method of Galen, the method of Realdus Columbus, the method of Galileo, the method of every genuine worker in science either in the past or the present. On the other hand, judged strictly by the standard of his own time, Bacon's ignorance of the progress which science had up to that time made is only to be equalled by his insolence toward men in comparison with whom he was the merest sciolist. Even when he had some hearsay knowledge of what has been done, his want of acquaintance with the facts and his abnormal deficiency in what I may call the scientific sense, prevent him from divining its importance. Bacon could see nothing remarkable in the chief contributions to science of Copernicus or of Kepler or of Galileo; Gilbert, his fellow-countryman, is the subject of a sneer; while Galen is bespattered with a shower of impertinences, which reach their climax in the epithets "puppy" and "plague."

I venture to think that if Francis Bacon, instead of spending his time in fabricating fine phrases about the advancement of learning, in order to play, with due pomp, the part which he assigned to himself of "trumpeter" of science, had put himself under Harvey's instructions, and had applied his quick wit to discover and methodize the logical process which underlaid the work of that consummate investigator, he would have employed his time to better purpose, and, at any rate, would not have deserved the just but sharp judgment which follows: "that his [Bacon's] method is impracticable cannot I think be denied, if we reflect, not only that it has never produced any result, but also that the process by which scientific truths have been established cannot be so presented as even to appear to be in accordance with it." I quote from one of Mr. Ellis' contributions to the great work of Bacon's most learned, competent, and impartial biographer, Mr. Spedding.

Few of Harvey's sayings are recorded, but Aubrey tells us that someone having enlarged upon the merits of the Baconian philosophy in his presence, "Yes," said Harvey, "he writes philosophy like a chancellor." On which pithy reply diverse persons will put diverse interpretations. The illumination of experience may possibly tempt a modern follower of Harvey to expound the dark saying thus: "So this servile courtier, this intriguing politician, this unscrupulous lawyer, this witty master of phrases proposes to teach me my business in the intervals of his. I have borne with Riolan; let me also be patient with him." At any rate, I have no better reading to offer.

In the latter half of the sixteenth and the beginning of the seventeenth centuries the future of physical science was safe enough in the hands of Gilbert, Galileo, Harvey, Descartes, and the noble army of investigators who flocked to their standard and followed up the advance of their leaders. I do not believe that their wonderfully rapid progress would have been one whit retarded if the *Novum Organon* had never seen the light; while, if Harvey's little *Exercise* had been lost, physiology would have stood still until another Harvey was born into the world.

THE "DEFENESTRATION" AT PRAGUE

THE THIRTY YEARS' WAR

A.D. 1618

SAMUEL R. GARDINER CHARLES F. HORNE

As the last great struggle between the contending sects of Europe for political as well as spiritual power the Thirty Years' War was one of the most important conflicts of the modern age. It was mainly carried on in the German states, but during its later stages all the great European powers were involved. The horrors of its battles and sieges have often been painted.

Among the direct causes of the war—the great general cause being the standing antagonism between Catholics and Protestants—was a clause in the Peace of Augsburg (1555) which remained a source of friction. It provided that any ecclesiastical prince who became Protestant must surrender the lands as well as the authority of his office. In many instances this clause was disregarded by the Protestants, who from the first felt it to be unjust. Until the accession of Rudolph II (1576) as Emperor of the Holy Roman Empire, there was no imperial intolerance, and Protestantism rapidly spread. But the harsh dealings of Rudolph with the Protestants provoked resentment. In 1607 Donauworth, a free Protestant city, was seized by the Catholic Duke of Bavaria. Next year the German Protestants formed the defensive Evangelical Union. Meanwhile Rudolph's policy only reacted in favor of the Protestant nobles. In 1611 his brother Matthias supplanted him as King of Bohemia, and in 1612 Rudolph died and Matthias succeeded to the imperial throne.

The outbreak of the Thirty Years' War followed upon a revolution in Bohemia, which was precipitated by Rudolph's attempt to evade the Royal Charter, extorted from him in 1609 by the estates. Its chief feature was a guarantee of freedom of conscience to Bohemians so long as they adhered to certain recognized creeds; but it also involved questions of authority over lands with respect to their use for religious purposes. The difficulties with the Royal Charter, which had led to Rudolph's downfall in Bohemia, were left to confront Matthias.

SAMUEL R. GARDINER

WHETHER it would have been possible in those days for a Catholic king to have kept a Protestant nation in working order we cannot say. At all events Matthias did not give the experiment a fair trial. He did not, indeed, attack the Royal Charter directly on the lands of the aristocracy. But he did his best to undermine it on his own. The Protestants of Braunau, on the lands of the Abbot of Braunau, and the Protestants of Klostergrab, on the lands of the Archbishop of Prague, built churches for themselves, the use of which was prohibited by the abbot and the archbishop. A dispute immediately arose as to the rights of ecclesiastical land-owners, and it was argued on the Protestant side that their lands were technically crown lands, and that they had therefore no right to close the churches. Matthias took the opposite view.

On his own estates Matthias found means to evade the charter. He appointed Catholic priests to Protestant churches, and allowed measures to be taken to compel Protestants to attend the Catholic service. Yet for a long time the Protestant nobility kept quiet. Matthias was old and infirm, and when he died they would, as they supposed, have an opportunity of choosing their next king, and it was generally believed that the election would fall upon a Protestant. The only question was whether the Elector Palatine or the Elector of Saxony would be chosen.

Suddenly in 1617 the Bohemian Diet was summoned. When the Estates of the kingdom met they were told that it was a mistake to suppose that the crown of Bohemia was elective. Evidence was produced that for some time before the election of Matthias the Estates had acknowledged the throne to be hereditary, and the precedent of Matthias was to be set aside as occurring in revolutionary times. Intimidation was used to assist the argument, and men in the confidence of the court whispered in the ears of those who refused to be convinced that it was to be hoped that they had at least two heads on their shoulders.

If ever there was a moment for resistance, if resistance was to be made at all, it was this. The arguments of the court were undoubtedly strong, but a skilful lawyer could easily have found technicalities on the other side, and the real evasion of the Royal Charter might have been urged as a reason why the court had no right to press technical arguments too closely. The danger was all the greater, as it was known that by the renunciation of all intermediate heirs the hereditary right fell upon Ferdinand of Styria, who had already stamped Protestantism out in his own dominions. Yet, in spite of this, the Diet did as it was bidden, and renounced the right of election by acknowledging Ferdinand as their hereditary king (1617).

The new King was more of a devotee and less of a statesman than Maximilian of Bavaria, his cousin on his mother's side. But their judgments of events were formed on the same lines. Neither of them was a mere ordinary bigot, keeping no faith with heretics. But they were both likely to be guided in their interpretation of the law by that which they conceived to be profitable to their church. Ferdinand was personally brave; but except when his course was very clear before him, he was apt to let difficulties settle themselves rather than come to a decision.

He had at once to consider whether he would swear to the Royal Charter. He consulted the Jesuits, and was told that, though it had been a sin to grant it, it was no sin to accept it now that it was the law of the land. As he walked in state to his coronation he turned to a nobleman who was by his side. "I am glad," he said, "that I have attained the Bohemian crown without any pangs of conscience." He took the oath without further difficulty.

The Bohemians were not long in feeling the effects of the change. Hitherto the hold of the house of Austria upon the country had been limited to the life of one old man. It had now, by the admission of the Diet itself, fixed itself forever upon Bohemia. The proceedings against the Protestants on the royal domains assumed a sharper character. The Braunau worshippers were rigorously excluded from their church. The walls of the new church at Klostergrab were actually levelled with the ground.

The Bohemians had thus to resist in 1618, under every disadvantage, the attack which they had done nothing to meet in 1617. Certain persons named "defensors" had, by law, the right of summoning an assembly of representatives of the Protestant Estates. Such an assembly met on March 5th, and, having prepared a petition to Matthias, who was absent from the kingdom, adjourned to May 21st.

Long before the time of meeting came, an answer was sent from Matthias justifying all that had been done, and declaring the assembly illegal. It was believed at the time, though incorrectly, that the answer was prepared by Slavata and Martinitz, two members of the regency who had been notorious for the vigor of their opposition to Protestantism.

In the Protestant assembly there was a knot of men, headed by Count Henry of Thurn, which was bent on the dethronement of Ferdinand. They resolved to take advantage of the popular feeling to effect the murder of the two Regents, and so to place an impassable gulf between the nation and the King.

Accordingly, on the morning of May 23d, the "beginning and cause," as a contemporary calls it, "of all the coming evil," the first day, though men as yet knew it not, of thirty years of war, Thurn sallied forth at the head of a band of noblemen and their followers, all of them with arms in their hands. Trooping into the room where the Regents were seated, they charged the obnoxious two with being the authors of the King's reply. After a bitter altercation both Martinitz and Slavata were dragged to a window which overlooked the fosse below from a dizzy height of some seventy feet. Martinitz, struggling against his enemies, pleaded hard for a confessor. "Commend thy soul to God," was the stern answer. "Shall we allow the Jesuit scoundrels to come here?" In an instant he was hurled out, crying, "Jesus, Mary!" "Let us see," said someone mockingly, "whether his Mary will help him." A moment later he added, "By God, his Mary has helped him." Slavata followed, and then the secretary Fabricius. By a wonderful preservation, in which pious Catholics discerned the protecting hand of God, all three crawled away from the spot without serious hurt.

There are moments when the character of a nation or party stands revealed as by a lightning flash, and this was one of them. It is not in such a way as this that successful revolutions are begun.

The first steps to constitute a new government were easy. Thirty directors were appointed, and the Jesuits were expelled from Bohemia. The Diet met and ordered soldiers to be levied to form an army. But to support this army money would be needed, and the existing taxes were insufficient. A loan was accordingly thought of, and the nobles resolved to request the towns to make up the sum, they themselves contributing nothing. The project falling dead upon the resistance of the towns, new taxes were voted, but no steps were taken to collect them, and the army was left to depend in a great measure upon chance.

Would the princes of Germany come to the help of the directors? John George of Saxony told them that he deeply sympathized with them, but that rebellion was a serious matter. To one who asked him what he meant to do he replied, "Help to put out the fire."

There was more help for them at Heidelberg than at Dresden. Frederick IV had died in 1610, and his son, the young Frederick V, looked up to Christian of Anhalt as the first statesman of his age. By his marriage with Elizabeth, the daughter of James I of England, he had contracted an alliance which gave him the appearance rather than the reality of strength. He offered every encouragement to the Bohemians, but for the time held back from giving them actual assistance.

CHARLES F. HORNE[1]

Ferdinand had crushed Protestantism in every estate he owned. In 1615 he and Matthias began, or at least permitted, measures for its repression in Bohemia. There were tumults, uprisings, and on May 23, 1618, a party of angry citizens of Prague burst into the council hall, seized Slavata and Martinitz, the two most obnoxious of the Catholic leaders, and hurled them from the window. It was an ancient form of Bohemian punishment, which had been used by Ziska and by others. The window this time was over eighty feet from the ground, yet the fall did not prove fatal. The men landed on a soft rubbish heap below, and one was unhurt; the other, though much injured, survived. Their secretary was hurled after them, and is said to have apologized to his masters, even as he landed, for his unavoidable discourtesy in alighting upon them.

This semicomic tragedy opened the Thirty Years' War. At first the struggle was confined to Bohemia and Austria. The other states, secure in the fact that four-fifths of the populace of the empire was Protestant, looked on with seeming indifference. The Bohemians drove the scattered imperial troops from their country.

[1] From *The Story of the Greatest Nations*, by permission of F. R. Niglutsch.

Meanwhile Matthias died, and Ferdinand was elected to the imperial throne as Ferdinand II (1619–1637). The Bohemians besieged him in Vienna. The Protestant Austrian nobles turned against him, and a deputation forced its way into the presence of the helpless Emperor, and insisted on his signing for them a grant of political and religious liberty. Ferdinand resolutely refused; the deputation grew threatening. One fierce noble seized the Emperor roughly by the coat front, crying, with an offensive nickname for Ferdinand, "Sign it, Nandel!" A trumpet from the castle yard interrupted them. It signalled the arrival of a body of imperial troops, who had slipped through the lines of the besiegers, and come to the Emperor's rescue.

The Austrian nobles withdrew. Spanish and Cossack troops were called by Ferdinand into the country to crush all opposition. The Bohemians, wasted by famine and plague, retreated into their own land, and the war continued there. The people offered the Bohemian throne to Frederick, the elector of the Rhenish Palatinate, and a son-in-law of the English King, James I.

Frederick accepted, went to Bohemia in state, and tried to draw the other Protestant princes to his help. But he was a Calvinist, so the Lutherans refused to join him. His new subjects were mainly Lutherans also, and his impolitic effort to enforce his religious views upon Prague soon roused the citizens to a state of revolt against him.

The Catholic princes of the empire had long been united in a "League," with Bavaria at its head. Bavaria was, next to Austria, the most powerful state of the empire, and it had become the stronghold of the Roman faith in Germany. Now, the army of this League, under its chief, Maximilian of Bavaria, offered its services to the Emperor against the disunited and wavering Bohemians. A portion of the Bohemian army was defeated at the battle of White Mountain, just outside of Prague. Frederick, the newly elected Bohemian King, saw his troops come fleeing back to the town, and their panic seems to have seized him also. Abandoning the strong walled city, he swept such of his possessions together as he could and fled in haste from Bohemia. "The Winter King" his enemies called him in derision, because his kingship had lasted but one short winter.

The citizens, disheartened by his flight, terrified by the overwhelming forces arrayed against them, surrendered to Ferdinand. Executions, proscriptions, banishments, followed without number. Every person of the land was compelled to accept Catholicism. Many burned their homes with their own hands, and fled to other countries. Seldom has liberty been so utterly trampled under foot; seldom has a land been so completely subjugated. The Bohemians, who had been one of the most intellectual, energetic peoples of Europe, here practically disappear from history as a separate nation.

We turn now to the second period of this deplorable war. Its scene shifts to the domain of the unhappy Frederick upon the Rhine. He himself fled to Holland, but his land was considered as forfeited, and was deliberately desolated by Spanish troops in the service of the Emperor. The Bohemians had employed a well-known leader of mercenary troops, Count Mansfeld. When their cause was lost, Mansfeld, with most of his army, amused the Catholic forces by negotiations, till he saw his opportunity, when he slipped away from them, and led his army to the Rhine. There he continued the war in Frederick's name, though really for his own sake. His troops supported themselves by pillaging the country, and the wretched inhabitants of Frederick's Palatinate were treated almost as mercilessly by their pretended friends as by their open foes.

The peasants of Upper Austria also rebelled against Ferdinand's efforts to force his religion upon them. For a time it seemed they would be as successful as the Swiss mountaineers had been. Under a peasant named Fadinger they gained several impressive victories; but he was killed, and their cause collapsed into ruin. In its last stages their struggle was taken up by an unknown leader, who was called simply "the Student." But it was too late. Remarkable and romantic as was the Student's career, his exploits and victories could not save the cause, and he perished at the head of his followers.

Meanwhile, the war along the Rhine assumed more and more the savage character that made it so destructive to the land. Mansfeld, driven from the Palatinate, supported his ferocious troops almost entirely by plundering. Tilly, the chief general of the Catholic League, followed similar tactics, and, wherever they passed, the land lay ruined behind them. Some of the lesser Protestant princes joined Mansfeld, but Tilly proved a great military leader, and his opponents were slowly crowded back into Northern Germany. The Emperor forced his religion upon the Rhine districts, as he had upon Bohemia and Austria. The Protestant world at last began to take alarm. Both England and Holland lent Mansfeld support. The King of Denmark, drawing as many of the Protestant German princes as possible to his side, joined vigorously in the contest.

This Danish struggle may be considered the third period of the war. It lasted from about 1625 to 1629, and introduces one of the two most remarkable men of the period.

Albert of Waldstein, or Wallenstein, as he is generally called, was a native of Bohemia, who joined the Catholics, and won military fame and experience fighting on the imperial side in the Bohemian war. He acquired vast wealth through marriage and the purchase of the confiscated Protestant estates. Proving a remarkably capable financial manager, he was soon the richest subject in the empire, and was created Duke of Friedland, a district of Bohemia.

All of these successes were to Wallenstein mere preliminary steps to an even more boundless ambition. He studied the political outlook, and his keen eye saw the possibility of vastly expanding Mansfeld's barbaric system of supporting his soldiers by plunder. The Emperor Ferdinand had but few troops of his own, and they were needed for quelling rebellion within his personal domains. For carrying on the war along the Rhine, he was entirely dependent upon the princes of the Catholic League and their army under Tilly.

Wallenstein now came forward and offered to supply the Emperor with a powerful imperial army which should not cost him a penny. This offer, coming from a mere private gentleman, sounded absurd; and for a time Wallenstein was put aside with contemptuous laughter. At last the Emperor told him, if he thought he could raise as many as ten thousand men, to go ahead. "If I have only ten thousand," said Wallenstein, "we must accept what people choose to give us. If I have thirty thousand, we can take what we like."

The answer makes plain his whole system. His troops supported and paid themselves at the expense of the neighborhood where they were quartered. If it was a district which upheld the Emperor they took "contributions to the necessity of the empire." If the land opposed him, no polite words were needed to justify its pillage. Within three months Wallenstein had nearly fifty thousand men under his standard, drawn to him by the tempting offers of plunder that his agents held out. If the war had been terrible before, imagine the awful phase it now assumed, and the blighting curse that fell upon unhappy Germany!

Modern justice can find little to choose thereafter between the methods of the opposing armies. We speak, therefore, only of the martial genius which Wallenstein displayed. He completely outmanœuvred Mansfeld, defeated him, and drove him to flight and death. Then Wallenstein and Tilly proceeded to destroy the high military reputation of the Danish King. He was overcome in battle after battle, and his land so completely devastated that he prayed for peace on any terms.

Peace seemed indeed at hand. The remaining Lutheran states of Saxony and Brandenburg, which had been neutral and were as yet almost unharmed, dared not interfere. The Emperor Ferdinand might have arranged everything as he chose had he used his power with moderation. But his hopes had grown with his fortunes, and he seems to have planned the establishment of such an absolute power over Germany as had been the aim of his ancestor, Charles V. Ferdinand passed laws and gave decrees, without any pretence of calling a council or seeking the approval of the princes. His general, Wallenstein, was given one of the conquered states as his dukedom; and Wallenstein declared openly that his master had no further need of councils; the time had come for Germany to be governed as were France and Spain.

The Catholic princes, with Maximilian of Bavaria at their head, became frightened by the giant they themselves had created, and began to take measures for their own preservation. They demanded that Wallenstein be removed from his command. The Emperor, perhaps himself afraid of his too powerful general, finally consented.

There still remained, however, the serious question whether

Wallenstein would accept his dismissal. His huge and ever-growing army was absolutely under his control. His influence over the troops was extraordinary. A firm believer in astrology, he asserted that the stars promised him certain success, and his followers believed him. Tall and thin, dark and solemn, silent and grim, wearing a scarlet cloak and a long, blood-red feather in his hat, he was declared by popular superstition to be in league with the devil, invulnerable and unconquerable. No evil act of his soldiery did he ever rebuke. Only two things he demanded of them—absolute obedience and unshaken daring. The man who flinched or disobeyed was executed on the instant. Otherwise the marauders might desecrate God's earth with whatsoever hideous crimes they would. His troops laughed at the idea of being Catholics or Protestants, Germans or Bohemians; they were "Wallensteiners" and nothing else.

Even Ferdinand would scarcely have dared oppose his overgrown servant had not Wallenstein failed in an attempt to capture Stralsund. This little Baltic seaport held out against the assaults of his entire army. Wallenstein vowed that he would capture it "though it were fastened by chains to heaven." But each mad attack of his wild troopers was beaten back from the walls by the desperate townsfolk; and at last, with twelve thousand of his men dead, he retreated from before the stubborn port. A superstitious load was lifted from the minds even of those who pretended to be his friends. Wallenstein was not unconquerable.

He accepted the Emperor's notice of removal with haughty disdain. He said he had already seen it in the stars that evil men had sowed dissension between him and his sovereign, but the end was not yet. He retired to his vast estates in Bohemia, and lived at Prague with a magnificence exceeding that of any court in Germany. His table was always set for a hundred guests. He had sixty pages of the noblest families to wait on him. For chamberlains and other household officials, he had men who came from similar places under the Emperor.

Meanwhile a new defender had sprung up for exhausted Protestantism. Gustavus Adolphus, King of Sweden, invaded Germany in 1630 and called on the Protestants to help him in the fight to save their faith. All Europe had grown afraid of the tremendous and increasing power of the Hapsburg Emperor. Not only was Protestant England in league with the Swedes, but Catholic France, under its shrewd minister, Richelieu, also upheld them. Still the burden of actual fighting fell upon Gustavus Adolphus, who proved himself the greatest military leader of the age, and, in the eyes of Protestant Europe, the noblest and sublimest man since Luther.

It is not our province to analyze the motives of the Swedish King, the "Lion of the North," as he is called. How much he was actuated by ambition, how much by religion, perhaps he himself might have found it hard to say. His coming marks the turning-point of the contest; his brilliant achievements constitute the fourth period of the war.

Tilly opposed him with the army of the Catholic League—Tilly, the victor of thirty desperate battles. The Emperor and his court laughed, and, thinking of the Bohemian King and the Dane, said: "Another of these snow kings has come against us. He, too, will melt in our southern sun."

The Protestant princes hesitated, fearing to join Gustavus; he was hampered on every side. Tilly in his very face stormed the great Protestant city of Magdeburg, and sacked it with such merciless brutalities as raised a cry of horrified disgust, even in that age of atrocities. "Never was such a victory," wrote Tilly to the Emperor, "since the storming of Troy or of Jerusalem. I am sorry you and the ladies of the court were not there to enjoy the spectacle." A heap of blackened ruins, hiding a few hundred famished and broken outcasts, was all that remained of a splendid and prosperous city of forty thousand souls.

Tilly's object in this bloody deed seems to have been to terrify the rest of Protestant Germany into submission. If so, he failed of his purpose. Gustavus promptly abandoned gentle measures, and by a threat of force compelled the Saxon elector to join him. He then met Tilly in a fierce battle near Leipsic and utterly defeated him. Tilly fled, and his army was almost annihilated, the fugitives who escaped the Swedes falling victims to the vengeance of the enraged Protestant peasantry. Few men who had taken part in the sack of Magdeburg lived long to boast of their achievement.

Gustavus swept victoriously through all the Rhineland. One

Catholic prince or bishop after another was defeated. The advance soon became little more than a triumphal procession, city after city opening its gates to welcome him. The Saxon army conquered Bohemia; Gustavus reached Bavaria.

There on the southern bank of the River Lech the Bavarian army under Tilly and Prince Maximilian was drawn to oppose the passage of the Protestant troops. It seemed impossible to cross the broad and deep stream in the face of such a force and such a general. Gustavus kept up a tremendous cannonade for three days. He burned great fires along the shore, that the smoke might conceal his movements. Tilly was struck down by a cannon-ball, the whole Bavarian army fell into confusion, and the Swedes rushed across the river almost unopposed. Maximilian fled with his army; and Bavaria, which as yet had escaped the horrors of the war, was in its turn plundered by an enemy.

The stars in their courses seemed indeed to fight for Wallenstein. From the moment that he was deprived of his command, the triumphant cause of the Emperor had fallen, fallen until now it lay in utter ruin. The Saxons held Bohemia; all Western Germany was in Gustavus' hands; nothing interposed between the conquerors and defenceless Austria—nothing but Wallenstein.

Messenger after messenger sped from the Emperor to his offended general, entreating him to reaccept his command. Wallenstein dallied, and postponed his consent, until he had wrung from his despairing sovereign such terms as never general secured before or since. Practically Wallenstein became as exalted in authority as the Emperor himself, and wholly independent of his former master. He was to carry on the war or to make peace entirely as he saw fit, without interference of any sort. Certain provinces of Austria were given him to hold as a guarantee of the Emperor's good faith.

The mere raising of the great general's standard drew around him another army of "Wallensteiners," with whom he marched against Gustavus. Two of the ablest military leaders in history were thus pitted against each other. There were clever marches and countermarches, partial, indecisive attacks, and at last a great culminating battle at Luetzen, in Saxony, November 6, 1632.

Gustavus won; but he perished on the field. He was always exposing himself in battle, and at Lutzen he galloped across in front of his army from one wing to another. A shot struck him —a traitor shot, say some, from his own German allies. He fell from his horse, and a band of the opposing cavalry encircled and slew him, not knowing who he was. His Swedes, who adored him, pressed furiously forward to save or avenge their leader. The Wallensteiners, after a desperate struggle, broke and fled before the resistless attack.

Wallenstein himself, his hat and cloak riddled with bullets, rushed in vain among his men, taunting them furiously with their cowardice. It was only the night and the death of Gustavus that prevented the Swedes from reaping the full fruits of their victory. The imperial troops retreated unpursued. Wallenstein held a savage court-martial, and executed all of his men whom he could prove had been among the first in flight.

From this time the war enters on its fifth stage. Wallenstein did little more fighting. He withdrew his troops into Bohemia, and it is hard to say what purposes simmered in his dark and inscrutable brain. He certainly was no longer loyal to the Emperor; probably the Emperor plotted against him. Wallenstein seems to have contemplated making himself king of an independent Bohemian kingdom. At any rate, he broke openly with his sovereign, and at a great banquet persuaded his leading officers to sign an oath that they would stand by him in whatever he did. Some of the more timid among them warned the Emperor, and with his approval formed a trap for Wallenstein. The general's chief lieutenants were suddenly set upon and slain; then the murderers rushed to Wallenstein's own apartments. Hearing them coming, he stood up dauntlessly, threw wide his arms to their blows, and died as silent and mysterious as he had lived. His slayers were richly rewarded by Ferdinand.

All Germany was weary of the war. The contending parties had fought each other to a standstill; and, had Germany alone been concerned, peace would certainly have followed. But the Swedes, abandoning Gustavus' higher policy, continued the war for what increase of territory they could get; and France helped herself to what German cities she could in Alsace and Lorraine.

So the war went on, the German princes taking sides now with this one, now the other, and nobody apparently ever thinking of the poor peasantry.

The spirit of the brutal soldiery grew ever more atrocious. Their captives were tortured to death for punishment or for ransom, or, it is to be feared, for the mere amusement of the bestial captors. The open country became everywhere a wilderness. The soldiers themselves began starving in the dismal desert.

The Emperor, Ferdinand II, the cause of all this destruction, died in 1637, and was succeeded by his son, Ferdinand III (1637–1657). The war still continued, though in a feeble, listless way, with no decisive victories on either side, until the peace of Westphalia, in 1648. This peace placed Protestants and Catholics on an equal footing of toleration throughout the empire. It gave Sweden what territory she wanted in the north, and France what she asked toward the Rhine. Switzerland and Holland were acknowledged as independent lands. The importance of the smaller princes was increased, they, too, becoming practically independent, and the power of the emperors was all but destroyed. From this time the importance of the Hapsburgs rested solely on their personal possessions in Austria, Hungary, and Bohemia. The title of emperor remained little better than a name.

Indeed, Germany itself had become scarcely more than a name. During those terrible thirty years the population of the land is said to have dwindled from fifteen millions to less than five millions. In the Palatinate less than fifty thousand people remained, where there had been five hundred thousand. Whole districts everywhere lay utterly waste, wild, and uninhabited. Men killed themselves to escape starvation, or slew their brothers for a fragment of bread. A full description of the horrors of that awful time will never be written; much has been mercifully obliterated. The material progress of Germany, its students say, was retarded by two centuries' growth. To this day the land has not fully recovered from the exhaustion of that awful war.

FIRST AMERICAN LEGISLATURE

A.D. 1619

CHARLES CAMPBELL

As a distinctly American event the beginning of formal legislation in this country has special interest, no less for the general reader than for students of legal history. None of the early institutions of the fathers is more important than that which developed into the State legislature.

At the opening of 1609 the Virginia colony, which was not then in a flourishing condition, asked and obtained from King James I a new charter. The territory was now greatly enlarged, the powers of local government increased, and Virginia soon entered upon its permanent career.

In 1617 "a party of greedy and unprincipled adventurers" in England succeeded in having an agent of their own appointed deputy governor. This was Samuel Argall. Lord Delaware, the Governor, dying in 1618, Argall became virtual dictator, and under his arbitrary and self-seeking rule the people suffered. Meanwhile others, in England, were at work in the interest of the Virginia Company, under whose auspices, from the granting of the new charter, the colony had existed. Sir Edwin Sandys, in 1618, was made treasurer and actual governor of the Virginia Company. Through the efforts of Sandys and others in England, Sir George Yeardley, who had governed Virginia in 1616, was sent in 1619 to supersede Argall.

This year "was remarkable in the annals of the colony. It is hardly an exaggeration to say that it witnessed the creation of Virginia as an independent community." From that year Sandys and his followers maintained their ascendency, and a high degree of energy and statesmanlike wisdom marked the administration of the colonial government. The calling of the first assembly was one of the principal acts of Yeardley's administration.

SIR THOMAS SMITH, treasurer or governor of the Virginia Company, was displaced in 1618, and succeeded by Sir Edwin Sandys. This enlightened statesman and exemplary man was born in Worcestershire in 1561, being the second son of the Archbishop of York. Educated at Oxford under the care of "the judicious Hooker," he obtained a prebend in the church of York. He afterward travelled in foreign countries, and published his observations in a work entitled *Europæ Speculum; or,*

A View of the State of Religion in the Western World. He resigned his prebend in 1602, was subsequently knighted by James, in 1603, and employed in diplomatic trusts. His appointment as treasurer gave great satisfaction to the colony; for free principles were now, under his auspices, in the ascendent. His name is spelled sometimes "Sandis," sometimes "Sands."

When Argall, in April, 1619, stole away from Virginia, he left for his deputy Captain Nathaniel Powell, who had come over with Captain Smith in 1607, and had evinced courage and discretion. He was one of the writers from whose narratives Smith compiled his *General History*. Powell held this office only about ten days, when Sir George Yeardley, recently knighted, arrived as Governor-General, bringing with him new charters for the colony. John Rolfe, who had been secretary, now lost his place, probably owing to his connivance at Argall's malpractices, and was succeeded by John Pory. He was educated at Cambridge, where he took the degree of master of arts in April, 1610. It is supposed that he was a member of the House of Commons. He was much of a traveller, and was at Venice in 1613, at Amsterdam in 1617, and shortly after at Paris. By the Earl of Warwick's influence he now procured the place of secretary of the colony of Virginia, having come over in April, 1619, with Sir George Yeardley, who appointed him one of his council.

In June Governor Yeardley summoned the first legislature that ever met in America. It assembled at James City or Jamestown on Friday, July 30, 1619, upward of a year before the Mayflower left England with the Pilgrims. A record of the proceedings is preserved in the London State Paper Office, in the form of a report from the speaker, John Pory.

John Pory, secretary of the colony, was chosen speaker, and John Twine, clerk. The Assembly sat in the choir of the church, the members of the council sitting on either side of the Governor, and the speaker right before him, the clerk next the speaker, and Thomas Pierse, the sergeant, standing at the bar. Before commencing business, prayer was said by Mr. Bucke, the minister.

Each burgess then, as called on, took the oath of supremacy. When the name of Captain Ward was called, the speaker objected to him as having seated himself on land without authority. Objections were also made to the burgesses appearing to represent Captain Martin's patent, because they were, by its terms, exempted from any obligation to obey the laws of the colony. Complaint was made by Opochancano that corn had been forcibly taken from some of his people in the Chesapeake by Ensign Harrison, commanding a shallop belonging to this Captain John Martin, "master of the Ordinance."

The speaker read the commission for establishing the council of state and the General Assembly, and also the charter brought out by Sir Thomas Yeardley. This last was referred to several committees for examination, so that if they should find anything "not perfectly squaring with the state of the colony, or any law pressing or binding too hard," they might by petition seek to have it redressed, "especially because this great charter is to bind us and our heirs forever." Mr. Abraham Persey was the Cape merchant. The price at which he was to receive tobacco, "either for commodities or upon bills," was fixed at three shillings for the best and eighteen pence for the second-rate.

After inquiry the burgesses from Martin's patent were excluded, and the Assembly "humbly demanded" of the Virginia Company an explanation of that clause in his patent entitling him to enjoy his lands as amply as any lord of a manor in England, adding, "the least the Assembly can allege against this clause is that it is obscure and that it is a thing impossible for us here to know the prerogatives of all the manors in England." And they prayed that the clause in the charter guaranteeing equal liberties and immunities to grantees, might not be violated, so as to "divert out of the true course the free and public current of justice." Thus did the first Assembly of Virginia insist upon the principle of the Declaration of Rights of 1776, that "no man or set of men are entitled to exclusive or separate emoluments or privileges from the community, but in consideration of public services."

Certain instructions sent out from England were "drawn into laws" for protection of the Indians from injury, and regulating intercourse with them, and educating their children, and preparing some of the most promising boys "for the college intended for them; that from thence they may be sent to that work of conversion"; for regulating agriculture, tobacco, and sassafras, then the chief merchantable commodities raised. Upon Captain Powell's petition, "a lewd and treacherous servant of his" was sentenced to stand for four days with his ears nailed to the pillory, and be whipped each day. John Rolfe complained that Captain Martin had made unjust charges against him, and cast "some aspersion upon the present government, which is the most temperate and just that ever was in this country—too mild, indeed, for many of this colony, whom unwonted liberty hath made insolent, and not to know themselves."

On the last day of the session were enacted such laws as issued "out of every man's private conceit." "It shall be free for every man to trade with the Indians, servants only excepted upon pain of whipping, unless the master will redeem it off with the payment of an angel." "No man to sell or give any of the greater hoes to the Indians, or any English dog of quality, as a mastiff, greyhound, bloodhound, land or water spaniel." "Any man selling arms or ammunition to the Indians, to be hanged so soon as the fact is proved." All ministers shall duly "read divine service, and exercise their ministerial function according to the ecclesiastical laws and orders of the Church of England, and every Sunday, in the afternoon, shall catechize such as are not ripe to come to the communion." All persons going up or down the James River were to touch at James City, "to know whether the Governor will command them any service." "All persons whatsoever, upon the Sabbath days, shall frequent divine service and sermons, both forenoon and afternoon; and all such as bear arms shall bring their pieces, swords, powder, and shot."

Captain Henry Spellman, charged by Robert Poole, interpreter, with speaking ill of the Governor "at Opochancano's court," was degraded from his rank of captain, and condemned to serve the colony for seven years as interpreter to the Governor. Paspaheigh, embracing three hundred acres of land, was also called Argallstown, and was part of the tract appropriated to the Governor. To compensate the speaker, clerk, sergeant, and provost-marshal, a pound of the best tobacco was levied from every male above sixteen years of age.

The Assembly prayed that the treasurer, council, and company would not "take it in ill part if these laws, which we have now brought to light, do pass current, and be of force till such time as we may know their further pleasure out of England; for otherwise this people (who now at length have got their reins of former servitude into their own swindge) would, in short time, grow so insolent as they would shake off all government, and there would be no living among them." They also prayed the company to "give us power to allow or disallow of their orders of court, as his majesty hath given them power to allow or reject *our* laws." So early did it appear that, from the necessity of the case, the colony must in large part legislate for itself, and so early did a spirit of independence manifest itself.

Owing to the heat of the weather several of the burgesses fell sick and one died, and thus the Governor was obliged abruptly, on August 4th, to prorogue the Assembly till March 1st. There being as yet no counties laid off, the representatives were elected from the several towns, plantations, and hundreds, styled boroughs, and hence they were called burgesses.

INTRODUCTION OF NEGROES INTO VIRGINIA

SPREAD OF SLAVERY AND THE CULTIVATION OF TOBACCO

A.D. 1619

CHARLES CAMPBELL JOHN M. LUDLOW

It was not till one hundred twenty years after the beginning of negro slavery in Spanish America that it was introduced in any part of the present United States. From its first introduction in Virginia (1619) the system grew and spread until it became one of the most prominent features of American society. The comprehensive view of its growth and decline presented by Mr. Ludlow, a well-known English writer, has therefore a special value here. From him and from the Virginia historian Mr. Campbell we get two widely diverging views upon the subject.

Along with the adoption and increase of slavery in Virginia went rapid progress in the cultivation there of tobacco, which had begun in 1612. Tobacco proved to be a staple of the first importance. It was destined to exert a controlling influence on the growth and prosperity of the colony. It was not long before this industry, by reason of the great profits which it returned, overshadowed every other.

CHARLES CAMPBELL

IN the month of August, 1619, a Dutch man-of-war visited Jamestown and sold the settlers twenty negroes, the first introduced into Virginia. Some time before this, Captain Argall, the deputy governor of Virginia, sent out on a "filibustering" cruise to the West Indies a ship called the Treasurer, manned "with the ablest men in the colony." She returned to Virginia, after some ten months, with her booty, which consisted of captured negroes, who were not left in Virginia, because Captain Argall had gone back to England, but were put on the Earl of Warwick's plantation in the Somer Islands.

It is probable that the planters who first purchased negroes reasoned but little on the morality of the act, or, if any scruples of conscience presented themselves, they could be readily silenced by reflecting that the negroes were heathens, descendants of Ham, and consigned by divine appointment to perpetual bondage. The planters may, if they reasoned at all on the subject, have supposed that they were even performing a humane act in releasing these Africans from the noisome hold of the ship. They might well believe that the condition of the negro slave would be less degraded and wretched in Virginia than it had been in his native country. This first purchase was not probably looked upon as a matter of much consequence, and for several years the increase of the blacks in Virginia was so inconsiderable as not to attract any special attention. The condition of the white servants of the colony, many of them convicts, was so abject that men accustomed to see their own race in bondage could look with more indifference at the worse condition of the slaves.

The negroes purchased by the slavers on the coast of Africa were brought from the interior, convicts sold into slavery, children sold by heathen parents destitute of natural affection, kidnapped villagers, and captives taken in war, the greater part of them born in hereditary bondage. The circumstances under which they were consigned to the slave-ship evince the wretchedness of their condition in their native country, where they were the victims of idolatry, barbarism, and war. The negroes imported were usually between the ages of fourteen and thirty, two-thirds of them being males. The new negro, just transferred from the wilds of a distant continent, was indolent, ignorant of the modes and implements of labor, and of the language of his master and, perhaps, of his fellow-laborers. To tame and domesticate, to instruct in the modes of industry, and to reduce to subordination and usefulness a barbarian, gross, obtuse, perverse, must have demanded persevering efforts and severe discipline.

While the cruel slave trade was prompted by a remorseless cupidity, an inscrutable Providence turned the wickedness of men into the means of bringing about beneficent results. The system of slavery doubtless entailed many evils on slave and slaveholder, and, perhaps, the greater on the latter. These evils are the tax paid for the elevation of the negro from his aboriginal condition.

Among the vessels that came over to Virginia from England about this time is mentioned a bark of five tons. A fleet sent out by the Virginia Company brought over, in 1619, more than twelve hundred settlers. The planters at length enjoyed the blessings of property in the soil and the society of women. The wives were sold to the colonists for one hundred twenty pounds of tobacco, and it was ordered that this debt should have precedence of all others. The price of a wife afterward became higher. The bishops in England, by the King's orders, collected nearly fifteen hundred pounds to build a college or university at Henrico, intended in part for the education of Indian children.

In July, 1620, the population of the colony was estimated at four thousand. One hundred "disorderly persons" or convicts sent over during the previous year by the King's order were employed as servants. For a brief interval the Virginia Company had enjoyed freedom of trade with the Low Countries, where they sold their tobacco; but in October, 1621, this was prohibited by an order in council; and from this time England claimed a monopoly of the trade of her plantations, and this principle was gradually adopted by all the European powers as they acquired transatlantic settlements.

Many new settlements were now made on the James and York rivers; and the planters, being supplied with wives and servants, began to be more content, and to take more pleasure in cultivating their lands. The brief interval of free trade with Holland had enlarged the demand for tobacco, and it was cultivated more extensively.

Sir George Yeardley's term of office having expired, the Company's council, upon the recommendation of the Earl of Southampton, appointed Sir Francis Wyat governor, a young gentleman of Ireland, whose education, family, fortune, and integrity well qualified him for the place. He arrived in October, 1621, with a fleet of nine sail, and brought over a new frame of government constituted by the company, and dated July 24, 1621, establishing a council of state and a general assembly.

Wyat brought with him also a body of instructions intended

for the permanent guidance of the governor and council. Among other things he was to cultivate corn, wine, and silk; to search for minerals, dyes, gums, and medical drugs, and to draw off the people from the excessive planting of tobacco; to take a census of the colony; to put apprentices to trades and not let them forsake them for planting tobacco or any such useless commodity; to build water-mills, to make salt, pitch, tar, soap and ashes; to make oil of walnuts, and employ apothecaries in distilling lees of beer; to make small quantity of tobacco, and that very good.

In 1615 twelve different commodities had been shipped from Virginia; sassafras and tobacco were now the only exports. During the year 1619 the company in England imported twenty thousand pounds of tobacco, the entire crop of the preceding year. James I endeavored to draw a "prerogative" revenue from what he termed a pernicious weed, and against which he had published his *Counterblast;* but he was restrained from this illegal measure by a resolution of the House of Commons. In 1607 he sent a letter forbidding the use of tobacco at St. Mary's College, Cambridge.

Smoking was the first mode of using tobacco in England, and when Sir Walter Raleigh first introduced the custom among people of fashion, in order to escape observation he smoked privately in his house (at Islington), the remains of which were till of late years to be seen, as an inn, long known as the Pied Bull. This was the first house in England in which tobacco was smoked, and Raleigh had his arms emblazoned there, with a tobacco-plant on the top. There existed also another tradition in the parish of St. Matthew, Friday Street, London, that Raleigh was accustomed to sit smoking at his door in company with Sir Hugh Middleton. Sir Walter's guests were entertained with pipes, a mug of ale, and a nutmeg, and on these occasions he made use of his tobacco-box, which was of cylindrical form, seven inches in diameter and thirteen inches long; the outside of gilt leather, and within a receiver of glass or metal, which held about a pound of tobacco. A kind of collar connected the receiver with the case, and on every side the box was pierced with holes for the pipes. This relic was preserved in the museum of Ralph Thoresby, of Leeds, in 1719, and about 1843 was added, by the late Duke of Sussex, to his collection of the smoking-utensils of all nations.

Although Raleigh first introduced the custom of smoking tobacco in England, yet its use appears to have been not entirely unknown before, for one Kemble, condemned for heresy in the time of Queen Mary the Bloody, while walking to the stake smoked a pipe of tobacco. Hence the last pipe that one smoked was called the Kemble pipe.

The writer of a pamphlet, supposed to have been Milton's father, describes many of the playbooks and pamphlets of that day, 1609, as "conceived over night by idle brains, impregnated with tobacco smoke and mulled sack, and brought forth by the help of midwifery of a candle next morning." At the theatres in Shakespeare's time the spectators were allowed to sit on the stage, and to be attended by pages, who furnished them with pipes and tobacco.

About the time of the settlement of Jamestown, in 1607, the characteristics of a man of fashion were, to wear velvet breeches, with panes or slashes of silk, an enormous starched ruff, a gilt-handled sword, and a Spanish dagger; to play at cards or dice in the room of the groom-porter, and to smoke tobacco in the tilt-yard, or at the playhouse.

The peers engaged in the trial of the Earls of Essex and Southampton smoked much while they deliberated on their verdict. It was alleged against Raleigh that he smoked tobacco on the occasion of the execution of the Earl of Essex, in contempt of him; and it was perhaps in allusion to this circumstance that when Raleigh was passing through London to Winchester, to stand his trial, he was followed by the execrations of the populace, and pelted with tobacco-pipes, stones, and mud. On the scaffold, however, he protested that during the execution of Essex he had retired far off into the armory, where Essex could not see him, although he saw Essex, and shed tears for him. Raleigh used tobacco on the morning of his own execution.

As early as the year 1610 tobacco was in general use in England. The manner of using it was partly to inhale the smoke and blow it out through the nostrils, and this was called "drinking tobacco," and this practice continued until the latter part of the reign of James I. In 1614 the number of tobacco-houses in or near London was estimated at seven thousand. In 1620 was chartered the Society of Tobacco-pipe Makers of London; they bore on their shield a tobacco-plant in full blossom.

The *Counterblast to Tobacco*, by King James I, if in some parts absurd and puerile, yet is not without a good deal of just reasoning and good sense; some fair hits are made in it, and those who have ridiculed that production might find it not easy to controvert some of its views. King James, in his *Counterblast*, does not omit the opportunity of expressing his hatred toward Sir Walter Raleigh. He continued his opposition to tobacco as long as he lived, and in his ordinary conversation oftentimes argued and inveighed against it.

The Virginia tobacco in early times was imported into England in the leaf, in bundles; the Spanish or West Indian tobacco in balls. Molasses or other liquid preparation was used in preparing those balls. Tobacco was then, as now, adulterated in various ways. The nice retailer kept it in what were called lily-pots; that is, white jars. It was cut on a maple block; juniper-wood, which retains fire well, was used for lighting pipes, and among the rich, silver tongs were employed for taking up a coal of it. Tobacco was sometimes called "the American Silver-Weed."

The Turkish vizier thrust pipes through the noses of smokers; and the Shah of Persia cropped the ears and slit the noses of those who made use of the fascinating leaf. The *Counterblast* says of it: "And for the vanity committed in this filthy custom, is it not both great vanity and uncleanness, that at the table—a place of respect of cleanliness, of modesty—men should not be ashamed to sit tossing of tobacco-pipes and puffing of smoke, one at another, making the filthy smoke and stink thereof to exhale athwart the dishes, and infect the air, when very often men who abhor it are at their repast? Surely smoke becomes a kitchen far better than a dining-chamber; and yet it makes the kitchen oftentimes in the inward parts of man, soiling and infecting them with an unctuous and oily kind of soot, as hath been found in some great tobacco-takers that after their deaths were opened."

The *Counterblast to Tobacco* was first printed in quarto, without name or date, at London, 1616. In the frontpiece were engraved the tobacco-pipes, cross-bones, death's-head, etc. It is not improbable that it was directly intended to foment the popular prejudice against Sir Walter Raleigh, who was put to death in the same year (1616). James alludes to the introduction of the use of tobacco and to Raleigh as follows: "It is not so long since the first entry of this abuse among us here, as that this present age cannot very well remember both the first author and the form of the first introduction of it among us. It was neither brought in by king, great conqueror, nor learned doctor of physic. With the report of a great discovery for a conquest, some two or three savage men were brought in together with this savage custom; but the pity is, the poor wild barbarous men died, but that vile barbarous custom is still alive, yea, in fresh vigor, so as it seems a miracle to me how a custom springing from so vile a ground, and brought in by a father so generally hated, should be welcomed upon so slender a warrant."

The King thus reasons against the Virginia staple: "Secondly, it is, as you use or rather abuse it, a branch of the sin of drunkenness, which is the root of all sins, for as the only delight that drunkards love any weak or sweet drink, so are not those (I mean the strong heat and fume) the only qualities that make tobacco so delectable to all the lovers of it? And as no man loves strong heavy drinks the first day (because *nemo repente fuit turpissimus*), but by custom is piece and piece allured, while in the end a drunkard will have as great a thirst to be drunk as a sober man to quench his thirst with a draught when he hath need of it; so is not this the true case of all the great takers of tobacco, which therefore they themselves do attribute to a bewitching quality in it? Thirdly, is it not the greatest sin that all of you, the people of all sorts of this kingdom, who are created and ordained by God to bestow both your persons and goods for the maintenance both of the honor and safety of your King and commonwealth, should disable yourself to this shameful imbecility, that you are not able to ride or walk the journey of a Jew's Sabbath, but you must have a reeky coal brought you from the next poorhouse to kindle your tobacco with? whereas he cannot be thought able for any service in the wars that cannot endure ofttimes the want of meat, drink, and sleep; much more then must he endure the want of tobacco."

A curious tractate on tobacco, by Dr. Tobias Venner, was published at London in 1621. The author was a graduate of Oxford, and a physician at Bath, and is mentioned in the *Oxoniæ Athenienses.*

The amount of tobacco imported in 1619 into England from Virginia, being the entire crop of the preceding year, was, as before said, twenty thousand pounds. At the end of seventy years there were annually imported into England more than fifteen million of pounds of it, from which a revenue of upward of one hundred thousand pounds was derived.

In April, 1621, the House of Commons debated whether it was expedient to prohibit the importation of tobacco entirely; and they determined to exclude all save from Virginia and the Somer Isles. It was estimated that the consumption of England amounted to one thousand pounds *per diem.* This seductive narcotic leaf, which soothes the mind and quiets its perturbations, has found its way into all parts of the habitable globe, from the sunny tropics to the snowy regions of the frozen pole. Its fragrant smoke ascends alike to the blackened rafters of the lowly hut and the gilded ceilings of luxurious wealth.

JOHN M. LUDLOW

The first negro slaves were brought by Dutchmen for sale into Virginia in 1619. The New England public was at first opposed to the practice of negro slavery, and there is even a record of a slave, who had been sold by a member of the Boston Church, being ordered to be sent back to Africa (1645). Yet negro slaves were to be found in New England as early as 1638. Massachusetts and Connecticut recognized the lawfulness of slavery; Massachusetts, however, only when voluntary or in the case of captives taken in war. Rhode Island, more generous, made illegal the perpetual service of "black mankind," requiring them to be set free after two years, the period of white men's indentures—a condition which, however, would only tend to the working slaves to death in the allotted time. But although there was no importation of negroes on any considerable scale into New England, the ships by which the slave trade was mainly carried on were those from Massachusetts and Rhode Island, which carried rum to Africa, and brought back slaves to the West Indies and the southern colonies. In Maryland slavery had been established at once; in South Carolina it came into birth with the colony itself. The attempt to exclude it from Georgia failed.

The guilt of the institution cannot, however, be fairly charged on the colonists. Queen Elizabeth had been a partner in the second voyage of Sir John Hawkins, the first English slave-captain. James I chartered a slave-trading company (1618); Charles I a second (1631); Charles II a third (1663), of which the Duke of York was president, and again a fourth, in which he himself, as well as the Duke, was a subscriber. Nor did the expulsion of the Stuarts cause any change of feeling in this respect. England's sharpest stroke of business at the Peace of Utrecht (1713) was the obtaining for herself the shameful monopoly of the "Asiento"—the slave trade with the Spanish West Indies—undertaking "to bring into the West Indies of America belonging to his Catholic majesty, in the space of thirty years, one hundred forty-four thousand negroes," at the rate of forty-eight hundred a year, at a fixed rate of duty, with the right to import any further number at a lower rate. As nearly the whole shores of the Gulf of Mexico were still Spanish, England thus contributed to build up slavery in most of the future Southern States of the Union. Whether for foreign or for English colonies, it is reckoned that, from 1700 to 1750, English ships carried away from Africa probably a million and a half of negroes, of whom one-eighth never lived to see the opposite shore.

In the same spirit England dealt with her colonies. When Virginia imposed a tax on the import of negroes, the law had to give way before the interest of the African Company. The same course was followed many years later toward South Carolina, when an act of the provincial Assembly laying a heavy duty on imported slaves was vetoed by the crown (1761). Indeed, the title to a political tract published in 1745, *The African Slave Trade, the Great Pillar and Support of the British Plantation Trade in America*, appears fairly to express the prevalent feeling of the mother-country on the subject before the War of Independence. The most remarkable relaxation of the navigation laws in the eighteenth century was the throwing open the slave trade by the act "for extending and improving the trade to Africa," which, after reciting that "the trade to and from Africa is very advantageous to Great Britain, and necessary for the supplying the plantations and colonies thereunto belonging with a sufficient number of negroes at reasonable rates," enacted that it should be lawful "for all his majesty's subjects to trade and traffick to and from any port or place in Africa, between the port of Sallee in South Barbary and the Cape of Good Hope." By 1763 there were about three hundred thousand negroes in the North American colonies.

It seemed at first as if the black man would gain by the Revolution. The mulatto Attucks was one of the victims of the Boston Massacre, and was buried with honor among the "martyrs of liberty." At the first call to arms the negroes freely enlisted; but a meeting of the general officers decided against their enlistment in the new army of 1775. The free negroes were greatly dissatisfied. Lest they should transfer their services to the British, Washington gave leave to enlist them, and it is certain that they served throughout the war, shoulder to shoulder with white men. At the battle of Monmouth there were more than seven hundred black men in the field. Rhode Island formed a battalion of negroes, giving liberty to every slave enlisting, with compensation to his owner; and the battalion did good service. But Washington always considered the policy of arming slaves "a moot point," unless the enemy set the example; and though Congress recommended Georgia and South Carolina to raise three thousand negroes for the war, giving full "compensation to the proprietors of such negroes," South Carolina refused to do so, and Georgia had been already overrun by the British when the advice was brought.

Notwithstanding the early adoption of a resolution against the importation of slaves into any of the thirteen colonies (April 6, 1776), Jefferson's fervid paragraph condemning the slave trade, and by implication slavery, was struck out of the Declaration of Independence in deference to South Carolina and Georgia, and a member from South Carolina declared that "if property in slaves should be questioned there must be an end to confederation." The resolution of Congress itself against the slave trade bound no single State, although a law to this effect was adopted by Virginia in 1778, and subsequently by all the other States; but this was so entirely a matter of State concernment that neither was any prohibition of the trade contained in the Articles of Confederation, nor was any suffered to be inserted in the treaty of peace.

The feeling against slavery itself was strong in the North. Vermont, in forming a constitution for herself in 1777, allowed no slavery, and was punished for doing so when she applied for admission as a State with the consent of New York, from which she had seceded in 1781: the Southern States refusing to admit her for the present, lest the balance of power should be destroyed. Massachusetts and Pennsylvania, directly or indirectly, abolished slavery in 1780, New Hampshire in 1783. They were followed the next year by Connecticut and Rhode Island, so that by 1784 slavery would be practically at an end in New England and Pennsylvania. Other States—Virginia, Delaware, New Jersey—went no further than to pass laws for allowing voluntary emancipation. In strange contrast to these, Virginia is found in 1780 offering a negro by way of bounty to any white man enlisting for the war. The great Virginians of the day, however—Jefferson, Patrick Henry, George Mason—were opposed to slavery, and large numbers of slaves were emancipated in the State.

So much and no more did the black man get from the Americans. It seemed at first, when Lord Dunmore issued his proclamation offering freedom to all slaves who should join the British standard, as if they were to get much more from England. Accordingly, Governor Rutledge of South Carolina declared in 1780 that the negroes offered up their prayers in favor of England. But although Lord Dunmore persisted in recommending the arming and emancipation of the blacks, neither the ministry at home nor the British officers would enter into the plan. Lord George Germain authorized the confiscation and sale of slaves, even of those who voluntarily followed the troops. Indians were encouraged to catch them and bring them in; they were distributed as prizes and shipped to the West Indies, two thousand at one time, being valued at two hundred fifty silver dollars each. The English name became a terror to the black man, and when Greene took the command they flocked in numbers to his standard. The terms of the peace forbade the British troops to carry away "negroes or other property." Whichever side he might fight for, the poor black man earned no gratitude.

Yet in little more than three-quarters of a century the political complications arising out of the wrongs inflicted on him were to involve the States that had just won their independence in a civil war in comparison with which the struggle to throw off the yoke of the mother-country would appear almost as child's play.

ENGLISH PILGRIMS SETTLE AT PLYMOUTH

A.D. 1620

JOHN S. BARRY

No event in American history is more famous throughout the world, and none has been followed by results more potent in the making of this country, than the settlement of the Pilgrims at Plymouth. This pioneer company, which founded the second English colony in the New World, was composed of Puritans who had left the Church of England, and were known as Independents or Separatists.

In the later years of the sixteenth century the tyranny of the Ecclesiastical Commission drove multitudes of English churchmen into the ranks of the dissenters. At last this tyranny, and the threats of King James I, caused some of the Independents to leave the country.

An Independent Church, mainly composed of simple country people, was formed in 1606 at Scrooby, in Nottinghamshire. At its head were John Robinson, the pastor, and William Brewster, often called Elder Brewster, who was postmaster at Scrooby. Robinson was distinguished alike for his learning and his tolerant spirit. Another leader was William Bradford, then but seventeen years old. He was afterward Governor of Plymouth colony for thirty years, and was its historian.

For some time the members of this Church quietly endured persecution at the hands of the King's officers. Then they began to talk of fleeing to Holland, whither other dissenters had already escaped. In 1607 some of the Scrooby congregation unsuccessfully attempted the flight. A few months later they succeeded in reaching Amsterdam, where they intended to remain. But finding the English exiles there involved in theological disputes, they acted on Robinson's advice and sought a more peaceful home in Leyden.

Here, about three hundred in number, they arrived in 1609, soon after Spain had granted Holland the Twelve Years' Peace, after the long Netherland wars. For eleven years the Pilgrims, as they were already called, remained in their new home, living by various employments. During that time the colony increased to more than a thousand souls.

FOR several years the exiled Pilgrims abode at Leyden in comparative peace. So mutual was the esteem of both pastor and people that it might be said of them, "as of the Emperor Marcus Aurelius and the people of Rome: it was hard to judge whether he delighted more in having such a people, or they in having such a pastor." With their spiritual, their temporal interests were objects of his care, so that he was "every way as a common father to them." And when removed from them by death, as he was in a few years, they sustained "such a loss as they saw could not be easily repaired, for it was as hard for them to find such another leader and feeder as the Taborites to find another Ziska."

Eight years' residence, however, in a land of strangers, subjected to its trials and burdened with its sorrows, satisfied this little band that Holland could not be for them a permanent home. The "hardness of the place" discouraged their friends from joining them. Premature age was creeping upon the vigorous. Severe toil enfeebled their children. The corruption of the Dutch youth was pernicious in its influence. They were Englishmen, attached to the land of their nativity. The Sabbath, to them a sacred institution, was openly neglected. A suitable education was difficult to be obtained for their children. The truce with Spain was drawing to a close, and the renewal of hostilities was seriously apprehended. But the motive above all others which prompted their removal was a "great hope and inward zeal of laying some good foundation for the propagating and advancing of the Gospel of the Kingdom of Christ in these remote parts of the world; yea, though they should be but as stepping-stones to others for performing of so great a work."

For these reasons—and were they frivolous?—a removal was resolved upon. They could not in peace return to England. It was dangerous to remain in the land of their exile. Whither, then, should they go? Where should an asylum for their children be reared? This question, so vital, was first discussed privately, by the gravest and wisest of the Church; then publicly, by all. The "casualties of the seas," the "length of the voyage," the "miseries of the land," the "cruelty of the savages," the "expense of the outfit," the "ill-success of other colonies," and "their own sad experience" in their removal to Holland were urged as obstacles which must doubtless be encountered. But, as a dissuasive from discouragement, it was remarked that "all great and honorable actions are accompanied with great difficulties, and must both be enterprised and overcome with answerable courages. It was granted the dangers very great, but not invincible; for although there were many of them likely, yet they were not certain. Some of the things they feared might never befall them; others, by providence, care, and the use of good means might in a great measure be prevented; and all of them, through the help of God, by fortitude or patience might either be borne or overcome."

Whither should they turn their steps? Some, and "none of the meanest," were "earnest for Guiana." Others, of equal worth, were in favor of Virginia, "where the English had already made entrance and beginning." But a majority were for "living in a distinct body by themselves, though under the general government of Virginia." For Guiana, it was said, "the country was rich, fruitful, and blessed with a perpetual spring and a flourishing greenness"; and the Spaniards "had not planted there nor anywhere near the same." Guiana was the El Dorado of the age. Sir Walter Raleigh, its discoverer, had described its tropical voluptuousness in the most captivating terms; and Chapman, the poet, dazzled by its charms, exclaims:

> "Guiana, whose rich feet are mines of gold,
> Whose forehead knocks against the roof of stars,
> Stands on her tiptoe at fair England looking,
> Kissing her hands, bowing her mighty breast,
> And every sign of all submission making,
> To be the sister and the daughter both
> Of our most sacred maid."

Is it surprising that the thoughts of the exiles were enraptured in contemplating this beautiful land? Was it criminal to seek a pleasant abode? But as an offset to its advantages, its "grievous diseases" and "noisome impediments" were vividly portrayed; and it was urged that, should they settle there and prosper, the "jealous Spaniard" might displace and expel them, as he had already the French from their settlements in Florida; and this the sooner, as there would be none to protect them, and their own strength was inadequate to cope with so powerful an adversary.

Against settling in Virginia it was urged that, "if they lived among the English there planted, or under their government, they would be in as great danger to be persecuted for the cause of religion as if they lived in England, and it might be worse, and, if they lived too far off, they should have neither succor nor defence from them." Upon the whole, therefore, it was decided to "live in a distinct body by themselves, under the general government of Virginia, and by their agents to sue his majesty to grant them free liberty and freedom of religion."

Accordingly John Carver, one of the deacons of the Church, and Robert Cushman, a private member, were sent to England to treat with the Virginia Company for a grant of land, and to solicit of the King liberty of conscience. The friends from whom aid was expected, and to some of whom letters were written, were Sir Edwin Sandys, the distinguished author of the *Europæ Speculum;* Sir Robert Maunton, afterward secretary of state; and Sir John Wolstenholme, an eminent merchant and a farmer of the customs. Sir Ferdinando Georges seems also to have been interested in their behalf, as he speaks of means used by himself, before his rupture with the Virginia Company, to "draw into their enterprises some of those families that had retired into Holland, for scruple of conscience, giving them such freedom and liberty as might stand with their likings."

The messengers—"God going along with them"—bore a missive signed by the principal members of the Church, commending them to favor, and conducted their mission with discretion and propriety; but as their instructions were not plenary, they soon returned, bearing a letter from Sir Edwin Sandys, approving their diligence and proffering aid. The next month a second embassy was despatched, with an answer to Sir Edwin's letter, in which, for his encouragement, the exiles say: "We believe and trust the Lord is with us, and will graciously prosper our endeavors accordingly to the simplicity of our hearts therein. We are well weaned from the delicate milk of our mother-country and inured to the difficulties of a strange and hard land. The people are, for the body of them, industrious and frugal. We are knit together in a strict and sacred bond and covenant of the Lord, of the violation whereof we make great conscience, and by virtue whereof we hold ourselves strictly tied to all care of others' goods. It is not with us, as with others, whom small things can discourage, or small discontentments cause to wish themselves at home again."

For the information of the council of the company, the "requests" of the Church were sent, signed by nearly the whole congregation, and, in a letter to Sir John Wolstenholme, explanation was given of their "judgments" upon three points named by his majesty's privy council, in which they affirmed that they differed nothing in doctrine and but little in discipline from the French reformed churches, and expressed their willingness to take the oath of supremacy if required, "if that convenient satisfaction be not given by our taking the oath of allegiance."

The new agents, upon their arrival in England, found the Virginia Company anxious for their emigration to America, and "willing to give them a patent with as ample privileges as they had or could grant to any"; and some of the chief members of the company "doubted not to obtain their suit of the King for liberty in religion." But the last "proved a harder work than they took it for." Neither James nor his bishops would grant such a request. The "advancement of his dominions" and "the enlargement of the Gospel" his majesty acknowledged to be "an honorable motive"; and "fishing"—the secular business they expected to follow—"was an honest trade, the apostle's own calling"; but for any further liberties he referred them to the prelates of Canterbury and London. All that could be obtained from the King after the most diligent "sounding" was a verbal promise that "he would connive at them and not molest them, provided they conducted themselves peaceably; but to allow or tolerate them under his seal" he would not consent.

With this answer the messengers returned, and their report was discouraging to the hopes of the exiles. Should they trust their monarch's word, when bitter experience had taught them the ease with which it could be broken? And yet, reasoned some, "his word may be as good as his bond; for if he purposes to injure us, though we have a seal as broad as the house-floor, means will be found to recall or reverse it." In this as in other matters, therefore, they relied upon Providence, trusting that distance would prove as effectual a safeguard as the word of a prince which had been so often forfeited.

Accordingly other agents were sent to procure a patent, and to negotiate with such merchants as had expressed a willingness to aid them with funds. On reaching England these agents found a division existing in the Virginia Company, growing out of difficulties between Sir Thomas Smith and Sir Edwin Sandys; and disagreeable intelligence had been received from Virginia of disturbances in the colony which had there been established. For these reasons little could be immediately effected. At length, after tedious delays, and "messengers passing to and fro," a patent was obtained, which, by the advice of friends, was taken in the name of John Wincob, a gentleman in the family of the Countess of Lincoln; and with this document, and the proposals of Mr. Thomas Weston, one of the agents returned, and submitted the same to the Church for inspection. The nature of these proposals has never transpired, nor is the original patent —the first which the Pilgrims received—known to be in existence. Future inquirers may discover this instrument, as recently other documents have been rescued from oblivion. We should be glad to be acquainted with its terms, were it only to know definitely the region it embraced. But if ever discovered, we will hazard the conjecture that it will be found to cover territory now included in New York.

Upon the reception of the patent and the accompanying proposals, as every enterprise of the Pilgrims began from God—a day of fasting and prayer was appointed to seek divine guidance; and Mr. Robinson, whose services were ever appropriate, discoursed to his flock from the words in Samuel: "And David's men said unto him, See, we be afraid here in Judah: how much more if we come to Keilah, against the host of the Philistines?" Next followed a discussion "as to how many and who should go first." All were ready and anxious to embark; but funds were wanting to defray their expenses. It was concluded, therefore, that the youngest and strongest should be the pioneers of the Church, and that the eldest and weakest should follow at a future date. If the Lord "frowned" upon their proceedings the first emigrants were to return, but if he prospered and favored them they were to "remember and help over the ancient and poor." As the emigrants proved the minority, it was agreed that the pastor should remain in Holland, and that Mr. Brewster, the elder, should accompany those who were to leave. Each party was to be an absolute church in itself; and as any went or came they were to be admitted to fellowship without further testimonies. Thus the church at Plymouth was the first in New England established upon the basis of Independent Congregationalism.

Early the next spring Mr. Weston visited Leyden to conclude the arrangements for "shipping and money," and Messrs. Carver and Cushman returned with him to England to "receive the money and provide for the voyage." The latter was to tarry in London, and the former was to proceed to Southampton; Mr. Christopher Martin, of Billerrica, in Essex, was to join them; and from the "county of Essex came several others, as also from London and other places."

Pending these negotiations, the property of those who were to embark was sold, and the proceeds were added to the common fund, with which vessels, provisions, and other necessaries were to be obtained. But Mr. Weston already half repented his engagements, and, more interested in trade than in religion, he informed his associates that "sundry honorable lords and worthy gentlemen" were treating for a patent for New England, distinct from the Virginia patent, and advised them to alter their plans and ally with the new company. At the same time their agents sent word that "some of those who should have gone fell off and would not go; other merchants and friends that professed to adventure their money withdrew and pretended many excuses: some disliking they went not to Guiana; others would do nothing unless they went to Virginia; and many who were most relied on refused to adventure if they went thither." Such discouragements would have disheartened men of a less sanguine temperament, and for a time the Pilgrims were "driven to great straits"; but as the patent for New England had not passed the seals, it was deemed useless to linger longer in uncertainty, and they "resolved to adventure with that patent they had."

Their greatest hardship was the compact with the merchants. The Pilgrims were poor and their funds were limited. They had no alternative, therefore, but to associate with others; and, as often happens in such cases, wealth took advantage of their impoverished condition. By their instructions the terms on which their agents were to engage with the adventurers were definitely fixed, and no alteration was to be made without consultation. But time was precious; the business was urgent; it had already been delayed so long that many were impatient; and to satisfy the merchants, who drove their bargain sharply and shrewdly, some changes were made, and by ten tight articles the emigrants were bound to them for the term of seven years. At the end of this period, by the original compact, the houses and improved lands were to belong wholly to the planters; and each colonist having a family to support was to be allowed two days in each week to labor for their benefit. The last is a liberty enjoyed by "even a Wallachian serf or a Spanish slave"; and the refusal of the merchants to grant so reasonable a request caused great complaint; but Mr. Cushman answered peremptorily that, unless they had consented to the change, "the whole design would have fallen to the ground, and, necessity having no law, they were constrained to be silent." As it was, it threatened a seven years' check to the pecuniary prosperity of the colony; but as it did not interfere with their civil or religious rights, it was submitted to with the less reluctance, though never acceptable.

At this critical juncture, while the Pilgrims were in such perplexity, and surrounded by so many difficulties, the Dutch, who were perfectly acquainted with their proceedings, and who could not but be sensible that the patent they had obtained of the Virginia Company, if sanctioned by the government of England, would interfere seriously with their projected West India Company, and with their settlement at New Netherland, stepped forward with the proposals of the most inviting and apparently disinterested and liberal character. Knowing that but a portion of the Church were preparing to embark for America, and that all would be glad to emigrate in a body, overtures were made to Mr. Robinson, as pastor, that he and his flock, and their friends in England, would embark under the auspices of the Lords States-General, themselves should be transported to America free of expense, and cattle should be furnished for their subsistence on their arrival. These are the "liberal offers" alluded to in general terms by early Pilgrim writers, and which are uniformly represented as having originated with the Dutch, though recently it has been suggested, and even asserted, that the overtures came from the Pilgrims themselves. But there is an inherent improbability in this last representation, arising from the fact that much time had been spent in procuring a patent in England, and in negotiating with the adventurers for the requisite funds, and an avowed object with the Pilgrims in leaving Holland was to preserve their nationality. They had no motive, therefore, to originate such a proposition, though when made to them by the Dutch it may have proved so attractive that they were willing to accept it upon certain conditions, of which one was that the government of Holland should guarantee to protect them.

This concession was enough for the merchants to act upon. "They saw at once that so many families going in a body to New Netherland could hardly fail to form a successful colony." But the political part of the question they were unable to decide. They were ready to expend their capital in carrying the emigrants to New Netherland and in supplying them with necessaries; but they had no authority to promise that the Dutch government would afford to the colonists special protection after their arrival there. "They therefore determined to apply directly to the general government at The Hague."

The Prince of Orange was then in the zenith of his power; and to him, as stadtholder, the merchants repaired with a memorial, professedly in the name of the "English preacher at Leyden," praying that "the aforesaid preacher and four hundred families may be taken under the protection of the United Provinces, and that two ships-of-war may be sent to secure, provisionally, the said lands to this government, since such lands may be of great importance whenever the West India Company shall be organized."

The Stadtholder was too wary a politician to approbate immediately so sweeping a proposal, and referred it to the States-General. For two months it was before this body, where it was several times discussed; and finally, after repeated deliberations, it was resolved "peremptorily to reject the prayer of the memorialists." Nor can we doubt the wisdom of the policy which prompted this decision. It was well known in Holland that the English claimed the territory of New Netherland. The Dutch had hitherto been tolerated in settling there, because they had not openly interfered with the trade of the English. But should they now send over a body of English emigrants, under the tricolored flag, designed to found a colony for the benefit of the Batavian republic, the prudent foresaw that a collision would be inevitable, and might result disastrously to the interests of their nation. Mr. Robinson and his associates, though exiles, were Englishmen, and would be held as such in Holland or America. Hence, had the Pilgrims emigrated under the auspices of the Dutch, and had James I demanded of them the allegiance of subjects, they would have been compelled to submit, or the nation which backed them would have been forced into war. There was wisdom, therefore, in the policy which rejected the memorial of the merchants.

In consequence of the disaffection of Mr. Weston, there were complaints of his delay in providing the necessary shipping; but at last the Speedwell, of sixty tons—miserable misnomer—was purchased in Holland for the use of the emigrants; and the Mayflower, of a hundred eighty tons—whose name is immortal—was chartered in England, and was fitting for their reception. The cost of the outfit, including a trading stock of seventeen hundred pounds, was but twenty-four hundred pounds—about twelve thousand dollars of the currency of the United States! It marks the poverty of the Pilgrims that their own funds were inadequate to meet such a disbursement; and it marks the narrowness of the adventurers that they doled the sum so grudgingly, and exacted such securities for their personal indemnity. There were some generous hearts among the members of this company—true and tried friends of the exiles in their troubles—but many of them were illiberal and selfish, and had very little sympathy with the principles of their partners.

As the time of departure drew near, a day of public humiliation was observed—the last that the emigrants kept with their pastor—and on this memorable occasion Mr. Robinson discoursed to them from the words in Ezra: "And there, at the river, by Ahava, I proclaimed a fast, that we might humble ourselves before God, and seek of him a right way for us, and for our children, and for all of our substance." The catholic advice of this excellent man was worthy to be addressed to the *Founders of New England:*

"We are now ere long to part asunder; and the Lord only knoweth whether ever I shall live to see your faces again. But, whether he hath appointed this or not, I charge you, before him and his blessed angels, to follow me no further than I have followed Christ; and if God should reveal anything to you by any other instrument of his, be as ready to receive it as ever you were to receive any truth by my ministry; and I am confident that the Lord hath more light and truth yet to break forth out of his holy Word. For my part, I cannot but bewail the condition of the reformed churches, who are come to a period of religion, and will go no further than the instruments of their reformation. The Lutherans, for example, cannot be drawn to go beyond what Luther saw; and whatever part of God's will he hath further imparted to Calvin, they will rather die than embrace; and so the Calvinists stick where he left them. This is a misery much to be lamented, for, though they were precious shining lights in their times, God hath not revealed his whole will to them; and were they now living, they would be as ready and willing to embrace further lights as that they did receive.

"Remember also your church covenants, and especially that part of it whereby you promise and covenant with God and one with another, to receive whatsoever light or truth shall be made known to you from his written Word. But take heed what you receive for truth, and examine, compare, and weigh it well with the Scriptures. It is not possible that the Christian world should come so lately out of such thick anti-Christian darkness, and that full perfection of knowledge should break forth at once. Shake off, too, the name of Brownists, for it is but a nickname, and a brand to make religion odious, and the professors of it, to the Christian world. And be ready to close with the godly party of the kingdom of England, and rather study union than disunion —how near you may, without sin, close with them, than in the least manner to affect disunion or separation."

At the conclusion of this discourse those who were to leave were feasted at their pastor's house, where, after "tears," warm and gushing, from the fulness of their hearts, the song of praise and thanksgiving was raised; and "truly," says an auditor, "it was the sweetest melody that ever mine ears heard." But the parting hour has come! The Speedwell lies at Delfthaven, twenty-two miles south of Leyden, and thither the emigrants are accompanied by their friends, and by others from Amsterdam who are present to pray for the success of their voyage. "*So they left that goodly and pleasant city, which had been their resting-place near twelve years. But they knew they were Pilgrims, and looked not much on those things, and quieted their spirits.*"

The last night was spent "with little sleep by the most, but with friendly entertainment and Christian discourse, and other real expressions of true Christian love." On the morrow they sailed; "and truly doleful was the sight of that sad and mournful parting; to see what sighs and sobs and prayers did sound among them; what tears did gush from every eye, and pithy speeches pierced each other's hearts; that sundry of the Dutch strangers, that stood on the quay as spectators, could not refrain from tears. Yet comfortable and sweet it was to see such lively and true expressions of dear and unfeigned love. But the tide, which stays for no man, calling them away that were thus loth to depart, their reverend pastor, falling down on his knees, and they all with him, with watery cheeks, commended them with most fervent prayers to the Lord and his blessing; and then, with mutual embraces and many tears, they took their leave one of another, which proved to be *the last leave* to many of them."

At starting they gave their friends "a volley of small shot and three pieces of ordnance"; and so, "lifting up their hands to each other, and their hearts for each other to the Lord God," they set sail, and found his presence with them, "in the midst of the manifold straits he carried them through." Favored by a prosperous gale they soon reached Southampton, where lay the Mayflower in readiness with the rest of their company; and after a joyful welcome and mutual congratulations, they "fell to parley about their proceedings."

In about a fortnight the Speedwell, commanded by Captain Reynolds, and the Mayflower, commanded by Captain Jones — both having a hundred twenty passengers on board —were ready to set out to cross the Atlantic. Overseers of the provisions and passengers were selected; Mr. Weston and others were present to witness their departure; and the farewell was said to the friends they were to leave. But "not every cloudless morning is followed by a pleasant day." Scarcely had the two barks left the harbor ere Captain Reynolds complained of the leakiness of the Speedwell, and both put in at Dartmouth for repairs. At the end of eight precious days they started again, but had sailed "only a hundred leagues beyond the land's end" when the former complaints were renewed, and the vessels put in at Plymouth, where, "by the consent of the whole company," the Speedwell was dismissed; and as the Mayflower could accommodate but one hundred passengers, twenty of those who had embarked in the smaller vessel—including Mr. Cushman and his family—were compelled to return; and matters being ordered with reference to this arrangement, "another sad parting took place."

Finally, after the lapse of two more precious weeks, the Mayflower, "freighted with the destinies of a continent," and having on board one hundred passengers, resolute men, women, and children, "loosed from Plymouth"—"her inmates having been kindly entertained and courteously used by divers friends there dwelling"—and, with the wind "east-northeast, a fine small gale," was soon far at sea.

The particulars of this voyage, more memorable by far than the famed expedition of the Argonauts, and paralleled, if at all, only by the voyage of Columbus, are few and scanty. Though fair winds wafted the bark onward for a season, contrary winds and fierce storms were soon encountered, by which she was "shrewdly shaken" and her "upper works made very leaky." One of the main beams of the midship was also "bowed and cracked," but a passenger having brought with him "a large iron screw," the beam was replaced and carefully fastened, and the vessel continued on. During this storm John Howland, "a stout young man," was by a "heel of the ship thrown into the sea, but catching by the halliards, which hung overboard, he kept his hold, and was saved." "A profane and proud young seaman," also, "stout and able of body, who had despised the poor people in their sickness, telling them he hoped to help cast off half of them overboard before they came to their journey's end, and to make merry with what they had, was smitten with a grievous disease, of which he died in a desperate manner, and was himself the first thrown overboard, to the astonishment of all his fellows." One other death occurred—that of William Button, a servant of Dr. Fuller; and there was one birth, in the family of Stephen Hopkins, of a son, christened "Oceanus," who died shortly after the landing. The ship being leaky, and the passengers closely stowed, their clothes were constantly wet. This added much to the discomfort of the voyage, and laid a foundation for a portion of the mortality which prevailed the first winter.

"Land-ho!" This welcome cry was not heard until two months had elapsed, and the sandy cliffs of Cape Cod were the first points which greeted the eyes of the exiles. Yet the appearance of these cliffs "much comforted them, and caused them to rejoice together, and praise God, that had given them once again to see land." Their destination, however, was to "the mouth of the Hudson," and now they were much farther to the north, and within the bounds of the New England Company. They therefore "tacked to stand to the southward," but "becoming entangled among roaring shoals, and the wind shrieking upon them withal, they resolved to bear up again for the Cape," and the next day, "by God's providence, they got into Cape harbor," where, falling upon their knees, they "blessed the Lord, the God of heaven, who had brought them over the vast and furious ocean, and delivered them from all perils and miseries, therein, again to set their feet on the firm and stable earth, their proper element."

Morton, in his memorial, asserts that the Mayflower put in at this cape, "partly by reason of a storm by which she was forced in, but more especially by the fraudulency and contrivance of the aforesaid Mr. Jones, the master of the ship; for their intention and his engagement was to Hudson's river; but some of the Dutch having notice of their intention, and having thoughts about the same time of erecting a plantation there likewise, they fraudulently hired the said Jones, by delays, while they were in England, and now under the pretence of the sholes, etc., to disappoint them in their going thither. Of this plot betwixt the Dutch and Mr. Jones I have had *late and certain intelligence.*" The explicitness of this assertion has caused charge of treachery —brought by no one but Morton—to be repeated by almost every historian down to the present period; and it is only within a few years that its correctness has been questioned by writers whose judgment is entitled to respect. But notwithstanding the

plausibility of the arguments urged to disprove this charge, and even the explicit assertion that it is a "Parthian calumny," and a "sheer falsehood," we must frankly own that, in our estimation, the veracity of Morton yet remains unimpeached. Facts prove that the Dutch were contemplating permanent settlement of New Netherland, and the early Pilgrim writers assert that overtures were made to the Leyden Church by the merchants of Holland to join them in that movement, and the petition to the States-General, when presented by those merchants, was finally rejected, and the Mayflower commenced her voyage intending to proceed to the Hudson. Is it improbable that steps may have been taken to frustrate their intention, and that arrangements may even have been made with the captain of that vessel by Dutch agents in England, to alter her course, and land the emigrants farther to the north?

We are aware that one to whose judgment we have usually deferred has said that had the intelligence been early it would have been more certain. But every student of history knows that *late* intelligence is often more reliable and authentic than *early;* and if it be asked from what source did Morton obtain his information, we can only suggest that, up to 1664, New Netherlands remained under the dominion of the Dutch, and the history of that colony was in a great measure secret to the English. But several of the prominent settlers of Plymouth had ere this removed to Manhattan—as Isaac Allerton and Thomas Willet—and after the reduction of the country and its subjection to England, from these persons the *late* and *certain* intelligence may have been received, or from access to documents which were before kept private.

The harbor in which the Mayflower now lay is worthy of a passing glance. It is described by Major Grahame as "one of the finest harbors for ships of war on the whole Atlantic coast. The width and freedom from obstructions of every kind, at its entrance, and the extent of sea-room upon the land side, make it accessible to vessels of the largest class in almost all winds. This advantage, its capacity, depth of water, excellent anchorage, and the complete shelter it affords from all winds render it one of the most valuable harbors upon our coast, whether considered in a commercial or a military point of view."

If to the advantages here enumerated could have been added a fertile soil, and an extensive back country, suitably furnished with timber and fuel, the spot to which this gallant bark was led would have proved as eligible a site for a flourishing colony as could possibly have been desired. But these advantages were wanting; and though our fathers considered it an "extraordinary blessing of God" in directing their course for these parts, which they were at first inclined to consider "one of the most pleasant, most healthful, and most fruitful parts of the world," longer acquaintance and better information abundantly satisfied them of the insuperable obstacles to agriculture and commerce.

The Pilgrims were now ready to pass to the shore. But before taking this step, as the spot where they lay was without the bounds of their patent, and as signs of insubordination had appeared among their servants, an association was deemed necessary, and an agreement to "combine in one body and to submit to such government and governors as should by common consent" be selected and chosen. Accordingly, a compact was prepared, and signed before landing by all the males of the company who were of age; and this instrument was the constitution of the colony for several years. It was as follows:

"In the name of God, Amen. We whose names are underwritten, the loyal subjects of our dread sovereign lord, King James, by the grace of God, of Great Britain, France, and Ireland, King, defender of the faith, etc., having undertaken, for the glory of God, and the advancement of the Christian faith, and honor of our King and country, a voyage to plant the first colony in the northern parts of Virginia, do, by these presents, solemnly and mutually, in the presence of God and one another, covenant and combine ourselves together unto a civil body politic, for our better ordering and preservation, and furtherance of the ends aforesaid, and by virtue hereof to enact, constitute, and frame such just and equal laws, ordinances, acts, constitutions, and offices, from time to time, as shall be thought most meet and convenient for the general good of the colony; unto which we promise all due submission and obedience. In witness whereof we have hereunder subscribed our names, at Cape Cod, the 11th of November, in the year of the reign of our sovereign lord, King James of England, France, and Ireland, the 18th, and of Scotland the 54th, A.D. 1620."

While on the one hand much eloquence has been expended in expatiating on this compact, as if in the cabin of the May-flower had consciously and for the first time been discovered in an age of Cimmerian darkness the true principles of republicanism and equality; on the other hand, it has been asserted that the Pilgrims were "actuated by the most daring ambition," and that even at this early period they designed to erect a government absolutely independent of the mother-country. But the truth seems to be that, although the form of government adopted by the emigrants is republican in its character, and remarkably liberal, at the same time its founders acknowledged suitable allegiance to England, and regarded themselves as connected with the land of their nativity by political and social ties, both endearing and enduring. Left to themselves in a wilderness land, apart from all foreign aid, and thrown upon their own resources, with none to help or advise, they adopted that course which commended itself to their calm judgment as the simplest and best; and if, under such circumstances, their compact was democratic, it seems chiefly to intimate that self-government is naturally attractive to the mind, and is spontaneously resorted to in emergencies like the present. It is as unwise to flatter our ancestors by ascribing to them motives different from those which they themselves professed as it is unjust to prefer charges against them to which they are not obnoxious. They were honest, sincere, and God-fearing men; humble in their circumstances, and guided by their own judgment; but endowed with no singular prophetic vision, and claiming no preternatural political sagacity. They could penetrate the future no farther than to confide in the justice of God and the power of truth. The latter they knew must ultimately prevail, for the former was pledged to secure its triumph.

The first care of the exiles, having established their provisional government, was to provide for their shelter. Cautiously, therefore, for fear of harm, on the same day that the compact was signed, fifteen or sixteen men, well armed, were set ashore at Long Point to explore the country; and returning at night with a boat-load of juniper, which delighted them with its fragrance, they reported that they had found "neither persons nor habitations."

The stillness of the Sabbath was consecrated to worship—the first, probably, ever observed by Christians in Massachusetts—and on the morrow the shallop was drawn to the beach for repairs, and for the first time the whole company landed for refreshment. As the fitting of the shallop promised to be a difficult task, the adventurous, impatient of delay, were eager to prosecute a journey by land for discovery. "The willingness of the persons was liked, but the thing itself, in regard of the danger, was rather permitted than approved." Consent, however, was obtained, and sixteen were detailed under Captain Standish, their military leader, who had served in the armies both of Elizabeth and James; and William Bradford, Stephen Hopkins, and Edward Tilly, being joined with him as "advisers and counsellors," the party debarked at Stevens' Point, at the western extremity of the harbor, and marching in single file, at the distance of about a mile, five savages were espied, who, at their approach, hastily fled.

Compassing the head of East Harbor Creek the next day, and reaching a deep valley, fed with numerous springs, the exhausted travellers, whose provisions consisted but of "biscuit and Holland cheese, with a little bottle of aqua vitæ," eagerly halted by one of these springs, and "drank their first draught of New England water with as much delight as ever they drunk drink in all their lives." Passing thence to the shore, and kindling a beacon-fire, they proceeded to another valley, in Truro, in which was a pond, "a musket-shot broad and twice as long," near which the Indians had planted corn. Further on graves were discovered; and at another spot the ruins of a house, and heaps of sand filled with corn stored in baskets. With hesitancy—so scrupulous were they of wilfully wronging the natives—an old kettle, a waif from the ruins, was filled with this corn, for which the next summer the owners were remunerated. In the vicinity of the Pamet were the ruins of a fort, or palisade; and encamping for the night near the pond in Truro, on the following day they returned to the ship "weary and welcome" and their "Eschol" was added for their diminishing stores.

Ten days after, another expedition was fitted out, in which

twenty-five of the colonists and nine or ten of the sailors, with Jones at their head, were engaged; and visiting the mouth of the Pamet, called by them "Cold Harbor," and obtaining fresh supplies from the aboriginal granaries, after a brief absence, in which a few unimportant discoveries were made, the party returned. Here a discussion ensued. Should they settle at Cold Harbor or seek a more eligible site? In favor of the former it was urged that the harbor was suitable for boats, if not for ships; the corn land was good; it was convenient to their fishing-grounds; the location was healthy; winter was approaching; travelling was dangerous; their provisions were wasting; and the captain of the Mayflower was anxious to return. On the other hand, it was replied that a better place might be found; it would be a hinderance to move a second time; good spring-water was wanting; and lastly, at Agawam, now Ipswich, twenty leagues to the north, was an excellent harbor, better ground, and better fishing. Robert Coppin, their pilot, likewise informed them of "a great and navigable river and good harbour in the other headland of the bay, almost right over against Cape Cod," which he had formerly visited, and which was called "Thievish Harbor."

A third expedition, therefore, was agreed upon; and though the weather was unfavorable, and some difficulty was experienced in clearing Billingsgate Point, they reached the weather shore, and there "had better sailing." Yet bitter was the cold, and the spray, as it froze on them, gave them the appearance of being encased in glittering mail. At night their rendezvous was near Great Meadow Creek; and early in the morning, after an encounter with the Indians, in which no one was wounded, their journey was resumed, their destination being the harbor which Coppin had described to them, and which he assured them could be reached in a few hours' sailing. Through rain and snow they steered their course; but by the middle of the afternoon a fearful storm raged; the hinges of their rudder were broken; the mast was split, the sail was rent, and the inmates of the shallop were in imminent peril; yet, by God's mercy, they survived the first shock, and, favored by a flood tide, steered into the harbor. A glance satisfied the pilot that it was not the place he sought; and in an agony of despair he exclaimed: "Lord be merciful to us! My eyes never saw this place before!" In his frenzy he would have run the boat ashore among the breakers; but an intrepid seaman resolutely shouted, "About with her, or we are lost!" And instantly obeying, with hard rowing, dark as it was, with the wind howling fiercely, and the rain dashing furiously, they shot under the lee of an island and moored until morning.

The next day the island was explored—now known as Clarke's Island—and the clothing of the adventurers was carefully dried; but, excusable as it might have been under the circumstances in which they were placed to have immediately resumed their researches, the Sabbath was devoutly and sacredly observed.

On Monday, December 11th, O. S., a landing was effected upon Forefather's Rock. The site of this stone was preserved by tradition, and a venerable contemporary of several of the Pilgrims, whose head was silvered with the frost of ninety-five winters, settled the question of its identity in 1741. Borne in his arm-chair by a grateful populace, Elder Faunce took his last look at the spot so endeared to his memory, and, bedewing it with tears, he bade it farewell. In 1774 this precious boulder, as if seized with the spirit of that bustling age, was raised from its bed to be consecrated to Liberty, and in the act of its elevation it split in twain—an occurrence regarded by many as ominous of the separation of the colonies from England, and the lower part being left in the spot where it still lies, the upper part, weighing several tons, was conveyed, amid the heartiest rejoicings, to Liberty-pole Square, and adorned with a flag bearing the imperishable motto, "Liberty or Death." On July 4, 1834, the natal day of the freedom of the colonies, this part of the rock was removed to the ground in front of Pilgrim Hall, and there it rests, encircled with a railing, ornamented with heraldic wreaths, bearing the names of the forty-one signers of the compact in the Mayflower. Fragments of this rock are relics in the cabinets of hundreds of our citizens, and are sought with avidity even by strangers as memorials of a pilgrimage to the birthplace of New England.

On the day of landing the harbor was sounded and the land explored; and, the place inviting settlement, the adventurers returned with tidings of their success; the Mayflower weighed anchor to proceed to the spot; and ere another Sabbath dawned she was safely moored in the desired haven. Monday and Tuesday were spent in exploring tours; and on Wednesday, the 20th, the settlement at Plymouth was commenced—twenty persons remaining ashore for the night. On the following Saturday the first timber was felled; on Monday their storehouse was commenced; on Thursday preparations were made for the erection of a fort; and allotments of land were made to the families; and on the following Sunday religious worship was performed for the first time in their storehouse.

For a month the colonists were busily employed. The distance of the vessel—which lay more than a mile from the shore—was a great hinderance to their work; frequent storms interrupted their operations; and by accident their storehouse was destroyed by fire, and their hospital narrowly escaped destruction. The houses were arranged in two rows, on Leyden street, each man building his own. The storehouse was twenty feet square; the size of the private dwellings we have no means of determining. All were constructed of logs, with the interstices filled with sticks and clay; the roofs were covered with thatch; the chimneys were of fragments of wood, plastered with clay; and oiled paper served as a substitute for glass for the inlet of light.

The whole of this first winter was a period of unprecedented hardship and suffering. Mild as was the weather, it was far more severe than that of the land of their birth; and the disease contracted on shipboard, aggravated by colds caught in their wanderings in quest of a home, caused a great and distressing mortality to prevail. In December six died; in January, eight; in February, seventeen; and in March, thirteen; a total of forty-four in four months—of whom twenty-one were signers of the compact. It is remarkable that the leaders of the colony were spared. The survivors were unwearied in their attentions to their companions; but affection could not avert the arrows of the Destroyer. The first burial-place was on Cole's Hill; and as an affecting proof of the miserable condition of the sufferers it is said that, knowing they were surrounded by warlike savages, and fearing their losses might be discovered and advantage be taken of their weakness to attack and exterminate them, the sad mounds formed by rude coffins hidden beneath the earth were carefully levelled and sowed with grain!

However rapidly we have sketched, in the preceding pages, the history of the Pilgrims from their settlement in Holland to their removal to America, no one can fail to have been deeply impressed with the inspiring lessons which that history teaches. As has been well said: "Their banishment to Holland was fortunate; the decline of their little company in the strange land was fortunate; the difficulties which they experienced in getting the royal consent to banish themselves to this wilderness was fortunate; all the tears and heartbreakings of that ever-memorable parting at Delfthaven had the happiest influence on the rising destinies of New England. All this purified the rank of the settlers. These rough touches of fortune brushed off the light, uncertain, selfish spirits. They made it a grave, solemn, self-denying expedition, and required of those who were engaged in it to be so too."

Touching also is the story of the "long, cold, dreary autumnal passage" in that "one solitary, adventurous vessel, the Mayflower, of a forlorn hope, freighted with the prospects of a future state and bound across the unknown sea." We behold it "pursuing with a thousand misgivings the uncertain, the tedious voyage. Suns rise and set, and winter surprises them on the deep, but brings them not the sight of the wished-for shore. The awful voice of the storm howls through the rigging. The laboring masts seem straining from their base; the dismal sound of the pumps is heard; the ship leaps, as it were, madly from billow to billow; the ocean breaks, and settles with engulfing floods over the floating deck, and beats with deadening, shivering weight against the staggering vessel."

Escaped from these perils, after a passage of sixty-six days, and subsequent journeyings until the middle of December, they land on the ice-clad rocks of Plymouth, worn out with suffering, weak and weary from the fatigues of the voyage, poorly armed, scantily provisioned, surrounded by barbarians, without prospect of human succor, without the help or favor of their king, with a useless patent, without assurance of liberty in religion, without shelter, and without means!

Yet resolute men are there: Carver, Bradford, Brewster, Standish, Winslow, Alden, Warren, Hopkins, and others. Female fortitude and resignation are there. Wives and mothers, with dauntless courage and unexampled heroism, have braved all these dangers, shared all these trials, borne all these sorrows, submitted to aii these privations. And there, too, is "chilled and shivering childhood, houseless but for a mother's arms, couchless but for a mother's breast."

But these sepulchres of the dead!—where lie Turner, Chilton, Crackston, Fletcher, Goodman, Mullins, White, Rogers, Priest, Williams, and their companions—these touch the tenderest and holiest chords. Husbands and wives, parents and children, have finished their pilgrimage, and mingled their dust with the dust of New England. Hushed as the unbreathing air, when not a leaf stirs in the mighty forest, was the scene at those graves where the noble and true were buried in peace. Deeply as they sorrowed at parting with those, doubly endeared to them by the remembrance of what they had suffered together, and by the fellowship of kindred griefs, they committed them to the earth calmly, but with hope." No sculptured marble, no enduring monument, no honorable inscription, marks the spot where they were laid. Is it surprising that local attachments soon sprung up in the breasts of the survivors, endearing them to the place of refuge and their sorrows? They had come "hither from a land to which they were never to return. Hither they had brought, and here they were to fix, their hopes and their affections." Consecrated by persecutions in their native land, by an exile in Holland of hardship and toil, by the perils of the occan voyage and its terrible storms, by their sufferings and wanderings in quest of a home, and by the heartrending trials of the first lonely winter—by all these was their new home consecrated and hallowed in their inmost thoughts; and forward to the future they looked with confidence in God and a cheerful reliance upon that beneficent Providence which had enabled them with patience to submit to his chastenings, and, Phœnix-like, to rise from the ashes of the dead and from the depths of the bitterest affliction and distress, with invincible courage, determined to subdue the wilderness before them, and to "fill this region of the great continent, which stretches almost from pole to pole," with freedom and intelligence, the arts and the sciences, flourishing villages, temples of worship, and the numerous blessings of civilized life, baptized in the fountain of the Gospel of Christ.

BIRTH OF MODERN SCIENTIFIC METHODS

BACON AND DESCARTES

A.D. 1620

GEORGE HENRY LEWES

Three centuries of modern thought have not sufficed to settle the dispute as to its own origin. Many Englishmen still claim insistently that Lord Bacon, in his *Advancement of Learning*, and still more positively in his later and greater work, the *Novum Organum* (1620) started modern scientific method. Present scientists themselves seem inclined to smile somewhat scornfully at the laurels thus placed on Bacon's brow. And as for Frenchmen, they simply refuse to hear the pompous Lord Chancellor mentioned at all. To them René Descartes is the only genuine originator of all modern philosophy. The publication of his *Discourse on Method* (1637) marks for them the epoch which separates two worlds of thought.

Fortunately, George Henry Lewes, himself a celebrated English critic and the author of a system of philosophy, presents us the two rivals side by side, seeking to explain and balance the honors due to each.

It is very certain that somewhere about this period did originate that mathematical exactitude of method in both thought and experiment which has produced modern science. And modern science has, in its brief but marvellous career of three centuries, altered the face of the globe. It has taught man more than ancient science did in all the preceding centuries; it has touched even our deepest faiths.

Whether its success has been due mainly to the abstract reasoners like Copernicus and the philosophers, or to the practical experimenters like Galileo and Harvey, is perhaps scarcely a practical question.

IN the evolution of philosophy, as in the evolution of an organism, it is impossible to fix with any precision a period of origin, because every beginning is also a termination, and presumes the results of a whole series of preceding evolutions. As Mr. Spedding felicitously says, our philosophy "was born about Bacon's time, and Bacon's name, as the brightest which presided at the time of its birth, has been inscribed upon it:

"Hesperus that led
The starry host rode brightest."

"Not that Hesperus did actually lead the other stars; he and they were moving under a common force, and they would have moved just as fast if he had been away; but because he shone brightest, he looked as if he led them." Bacon and Descartes are generally recognized as the "Fathers of Modern Philosophy," though they themselves were carried along by the rapidly swelling current of their age, then decisively setting in the direction of science. It is their glory to have seen visions of the coming greatness, to have expressed in terms of splendid power the thoughts which were dimly stirring the age, and to have sanctioned the new movement by their authoritative genius. The destruction of scholasticism was complete. They came to direct the construction of a grander temple.

There are in these two thinkers certain marked features of resemblance, and others equally marked of difference. We see their differences most strikingly in their descendants. From Bacon lineally descended Hobbes, Locke, Diderot, D'Alembert, Condillac, Cabanis, and our Scotch school. From Descartes descended Spinoza, Malebranche, Leibnitz, Fichte, Schelling, and Hegel. The inductive method predominated in one school, the deductive in the other. These differences we shall recognize more fully later on; at present we may fix our minds on the two great points of resemblance: 1st, the decisive separation of philosophy from theology; 2d, the promulgation of a new method.

The separation of philosophy from theology is made emphatic in the rejection of final causes by both Bacon and Descartes. Perhaps the most effective of their novelties was the effort of Descartes to explain the system of the world by matter and motion only, thus quietly setting aside all causes and metaphysical entities which had hitherto been invoked. The hypothesis of vortices was indeed soon disclosed to be untenable; but the scientific attitude from which that hypothesis proceeded was never afterward relinquished. It was a bold attempt at the application of the objective method, and was only defective in its restriction to cosmology, and its exclusion of biology, which was still left to the subjective method, as I shall presently notice.

The second point on which Bacon and Descartes resemble each other is in their conception of the results to be achieved by a totally new method. Coming as they did on the top of the revolutionary wave which had washed away the old methods, seeing as they saw the striking results of physical research, and foreseeing yet more glorious conquests from the spirit which achieved those results, they yielded themselves to the pleasant illusion that a new method would rapidly solve all problems. Bacon, as the more magnificent and imaginative mind, had grander visions and more enthusiastic faith; but Descartes also firmly believed that the new method was to do wonders. Indeed, it is interesting to note how these great intellects seem quite unconscious of their individual superiority, and are ready to suppose that their method will equalize all intellects. It reminds us of Sydney Smith maintaining that any man might be witty if he tried. Descartes affirms that "it is not so essential to have a fine understanding as to apply it rightly. Those who walk slowly make greater progress if they follow the right road than those who run swiftly on a wrong one." To the same effect Bacon: "A cripple on the right path will beat a racer on the wrong one." This is true enough, but is beside the question. Equipped with good or bad instruments, the superiority of one worker over another is always made manifest; and it is precisely in the right use of a good method that the scientific genius is called upon for its delicate and patient skill.

Into the vexed questions of Bacon's conduct, both with regard to Essex and with regard to bribery, I cannot enter here; but referring the curious to his biographers and critics, I will simply note that he was born in 1561; was educated at Trinity College, Cambridge, where he learned to distrust the Aristotelianism of his masters, and planned his own vast scheme of reform; went to Paris; sat in Parliament as member for Middlesex; was successively appointed of the Privy Council, and lord chancellor; was created Viscount Verulam; was impeached and condemned for corruption as a judge; and died in the spring of 1626. "For my name and memory," said the dying man, "I leave it to men's charitable speeches, and to foreign nations, and the next age."

Posterity has been generous; the fame of Bacon is immense. Admirers have not always been unanimous as to his special claims; but there has been no lack of enthusiasm, no questioning of his genius. He has been lauded for achievements in which he had no part, and has been adorned with titles to which he had doubtful pretensions; while his most important services have been overlooked. But the general recognition of his greatness, and our national pride in it, have not prevented certain attacks on his reputation, which have been answered in a rather angry spirit; and thus from one cause and another there is great difficulty in arriving at any candid and thorough appreciation of the work he did. It seems to some persons that Bacon did very little in rising against the philosophy of his day, and pointing out a new path; and to others it seems that he did nothing of the kind. But whoever looks closely into the writings of Bacon's predecessors will see that what now seems obvious and trivial was then startling and important. As M. Rémusat felicitously says, "*Il fallait du génie pour avoir ce bon sens.*" And to those who deny that Bacon did head the revolution, I would oppose not simply the testimony of nearly three centuries, but the testimony of Gassendi, who, both as contemporary and as foreigner, was capable of judging the effect then produced. It is indeed apparent to anyone familiar with the writings of some of Bacon's immediate predecessors, especially Galileo, that there was little novelty in his denunciations of the erroneous method then popular, or in his exhortations to pursue observation, experiment, and induction. But it is not less apparent that he had wider and profounder views of the philosophy of method than any of them, and that the popular opinion does not err in attributing to him the glory of heading the new era.

In England he is commonly regarded as the "Father of Experimental Philosophy" and the originator of the inductive method. Men profess themselves followers of the "Baconian philosophy," sometimes confounding that with a servile attention to facts and a most unscientific scorn of theories; at other times implying that by the Baconian method is to be understood the one on which science has successfully been pursued. A rigorous investigation of Bacon's claims will disclose the truth of his own statement, that he was rather one who sounded the trumpet-call than one who marshalled the troops. He insisted on the importance of experiment, but he could not teach what he did not himself understand—the experimental method. He exhorted men to study nature; but he could not give available directions for that study. He had fervent faith in the possible conquests of science; but never having thoroughly mastered any one science, he was incapable of appreciating the real conditions of research. He saw clearly enough the great truth that the progress of research must be gradual, but he did not see what were the necessary grades, he did not see the kind of inquiries, and the order they must follow before discoveries could be made.

That he had really but vague and imperfect conceptions of scientific method is decisively shown by his contemptuous rejection of Copernicus, Galileo, and Gilbert, and by his own plan of investigation into heat. One sentence alone would suffice to show this, namely, his sneer at Copernicus as "a man who thinks nothing of introducing fictions of any kind into nature, provided his calculations turn out well." Bacon did not understand, what Copernicus profoundly saw, that the only value of an hypothesis was its reconciliation of calculations with observations. In his plan for an inquisition into the nature of heat, we see a total misconception of the scientific process; not only does he set about in a laboriously erroneous way, but he seeks that which science proclaims inaccessible, the nature of heat. It is true that he arrives at a hypothesis which bears some resemblance to the hypothesis now accepted, namely, that heat is a mode of motion —"an expansive and restrained motion, modified in certain ways, and exerted in the smaller particles of the body." But those who have been eager to credit him with an anticipation of modern views on the strength of this definition, have overlooked the fact that it is incapable of explaining a single process, includes none of the ascertained laws of phenomena, and is itself an example of the illicit generalization which Bacon elsewhere condemns. It was with some justification, therefore, that Harvey, who knew what science was, and knew better than most men how discoveries were made, said of him that he wrote of science like a lord chancellor.

Indeed, it is to mistake his position and his greatness altogether to attribute his influence on philosophy, which is undeniable, to an influence on science which is more than questionable. Bacon was a philosopher; but because with him philosophy, separating itself from the bondage of theology, claimed to ally itself with science, and sought its materials in the generalities of science, those writers who have never made a very accurate distinction between the two, but have confounded philosophy with metaphysics, and science with physics, have naturally regarded Bacon as the precursor of Newton, Laplace, Faraday, and Liebig. It is in vain that critics oppose such a claim by asserting what is undeniable, that the great discoveries in modern science were neither made on Bacon's method nor under any direct guidance from him—that Copernicus, Galileo, and Kepler preceded him, that Harvey and Newton ignored him—stanch admirers have their answer ready; they know that Bacon was the herald of the new era, and they believe that it was his trumpet-call which animated the troops and led them to victory.

Having thus indicated his position, it will be necessary to give a brief outline of the method which he confidently believed was to be infallible and applicable in all inquiries. This was imperatively needed: "for let a man look carefully into all that variety of books with which the arts and sciences abound, he will find everywhere endless repetitions of the same thing, varying in the method of treatment, but not new in substance, insomuch that the whole stock, numerous as it appears at first view, proves on examination to be but scanty. What was asserted once is asserted still, and what was a question once is a question still, and, instead of being resolved by discussion, is only fixed and fed."

He proposes his new method, that thereby "the intellect may be raised and exalted and made capable of overcoming the difficulties and obscurities of nature. The art which I introduce with this view (which I call the 'Interpretation of Nature') is a kind of logic, though the difference between it and the ordinary logic is great, indeed immense. For the ordinary logic professes to contrive and prepare helps and guards for the understanding, as mine does; and in this one point they agree. But mine differs from it in three points: viz., in the end aimed at, in the order of demonstration, and in the starting-point of inquiry.

"But the greatest change I introduce is in the form itself of induction and the judgments made thereby. For the induction of which the logicians speak, which proceeds by simple enumeration, is a puerile thing; concluded at hazard, is always liable to be upset by a contradictory instance, takes into account only what is known and ordinary, and leads to no result. Now, what the sciences stand in need of is a form of induction which shall analyze experience and take it to pieces, and by a due process of exclusion and rejection lead to an inevitable conclusion."

"Now, my method, though hard to practise, is easy to explain; and it is this: I propose to establish progressive stages of certainty. The evidence of sense, helped and guarded by a certain process of correction, I retain; but the mental operation which follows the act of sense I for the most part reject; and instead of it I open and lay out a new and certain path for the mind to proceed in, starting directly from the simple sensuous perception."

The same dissatisfaction with mediæval philosophy expressed itself in Descartes. The incompetence of philosophers to solve the problems they occupied themselves with—the anarchy which reigned in the scientific world, where no two thinkers could agree upon fundamental points—the extravagance of the conclusions to which some accepted premises led, determined him to seek no more to slake his thirst at their fountains.

"And that is why, as soon as my age permitted me to quit my preceptors," he says, "I entirely gave up the study of letters; and resolving to seek no other science than that which I could find in myself, or else in the great book of the world, I employed the remainder of my youth in travel, in seeing courts and camps, in frequenting people of diverse humors and conditions, in collecting various experiences, and above all in endeavoring to draw some profitable reflection from what I saw. For it seemed to me that I should meet with more truth in the reasonings which each man makes in his own affairs, and which, if wrong, would be speedily punished by failure, than in those reasonings which the philosopher makes in his study, upon speculations which produce no effect, and which are of no consequence to him, except perhaps that he will be more vain of them the more remote they are from common-sense, because he would then have been forced to employ more ingenuity and subtlety to render them plausible."

For many years he led a roving, unsettled life; now serving in the army, now making a tour, now studying mathematics in solitude, now conversing with scientific men. One constant purpose gave unity to those various pursuits. He was elaborating his answers to the questions which perplexed him; he was preparing his method.

When only twenty-three he conceived the design of a reformation in philosophy. He was at that time residing in his winter quarters at Neuburg, on the Danube. His travels soon afterward commenced, and at the age of thirty-three he retired into Holland, there in silence and solitude to arrange his thoughts into a consistent whole. He remained there eight years; and so completely did he shut himself from the world that he concealed from his friends the very place of his residence.

When the results of this meditative solitude were given to the world in the shape of his celebrated *Discourse on Method*, and his *Meditations*—to which he invented replies—the sensation produced was immense. It was evident to all men that an original thinker had arisen; and although this originality could not but rouse much opposition, from the very fact of being original, yet Descartes gained the day. His name became European. His controversies were European quarrels. Charles I of England invited him over, with the promise of a liberal appointment; and the invitation would probably have been accepted had not the civil war broken out. He afterward received a flattering invitation from Christina of Sweden, who had read some of his works with great satisfaction, and wished to learn from himself the principles of his philosophy.

He accepted it, and arrived in Stockholm in 1649. His reception was most gratifying, and the Queen was so pleased with him as earnestly to beg him to remain with her, and give his assistance toward the establishment of an academy of sciences. But the delicate frame of Descartes was ill fitted for the severity of the climate, and a cold, caught in one of his morning visits to Christina, produced inflammation of the lungs, which carried him off.

Christina wept for him, had him interred in the cemetery for foreigners, and placed a long eulogium upon his tomb. His remains were subsequently (1666) carried from Sweden into

France, and buried with great ceremony in Ste. Geneviève du Mont.

Descartes was a great thinker; but having said this, we have almost exhausted the praise we could bestow upon him as a man. In disposition he was timid to servility. When promulgating his proofs of the existence of the Deity, he was in evident alarm lest the Church should see something objectionable in them. He had also written an astronomical treatise; but hearing of the fate of Galileo, he refrained from publishing, and always used some chicane in speaking of the world's movement. He was not a brave man, nor was he an affectionate man. But he was even-tempered, placid, and studious not to give offence.

It has already been indicated that the great work performed by Descartes was, like that of Bacon, the promulgation of a new method. This was rendered necessary by their separation from the ancient philosophy and their exclusion of authority. If inquiry is to be independent, if reason is to walk alone, in what direction must she walk? Having relinquished the aid of the Church, there were but two courses open: the one to tread once more in the path of the ancients, and to endeavor by the ancient methods to attain the truth; or else to open a new path, to invent a new method. The former was barely possible. The spirit of the age was deeply imbued with a feeling of opposition against the ancient methods; and Descartes himself had been painfully perplexed by the universal anarchy and uncertainty which prevailed. The second course was therefore chosen.

Uncertainty was the disease of the epoch. Scepticism was widespread, and even the most confident dogmatism could offer no criterion of certitude. This want of criterion we saw leading, in Greece, to scepticism, Epicureanism, Stoicism, the New Academy, and finally leading the Alexandrians into the province of faith, to escape from the dilemma. The question of a criterion had long been the vital question of philosophy. Descartes could get no answer to it from the doctors of his day. Unable to find firm ground on any of the prevalent systems, distracted by doubts, mistrusting the conclusions of his own understanding, mistrusting the evidences of his senses, he determined to make a *tabula rasa*, and reconstruct his knowledge. He resolved to examine the premises of every conclusion, and to believe nothing but upon the clearest evidence of reason; evidence so convincing that he could not by any effort refuse to assent to it.

He has given us the detailed history of his doubts. He has told us how he found that he could plausibly enough doubt of everything except of his own existence. He pushed his scepticism to the verge of self-annihilation. There he stopped; there in self, in his consciousness, he found at last an irresistible fact, an irreversible certainty.

Firm ground was discovered. He could doubt the existence of the external world, and treat it as a phantasm; he could doubt the existence of a God, and treat the belief as a superstition; but of the existing of his thinking, doubting mind no sort of doubt was possible. He, the doubter, existed if nothing else existed. The existence that was revealed in his own consciousness was the primary fact, the first indubitable certainty. Hence his famous "*Cogito, ergo sum*" ("I think, therefore I am").

It is somewhat curious, and, as an illustration of the frivolous verbal disputes of philosophers, not a little instructive, that this celebrated "*Cogito, ergo sum,*" should have been frequently attacked for its logical imperfection. It has been objected, from Gassendi downward, that to say, "I think, therefore I am," is a begging of the question; since existence has to be proved identical with thought. Certainly, if Descartes had intended to prove his own existence by reasoning, he would have been guilty of the *petitio principii* Gassendi attributes to him, viz., that the major premise, "that which thinks exists," is assumed, not proved. But he did not intend this. What was his object? He has told us that it was to find a starting-point from which to reason—to find an irreversible certainty. And where did he find this? In his own consciousness. Doubt as I may, I cannot doubt of my own existence, because my very doubt reveals to me a something which doubts. You may call this an assumption, if you will: I will point out the fact as one above and beyond all logic; which logic can neither prove nor disprove; but which must always remain an irreversible certainty, and as such a fitting basis of philosophy.

I exist. No doubt can darken such a truth; no sophism can confute this clear principle. This is a certainty, if there be none other. This is the basis of all science. It is in vain to ask for a proof of that which is self-evident and irresistible. I exist. The consciousness of my existence is to me the assurance of my existence.

Had Descartes done no more than point out this fact he would have no claim to notice here; and we are surprised to find many writers looking upon this "*Cogito, ergo sum,*" as constituting the great idea in his system. Surely it is only a statement of universal experience—an epigrammatic form given to the common-sense view of the matter. Any clown would have told him that the assurance of his existence was his consciousness of it; but the clown would not have stated it so well. He would have said, "I know I exist, because I feel that I exist."

Descartes therefore made no discovery in pointing out this fact as an irreversible certainty. The part it plays in his system is only that of a starting-point. It makes consciousness the basis of all truth. There is none other possible. Interrogate consciousness, and its clear replies will be science. Here we have a new basis and a new philosophy introduced. It was indeed but another shape of the old formula, "Know thyself," so differently interpreted by Thales, Socrates, and the Alexandrians; but it gave that formula a precise signification, a thing it had before always wanted. Of little use could it be to tell man to know himself. How is he to know himself? By looking inward? We all do that. By examining the nature of his thoughts? That had been done without success. By examining the process of his thoughts? That, too, had been accomplished, and the logic of Aristotle was the result.

The formula needed a precise interpretation; and that interpretation Descartes gave. Consciousness, said he, is the basis of all knowledge; it is the only ground of absolute certainty. Whatever it distinctly proclaims must be true. The process, then, is simple: examine your consciousness, and its clear replies. Hence the vital portion of his system lies in this axiom: All clear ideas are true: whatever is clearly and distinctly conceived is true. This axiom he calls the foundation of all science, the rule and measure of truth.

The next step to be taken was to determine the rules for the proper detection of these ideas; and these rules he has laid down as follows:

1. Never accept anything as true but what is evidently so; to admit nothing but what so clearly and distinctly presents itself as true that there can be no reason to doubt it.

2. To divide every question into as many separate questions as possible; that each part being more easily conceived, the whole may be more intelligible—(Analysis).

3. To conduct the examination with order, beginning by that of objects the most simple, and therefore the easiest to be known, and ascending little by little up to knowledge of the most complex—(Synthesis).

4. To make such exact calculations and such circumspections as to be confident that nothing essential has been omitted.

Consciousness, being the ground of all certainty, everything of which you are clearly and distinctly conscious must be true; everything which you clearly and distinctively conceive exists, if the idea of it involves existence.

In the four rules, and in this view of consciousness, we have only half of Descartes' system; the psychological half. It was owing to the exclusive consideration of this half that Dugald Stewart was led—in controverting Condorcet's assertion that Descartes had done more than either Galileo or Bacon toward experimental philosophy—to say that Condorcet would have been nearer the truth if he had pointed him out as the "Father of the Experimental Philosophy of the Mind." Perhaps the title is just; but Condorcet's praise, though exaggerated, was not without good foundation.

There is, in truth, another half of Descartes' system, equally important, or nearly so: we mean the deductive method. His eminence as a mathematician is universally recognized. He was the first to make the grand discovery of the application of algebra to geometry; and he made this at the age of twenty-three. The discovery that geometrical curves might be expressed by algebraical numbers, though highly important in the history of mathematics, only interests us here by leading us to trace his philosophical development. He was deeply engrossed in mathematics; he saw that mathematics were capable of a still further simplification and a far more extended application. Struck as he was with the certitude of mathematical reasoning, he began applying the principles of mathematical reasoning to the subject of metaphysics. His great object was, amid the scepticism and anarchy of his contemporaries, to found a system which should be solid and convincing. He first wished to find a basis of certitude—a starting-point: this he found in consciousness. He next wished to find a method of certitude: this he found in mathematics.

"Those long chains of reasoning," he tells us, "all simple and easy, which geometers use to arrive at their most difficult demonstrations, suggested to me that all things which came within human knowledge must follow each other in a similar chain; and that provided we abstain from admitting anything as true which is not so, and that we always preserve in them the order necessary to deduce one from the other, there can be none so remote to which we cannot finally attain, nor so obscure but that we may discover them." From these glimpses of the twofold nature of Descartes' method, it will be easy to see into his whole system: consciousness being the only ground of certitude, mathematics the only method of certitude.

We may say therefore that the deductive method was now completely constituted. The whole operation of philosophy henceforth consisted in deducing consequences. The premises had been found; the conclusions alone were wanting. This was held to be true of physics no less than of psychology. Thus, in his *Principia*, he announces his intention of giving a short account of the principal phenomena of the world, not that we may use them as reasons to prove anything; for he adds: "we desire to deduce effects from causes, not from effects; but only in order that out of the innumerable effects which we learn to be capable of resulting from the same causes, we may determine our minds to consider these rather than others."

SIEGE OF LA ROCHELLE

RICHELIEU RULES FRANCE

A.D. 1627

ANDREW D. WHITE

Through the work which Cardinal Richelieu, chief minister of Louis XIII, performed for that monarch and for France, the country was lifted from a state of comparative disorganization and weakness, and started on a fresh career, which led her to the foremost position among European nations.

At the death of Henry IV, in 1610, his son Louis XIII was but nine years old, and from 1624 to the end of the reign, in 1643, Richelieu directed the policy of France. By crushing the Huguenots as a political party he prepared the way for building up the power of the King. The Huguenots were aiming at an independent Protestant commonwealth within the kingdom. When Richelieu had defeated this project by his victory at La Rochelle he was free to undertake a readjustment of the relations between the throne and the grasping nobles. After accomplishing this he could turn his attention to foreign affairs.

In the last stage of the Thirty Years' War France under Richelieu played her part so well that the house of Austria was humbled, and, although the great Cardinal died before the end of the war, in the final settlement France received territorial and political benefits which greatly added to her prestige.

White, our eminent historian, educator, and diplomatist, has given to the world, in the following narrative and analysis, the best account of Richelieu's administration to be found in English.

THUS far the struggles of the world have developed its statesmanship after three leading types.

First of these is that based on faith in some great militant principle. Strong among statesmen of this type, in this time, stand Cavour, with his faith in constitutional liberty; Cobden, with his faith in freedom of trade; the third Napoleon, with his faith that the world moves, and that a successful policy must keep the world's pace.

The second style of statesmanship is seen in the reorganization of old states to fit new times. In this the chiefs are such men as Cranmer and Turgot.

But there is a third class of statesmen sometimes doing more brilliant work than either of the others. These are they who serve a state in times of chaos—in times when a nation is by no means ripe for revolution, but only stung by desperate revolt. These are they who are quick enough and firm enough to bind all the good forces of the state into one cosmic force, therewith to compress or crush all chaotic forces; these are they who throttle treason and stab rebellion; who fear not, when defeat must send down misery through ages, to insure victory by using weapons of the hottest and sharpest. Theirs, then, is a statesmanship which it may be well for the leading men of this land and time to be looking at and thinking of, and its representative man shall be Richelieu.

Never perhaps did a nation plunge more suddenly from the height of prosperity into the depth of misery than did France on May 14, 1610, when Henry IV fell dead by the dagger of Ravaillac. All earnest men, in a moment, saw the abyss yawning —felt the state sinking—felt themselves sinking with it. And they did what in such a time men always do: first all shrieked, then every man clutched at the means of safety nearest him. Sully, Henry's great minister, rode through the streets of Paris with big tears streaming down his face; strong men whose hearts had been toughened and crusted in the dreadful religious wars sobbed like children; all the populace swarmed abroad bewildered—many swooned—some went mad. This was the first phase of feeling.

Then came a second phase yet more terrible. For now burst forth that old whirlwind of anarchy and bigotry and selfishness and terror which Henry had curbed during twenty years. All earnest men felt bound to protect themselves, and seized the nearest means of defence. Sully shut himself up in the Bastille, and sent orders to his son-in-law, the Duke of Rohan, to bring in six thousand soldiers to protect the Protestants. All unearnest men, especially the great nobles, rushed to the court, determined now, that the only guardians of the state were a weak-minded woman and a weak-bodied child, to dip deep into the treasury which Henry had filled to develop the nation, and to wrench away the power which he had built to guard the nation.

In order to make ready for this grasp at the state treasure and power by the nobles, the Duke of Épernon—from the corpse of the King by whose side he was sitting when Ravaillac struck him—strides into the Parliament of Paris and orders it to declare the late Queen, Marie de' Medici, regent; and when this Parisian court, knowing full well that it had no right to confer the regency, hesitated, he laid his hand on his sword, and declared that, unless they did his bidding at once, his sword should be drawn from its scabbard. This threat did its work. Within three hours after the King's death the Paris Parliament, which had no right to give it, bestowed the regency on a woman who had no capacity to take it.

At first things seemed to brighten a little. The Queen Regent sent such urgent messages to Sully that he left his stronghold of the Bastille and went to the palace. She declared to him before the assembled court that he must govern France still. With tears she gave the young King into his arms, telling Louis that Sully was his father's best friend, and bidding him pray the old statesman to serve the state yet longer.

But soon this good scene changed. Mary had a foster-sister, Leonora Galligai, and Leonora was married to an Italian adventurer, Concini. These seemed a poor couple, worthless and shiftless, their only stock in trade Leonora's Italian cunning; but this stock soon came to be of vast account, for thereby she soon managed to bind and rule the Queen Regent—managed to drive Sully into retirement in less than a year—managed to make herself and her husband the great dispensers at court of place and pelf. Penniless though Concini had been, he was in a few months able to buy the Marquisate of Ancre, which cost him nearly a half a million livres; and, soon after, the post of first gentleman of the bedchamber, and that cost him nearly a quarter of a million; and, soon after that, a multitude of broad estates and high offices at immense prices. Leonora also was not idle; among her many gains was the bribe of three hundred thousand livres to screen certain financiers under trial for fraud.

Next came the turn of the great nobles. For ages the nobility of France had been the worst among her many afflictions. From age to age attempts had been made to curb them. In the fifteenth century Charles VII had done much to undermine their power, and Louis XI had done much to crush it. But strong as was the policy of Charles, and cunning as was the policy of Louis, they had made one omission, and that omission left France, though advanced, miserable. For these monarchs had not cut the root of the evil. The French nobility continued practically a serf-holding nobility.

Despite, then, the curb put upon many old pretensions of the nobles, the serf-owning spirit continued to spread a network of curses over every arm of the French government, over every acre of the French soil, and, worst of all, over the hearts and minds of the French people. Enterprise was deadened, invention crippled. Honesty was nothing, honor everything. Life was of little value. Labor was the badge of servility; laziness the very badge and passport of gentility. The serf-owning spirit was an iron wall between noble and not noble—the only unyielding wall between France and prosperous peace.

But the serf-owning spirit begat another evil far more terrible: it begat a substitute for patriotism—a substitute which crushed out patriotism just at the very emergencies when patriotism was most needed. For the first question which in any state emergency sprang into the mind of a French noble was not, How does this affect the welfare of the nation? but, How does this affect the position of my order? The serf-owning spirit developed in the French aristocracy an instinct which led them in national troubles to guard the serf-owning class first and the nation afterward, and to acknowledge fealty to the serf-owning interest first and to the national interest afterward.

So it proved in that emergency at the death of Henry. Instead of planting themselves as a firm bulwark between the state and harm, the Duke of Épernon, the Prince of Condé, the Count of Soissons, the Duke of Guise, the Duke of Bouillon, and many others, wheedled or threatened the Queen into granting pensions of such immense amounts that the great treasury filled by Henry and Sully with such noble sacrifices, and to such noble ends, was soon nearly empty.

But as soon as the treasury began to run low the nobles began a worse work. Mary had thought to buy their loyalty, but when they had gained such treasures their ideas mounted higher. A saying of one among them became their formula, and became noted: "The day of kings is past; now is come the day of the grandees."

Every great noble now tried to grasp some strong fortress or rich city. One fact will show the spirit of many. The Duke of Épernon had served Henry as governor of Metz, and Metz was the most important fortified town in France; therefore Henry, while allowing D'Épernon the honor of governorship, had always kept a royal lieutenant in the citadel, who corresponded directly with the ministry. But on the very day of the King's death D'Épernon despatched commands to his own creatures at Metz to seize the citadel, and to hold it for him against all other orders.

But at last even Mary had to refuse to lavish more of the national treasure and to shred more of the national territory among these magnates. Then came their rebellion.

Immediately Condé and several great nobles issued a proclamation denouncing the tyranny and extravagance of the court—calling on the Catholics to rise against the Regent in behalf of their religion—calling on the Protestants to rise in behalf of theirs—summoning the whole people to rise against the waste of their state treasure.

It was all a glorious joke. To call on the Protestants was wondrous impudence, for Condé had left their faith and had persecuted them. To call on the Catholics was not less impudent, for he had betrayed their cause scores of times; but to call on the whole people to rise in defence of their treasury was impudence sublime, for no man had besieged the treasury more persistently, no man had dipped into it more deeply, than Condé himself.

The people saw this and would not stir. Condé could rally only a few great nobles and their retainers, and therefore, as a last tremendous blow to the court, he and his followers raised the cry that the Regent must convoke the States-General.

Any who have read much in the history of France, and especially in the history of the French Revolution, know in part how terrible this cry was. By the court, and by the great privileged classes of France, this great assembly of the three estates of the realm was looked upon as the last resort amid direst calamities. For at its summons came stalking forth from the foul past the long train of Titanic abuses and satanic wrongs; and came surging up from the seething present the great hoarse cry of the people; then loomed up, dim in the distance, vast shadowy ideas of new truth and new right; and at the bare hint of these, all that was proud in France trembled.

This cry for the States-General, then, brought the Regent to terms at once, and, instead of acting vigorously, she betook herself to her old vicious fashion of compromising—buying off the rebels at prices more enormous than ever. By her treaty of Ste. Ménehould, Condé received a half a million of livres, and his followers received payments proportionate to the evil they had done.

But this compromise succeeded no better than the previous compromises. Even if the nobles had wished to remain quiet, they could not. Their lordship over a servile class made them independent of all ordinary labor and all care arising from labor; some exercise of mind and body they must have; Condé took this needed exercise by attempting to seize the city of Poitiers, and, when the burgesses were too strong for him, by ravaging the neighboring country. The other nobles broke the compromise in ways wonderfully numerous and ingenious. France was again filled with misery.

Dull as Regent Mary was, she now saw that she must call that dreaded States-General, or lose not only the nobles, but the people. Undecided as she was, she soon saw that she must do it at once; that if she delayed it, her great nobles would raise the cry for it again and again just as often as they wished to extort office or money. Accordingly, on October 14, 1614, she summoned the deputies of the three estates to Paris, and then the storm set in.

Each of the three orders presented its "portfolio of grievances" and its programme of reforms. It might seem, to one who has not noted closely the spirit which serf-mastering thrusts into a man, that the nobles would appear in the States-General, not to make complaints, but to answer complaints. It was not so. The noble order, with due form, entered complaint that theirs was the injured order. They asked relief from familiarities and assumptions of equality on the part of the people. Said the Baron de Sénecccé, "It is a great piece of insolence to pretend to establish any sort of equality between the people and the nobility": other nobles declared, "There is between them and us as much difference as between master and lackey."

To match these complaints and theories, the nobles made demands; demands that commoners should not be allowed to keep firearms, nor to possess dogs unless the dogs were hamstrung; nor to clothe themselves like nobles, nor to clothe their wives like the wives of nobles; nor to wear velvet or satin under a penalty of five thousand livres. And preposterous as such claims may seem to us, they carried them into practice. A deputy of the Third Estate having been severely beaten by a noble, his demands for redress were treated as absurd. One of the orators of the lower order having spoken of the French as forming one great family in which the nobles were the elder brothers and the commoners the younger, the nobles made a formal complaint to the King, charging the Third Estate with insolence insufferable. Next came the complaints and demands of the clergy. They insisted on the adoption in France of the decrees of the Council of Trent, and the destruction of the liberties of the Gallican Church.

But far stronger than these came the voice of the people: first spoke Montaigne, denouncing the grasping spirit of the nobles. Then spoke Savaron, stinging them with sarcasm, torturing them with rhetoric, crushing them with statements of facts.

But chief among the speakers was the president of the Third Estate, Robert Miron, provost of the merchants of Paris. His speech, though spoken across the great abyss of time and space and thought and custom which separates him from us, warms a true man's heart even now. With touching fidelity he pictured the sad life of the lower orders—their thankless toil, their constant misery; then with a sturdiness which awes us, he arraigned, first, royalty for its crushing taxation; next, the whole upper class for its oppressions, and then, daring death, he thus launched into popular thought an idea:

"It is nothing less than a miracle that the people are able to answer so many demands. On the labor of their hands depends the maintenance of your majesty, of the clergy, of the nobility, of the commons. What without their exertions would be the value of the tithes and great possessions of the Church, of the splendid estates of the nobility, or of our own house-rents and inheritances? With their bones scarcely skinned over, your wretched people present themselves before you, beaten down and helpless, with the aspect rather of death itself than of living men, imploring your succor in the name of Him who has appointed you to reign over them—who made you a man, that you might be merciful to other men—and who made you the father of your subjects, that you might be compassionate to these your helpless children. If your majesty shall not take means for that end, I fear lest despair should teach the sufferers that a soldier is, after all, nothing more than a peasant bearing arms; and lest, when the vine-dresser shall have taken up his arquebuse, he should cease to become an anvil only that he may become a hammer."

After this the Third Estate demanded the convocation of a general assembly every ten years, a more just distribution of taxes, equality of all before the law, the suppression of interior custom-houses, the abolition of sundry sinecures held by nobles, the forbidding to leading nobles of unauthorized levies of soldiery, some stipulations regarding the working clergy and the non-residence of bishops; and in the midst of all these demands, as a gold grain amid husks, they placed a demand for the emancipation of the serfs.

But these demands were sneered at. The idea of the natural equality in rights of all men—the idea of the personal worth of every man—the idea that rough-clad workers have prerogatives which can be whipped out by no smooth-clad idlers—these ideas were as far beyond serf-owners of those days as they were beyond slave-owners of our own days. Nothing was done. Augustin Thierry is authority for the statement that the clergy were willing to yield something. The nobles would yield nothing. The different orders quarrelled until one March morning in 1615, when, on going to their hall, they were barred out and told that the workmen were fitting the place for a court ball. And so the deputies separated—to all appearance no new work was done, no new ideas enforced, no strong men set loose.

So it was in seeming; so it was not in reality. Something had been done. That assembly planted ideas in the French mind which struck more and more deeply, and spread more and more widely, until, after a century and a half, the Third Estate met again and refused to present petitions kneeling; and when King and nobles put on their hats, the commons put on theirs, and when that old brilliant stroke was again made, and the hall was closed and filled with busy carpenters and upholsterers, the deputies of the people swore that great tennis-court oath which blasted French tyranny.

But something great was done immediately. To that suffering nation a great man was revealed; for when the clergy pressed their requests they chose as their orator a young man only twenty-nine years of age, the Bishop of Luçon, Armand Jean du Plessis de Richelieu.

He spoke well. His thoughts were clear, his words well pointed, his bearing firm. He had been bred a soldier, and so had strengthened his will; afterward he had been made a scholar and so had strengthened his mind. He grappled with the problems given him in that stormy assembly with such force that he seemed about to do something; but just then came that day of the court ball, and Richelieu turned away like the rest.

But men had seen him and heard him. Forget him they could not. From that tremendous farce, then, France had gained directly one thing at least, and that was a sight of Richelieu.

The year, after the States-General, wore away in the old vile fashion. Condé revolted again, and this time he managed to scare the Protestants into revolt with him. The daring of the nobles was greater than ever. They even attacked the young King's train as he journeyed to Bordeaux, and another compromise had to be wearily built in the Treaty of Loudun. By this Condé was again bought off—but this time only by a bribe of a million and a half of livres. The other nobles were also paid enormously, and on making a reckoning it was found that this compromise had cost the King four millions and the country twenty millions. The nation had also to give into the hands of the nobles some of its richest cities and strongest fortresses.

Immediately after this compromise Condé returned to Paris, loud, strong, jubilant, defiant, bearing himself like a king. Soon he and his revolted again; but just at that moment Concini happened to remember Richelieu. The young bishop was called and set at work.

Richelieu grasped the rebellion at once. In broad daylight he seized Condé and shut him up in the Bastille; other noble leaders he declared guilty of treason and degraded them; he set forth the crimes and follies of the nobles in a manifesto which stung their cause to death in a moment; he published his policy in a proclamation which ran through France like fire, warming all hearts of patriots, withering all hearts of rebels; he sent out three great armies: one northward to grasp Picardy, one eastward to grasp Champagne, one southward to grasp Berri. There is a man who can do something! The nobles yield in a moment; they *must* yield.

But just at this moment, when a better day seemed to dawn, came an event which threw France back into anarchy and Richelieu into the world again.

The young King, Louis XIII, was now sixteen years old. His mother the Regent and her favorite Concini had carefully kept him down. Under their treatment he had grown morose and seemingly stupid; but he had wit enough to understand the policy of his mother and Concini, and strength enough to hate them for it.

The only human being to whom Louis showed any love was a young falconer, Albert de Luynes, and with De Luynes he conspired against his mother's power and her favorite's life. On an April morning, 1617, the King and De Luynes sent a party of chosen men to seize Concini. They met him at the gate of the Louvre. As usual he is bird-like in his utterance, snake-like in his bearing. They order him to surrender; he chirps forth his surprise, and they blow out his brains. Louis, understanding the noise, puts on his sword, appears on the balcony of the palace, is saluted with hurrahs, and becomes master of his kingdom.

Straightway measures are taken against all supposed to be attached to the regency. Concini's wife, the favorite Leonora, is burned as a witch; Regent Mary is sent to Blois, and Richelieu is banished to his bishopric.

And now matters went from bad to worse. King Louis was no stronger than Regent Mary had been; King's favorite, De Luynes, was no better than Regent's favorite, Concini, had been. The nobles rebelled against the new rule as they had rebelled against the old. The King went through the same old extortions and humiliations.

Then came also to full development yet another vast evil. As far back as the year after Henry's assassination, the Protestants, in terror of their enemies, now that Henry was gone and the Spaniards seemed to grow in favor, formed themselves into a great republican league—a state within the state—regularly organized; in peace, for political effort, and in war, for military effort, with a Protestant clerical caste which ruled always with pride, and often with menace.

Against such a theocratic republic war must come sooner or later, and in 1617 the struggle began. Army was pitted against army; Protestant Duke of Rohan against Catholic Duke of Luynes. Meanwhile Austria and the foreign enemies of France, Condé and the domestic enemies of France fished in the troubled waters, and made rich gains every day. So France plunged into sorrows ever deeper and blacker. But in 1624 Marie de' Medici, having been reconciled to her son, urged him to recall Richelieu.

The dislike which Louis bore Richelieu was strong, but the dislike he bore toward compromises had become stronger. Into his poor brain at last began to gleam the truth that a serf-mastering caste, after a compromise, only whines more steadily and snarls more loudly; that at last, compromising becomes worse than fighting. Richelieu was called and set at work.

Fortunately for our studies of the great statesman's policy, he left at his death a *Political Testament*, which floods with light his steadiest aims and boldest acts. In that *Testament* he wrote this message:

"When your majesty resolved to give me entrance into your councils and a great share of your confidence, I can declare with truth that the Huguenots divided the authority with your majesty, that the great nobles acted not at all as subjects, that the governors of the provinces took on themselves the airs of sovereigns, and that the foreign alliances of France were despised. I promised your majesty to use all my industry, all the authority you gave me, to ruin the Huguenot party, to abase the pride of the high nobles, and to raise your name among foreign nations to the place where it ought to be."

Such were the plans of Richelieu at the outset. Let us see how he wrought out their fulfilment.

First of all, he performed daring surgery and cautery about the very heart of the court. In a short time he had cut out from that living centre of French power a number of unworthy ministers and favorites, and replaced them by men on whom he could rely. Then he began his vast work. His policy embraced three great objects: First, the overthrow of the Huguenot power; secondly, the subjugation of the great nobles; thirdly, the destruction of the undue might of Austria.

First, then, after some preliminary negotiations with foreign powers, he attacked the great politico-religious party of the Huguenots. These held, as their great centre and stronghold, the famous seaport of La Rochelle. He who but glances at the map shall see how strong was this position; he shall see two islands lying just off the west coast at that point, controlled by La Rochelle, yet affording to any foreign allies, whom the Huguenots might admit there, facilities for stinging France during centuries. The position of the Huguenots seemed impregnable. The city was well fortressed, garrisoned by the bravest of men, mistress of a noble harbor open at all times to supplies from foreign ports, and in that harbor rode a fleet, belonging to the city, greater than the navy of France. Richelieu saw well that here was the head of the rebellion. Here, then, he must strike it.

Strange as it may seem, his diplomacy was so skilful that he obtained ships to attack the Protestants in La Rochelle from the two great Protestant powers—England and Holland. With these he was successful. He attacked the city fleet, ruined it, and cleared the harbor.

But now came a terrible check. Richelieu had aroused the hate of that incarnation of all that was and is offensive in English politics—the Duke of Buckingham. Scandal-mongers were wont to say that both were in love with the Queen, and that the Cardinal, though unsuccessful in his suit, outwitted the Duke and sent him out of the kingdom; and that the Duke swore a great oath that if he could not enter France in one way, he would enter in another; and that he brought about a war and came himself as a commander. Of this scandal believe what you will, but—be the causes what they may—the English policy changed, and Charles I sent Buckingham with ninety ships to aid La Rochelle.

But Buckingham was flippant and careless; Richelieu careful when there was need, and daring when there was need. Buckingham's heavy blows were foiled by Richelieu's keen thrusts, and then, in his confusion, Buckingham blundered so foolishly and Richelieu profited by his blunders so shrewdly that the fleet returned to England without any accomplishment of its purpose. The English were also driven from that vexing position in the Isle of Ré.

Having thus sent the English home, for a time at least, he led King and nobles and armies to La Rochelle, and commenced the siege in full force. Difficulties met him at every turn; but the difficulty of all was that arising from the spirit of the nobility.

No one could charge the nobles of France with lack of bravery. The only charge was that their bravery was almost sure to shun every useful form, and to take every noxious form. The bravery which finds outlet in duels they showed constantly; the bravery which finds outlets in street fights they had shown from the day when the Duke of Orleans perished in a brawl, to the days when the "Mignons" of Henry III fought at sight every noble whose beard was not cut to suit them. The pride fostered by lording it over serfs, in the country, and by lording it over men who did not own serfs, in the capital, aroused bravery of this sort and plenty of it. But that bravery which serves a great good cause, which must be backed by steadiness and watchfulness, was not so plentiful. So Richelieu found that the nobles who had conducted the siege before he took command had, through their brawling propensities and lazy propensities, allowed the besieged to garner in the crops from the surrounding country, and master all the best points of attack.

But Richelieu pressed on. First he built an immense wall and earthwork, nine miles long, surrounding the city, and to protect this he raised eleven great forts and eighteen redoubts. Still the harbor was open, and into this the English fleet might return and succor the city at any time. His plan was soon made. In the midst of that great harbor of La Rochelle he sank sixty hulks of vessels filled with stone; then, across the harbor—nearly a mile wide and, in places, more than eight hundred feet deep—he began building over these sunken ships a great dike and wall; thoroughly fortified, carefully engineered, faced with sloping layers of hewn stone.

His own men scolded at the magnitude of the work; the men in La Rochelle laughed at it. Worse than that, the ocean sometimes laughed and scolded at it. Sometimes the waves, sweeping in from that fierce Bay of Biscay, destroyed in an hour the work of a week. The carelessness of a subordinate once destroyed in a moment the work of three months.

Yet it is but fair to admit that there was one storm which did not beat against Richelieu's dike. There set in against it no storm of hypocrisy from neighboring nations. Keen works for and against Richelieu were put forth in his day: works calm and strong for and against him have been issuing from the presses of France and England and Germany ever since; but not one of the old school of keen writers, or of the new school of calm writers, is known to have ever hinted that this complete sealing of the only entrance to a leading European harbor was unjust to the world at large or unfair to the besieged themselves.

But all other obstacles Richelieu had to break through or cut through constantly. He was his own engineer, general, admiral, prime minister. While he urged on the army to work upon the dike, he organized a French navy, and in due time brought it around to that coast and anchored it so as to guard the dike and to be guarded by it. Yet daring as all this work was, it was but the smallest part of his work. Richelieu found that his officers were cheating his soldiers in their pay and disheartening them; in the face of the enemy he had to reorganize the army and to create a new military system. He made the army twice as effective and supported it at two-thirds less cost than before. It was his boast in his *Testament* that, from a mob, the army became "like a well-ordered convent."

He found also that his subordinates were plundering the surrounding country, and thus rendering it disaffected; he at once ordered that what had been taken should be paid for, and that persons trespassing thereafter should be severely punished. He found also the great nobles who commanded in the army half-hearted and almost traitorous from sympathy with those of their own caste on the other side of the walls of La Rochelle, and from their fear of his increased power should he gain a victory. It was their common saying that they were fools to help him do it. But he saw the true point at once. He placed in the most responsible positions of his army men who felt for their cause, whose hearts and souls were in it—men not of the Dalgetty stamp, but of the Cromwell stamp. He found also—as he afterward said—that he had to conquer not only the kings of England and Spain, but also the King of France. At the most critical moment of the siege Louis defeated him, went back to Paris, allowed courtiers to fill him with suspicions. Not only Richelieu's place, but his life, was in danger, and he well knew it; yet he never left his dike and siege-works, but wrought on steadily until they were done; and then the King, of his own will, in very shame broke away from his courtiers and went back to his master.

And now a royal herald summoned the people of La Rochelle to surrender. But they were not yet half conquered. Even when they had seen two English fleets, sent to aid them, driven back from Richelieu's dike, they still held out manfully. The Duchess of Rohan, the Mayor Guiton, and the minister Salbert, by noble sacrifices and burning words, kept the will of the besieged firm as steel. They were reduced to feed on their horses; then on bits of filthy shellfish; then on stewed leather. They died in multitudes.

Guiton, the mayor, kept a dagger on the city council-table to stab any man who should speak of surrender; some, who spoke of yielding, he ordered to execution as seditious. When a friend showed him a person dying of hunger, he said: "Does that astonish you? Both you and I must come to that!" When another told him that multitudes were perishing he said, "Provided one remains to hold the city gate, I ask nothing more."

But at last even Guiton had to yield. After the siege had lasted more than a year, after five thousand were found remaining out of fifteen thousand, after a mother had been seen to feed her child with her own blood, the Cardinal's policy became too strong for him. The people yielded and Richelieu entered the city as master.

And now the victorious statesman showed a greatness of soul to which all the rest of his life was as nothing. He was a Catholic cardinal; the Rochellois were Protestants; he was a stern ruler; they were rebellious subjects who had long worried and almost impoverished him; all Europe, therefore, looked for a retribution more terrible than any in history.

Richelieu allowed nothing of the sort. He destroyed the old franchises of the city, for they were incompatible with that royal authority which he so earnestly strove to build. But this was all. He took no vengeance; he allowed the Protestants to worship as before; he took many of them into the public service, and to Guiton he showed marks of respect. He stretched forth that strong arm of his over the city and warded off all harm. He kept back greedy soldiers from pillage; he kept back bigot priests from persecution.

Years before this he had said, "The diversity of religions may indeed create a division in the other world, but not in this." At another time he wrote, "Violent remedies only aggravate spiritual diseases." And he was now so tested that these expressions were found to embody not merely an idea, but a belief. For when the Protestants in La Rochelle, though thus owing tolerance—and even existence—to a Catholic, vexed Catholics in a spirit most intolerant, even that could not force him to abridge the religious liberties he had given.

He saw beyond his time, not only beyond Catholics, but beyond Protestants. Two years after that great example of toleration in La Rochelle, Nicholas Antoine was executed for apostasy from Calvinism at Geneva. And for his leniency Richelieu received the titles of "Pope of the Protestants" and "Patriarch of the Atheists." But he had gained the first great object of his policy, and he would not abuse it: he had crushed the political power of the Huguenots forever.

Let us turn now to the second great object of his policy. He must break the power of the nobility: on that condition alone could France have strength and order, and here he showed his daring at the outset. "It is iniquitous," he was wont to tell the King, "to try to make an example by punishing the lesser offenders; they are but trees which cast no shade: it is the great nobles who must be disciplined."

It was not long before he had to begin this work—and with the highest—with no less a personage than Gaston, Duke of Orléans, favorite son of Mary, brother of the King. He who thinks shall come to a higher idea of Richelieu's boldness when he remembers that for many years after this Louis was childless and sickly, and that during all those years Richelieu might awake any morning to find Gaston—king.

In 1626 Gaston, with the Duke of Vendôme, half-brother of the King, the Duchess of Chevreuse, confidential friend of the Queen, the Count of Chalais, and the Marshal Ornano, formed a conspiracy after the old fashion. Richelieu had his hand at their lofty throats in a moment. Gaston, who was used only as a makeweight, he forced into the most humble apology and the most binding pledges; Ornano he sent to die in the Bastille; the Duke of Vendôme and the Duchess of Chevreuse he banished; Chalais he sent to the scaffold.

The next year he gave the grandees another lesson. The serf-owning spirit had fostered in France, through many years, a rage for duelling. Richelieu determined that this should stop. He gave notice that the law against duelling was revived, and that he would enforce it. It was soon broken by two of the loftiest nobles in France—by the Count of Bouteville Montmorency and the Count des Chapelles. They laughed at the law: they fought defiantly in broad daylight. Nobody dreamed that the law would be carried out against them. The Cardinal would, they thought, deal with them as rulers have dealt with serf-mastering lawbreakers from those days to these—invent some quibble and screen them with it. But his method was sharper and shorter. He seized both, and executed both on the Place de la Grève—the place of execution for the vilest malefactors.

No doubt that under the present domineering of the pettifogger caste there are hosts of men whose minds run in such small old grooves that they hold legal forms not a means, but an end; these will cry out against this proceeding as tyrannical. No doubt, too, that under the present palaver of the "sensationist" caste, the old ladies of both sexes have come to regard crime as mere misfortune: these will lament this proceeding as cruel. But for this act, if for no other, an earnest man's heart ought in these times to warm toward the great statesman. The man had a spine. To his mind crime was not mere misfortune: crime was *crime*.

Crime was strong; it would pay him well to screen it: it might cost him dear to fight it. But he was not a modern "smart" lawyer to seek popularity by screening criminals; nor a modern soft juryman, to suffer his eyes to be blinded by quirks and quibbles to the great purposes of law; nor a modern bland governor, who lets a murderer loose out of politeness to the murderer's mistress. He hated crime; he whipped the criminal; no petty forms and no petty men of forms could stand between him and a rascal. He had the sense to see that this course was not cruel, but merciful. In the eighteen years before Richelieu's administration, four thousand men perished in duels; in the ten years after Richelieu's death nearly a thousand thus perished; but during his whole administration, duelling was checked completely. Which policy was tyrannical? Which policy was cruel?

The hatred of the serf-mastering caste toward their new ruler grew blacker and blacker, but he never flinched. The two brothers Marillac, proud of birth, high in office, endeavored to stir revolt as in their good days of old. The first, who was keeper of the seals, Richelieu threw into prison; with the second, who was a marshal of France, Richelieu took another course. For this marshal had added to revolt things more vile and more insidiously hurtful: he had defrauded the government in army contracts. Richelieu tore him from his army and put him on trial. The Queen-Mother, whose pet he was, insisted on his liberation. Marillac himself blubbered that it "was all about a little straw and hay, a matter for which a master would not whip a lackey." Marshal Marillac was executed. So, when statesmen rule, fare all who take advantage of the agonies of a nation to pilfer a nation's treasure.

To crown all, the Queen-Mother began now to plot against Richelieu because he would not be her puppet, and he banished her from France forever.

The high nobles were now exasperated. Gaston fled the country, first issuing against Richelieu a threatening manifesto. Now awoke the Duke of Montmorency. By birth he stood next the King's family: by office, as constable of France, he stood next the King himself. Montmorency was defeated and taken. The nobles supplicated for him lustily: they looked on crimes of nobles resulting in deaths of plebeians as lightly as the English

House of Lords afterward looked on Lord Mohun's murder of Will Mountfort, or as another body of lords looked on Matt Ward's murder of Professor Butler: but Montmorency was executed. Says Richelieu in his *Memoirs,* "Many murmured at this act, and called it severe; but others, more wise, praised the justice of the King, who preferred the good of the state to the vain reputation of a hurtful clemency."

Nor did the great minister grow indolent as he grew old. The Duke of Épernon, who seems to have had more direct power of the old feudal sort than any other man in France, and who had been so turbulent under the regency, him Richelieu humbled completely. The Duke of Valette disobeyed orders in the army, and was executed as a common soldier would have been for the same offence. The Count of Soissons tried to see if he could not revive the good old turbulent times, and raised a rebel army; but Richelieu hunted him down like a wild beast. Then certain court nobles—pets of the King—Cinq-Mars and De Thou, wove a new plot, and, to strengthen it, made a secret treaty with Spain; but the Cardinal, though dying, obtained a copy of the treaty, through his agent, and the traitors expiated their treason with their blood.

But this was not all. The Parliament of Paris—a court of justice—filled with the idea that law is not a means, but an end, tried to interpose forms between the master of France and the vermin he was exterminating. That Parisian court might, years before, have done something. They might have insisted that the petty quibbles set forth by the lawyers of Paris should not defeat the eternal laws of retribution set forth by the Lawgiver of the Universe. That they had not done, and the time for legal forms had gone by. The Paris Parliament would not see this, and Richelieu crushed the Parliament. Then the court of aids refused to grant supplies, and he crushed that court. In all this the nation upheld him. Woe to the courts of a nation when they have forced the great body of plain men to regard legality as injustice! Woe to the councils of a nation when they have forced the great body of plain men to regard legislation as traffic! Woe thrice repeated to gentlemen of small pettifogging sort when they have brought such times, and God has brought a man to fit them!

There was now in France no man who could stand against the statesman's purpose. And so, having hewn through all that anarchy and bigotry and selfishness a way for the people, he called them to the work. In 1626 he summoned an assembly to carry out reforms. It was essentially a people's assembly. That anarchical States-General, domineered by great nobles, he would not call; but he called an "Assembly of Notables." In this was not one prince or duke, and two-thirds of the members came directly from the people. Into this body he thrust some of his own energy. Measures were taken for the creation of a navy. An idea was now carried into effect which many suppose to have sprung from the French Revolution; for the army was made more effective by opening its high grades to the commons.

A reform was also made in taxation, and shrewd measures were taken to spread commerce and industry by calling the nobility into them.

Thus did France, under his guidance, secure order and progress. Calmly he destroyed all the useless feudal castles which had so long overawed the people and defied the monarchy. He abolished also the military titles of grand admiral and high constable, which had hitherto given the army and navy into the hands of leading noble families. He destroyed some troublesome remnants of feudal courts, and created royal courts; in one year, that of Poitiers alone, punished for exactions and violence against the people, more than two hundred nobles. Greatest step of all, he deposed the hereditary noble governors, and placed in their stead governors taken from the people—"Intendants"—responsible to the central authority alone.

We are brought now to the third great object of Richelieu's policy. He saw from the beginning that Austria and her satellite Spain must be humbled if France was to take her rightful place in Europe.

Hardly, then, had he entered the council, when he negotiated a marriage of the King's sister with the son of James I of England; next he signed an alliance with Holland; next he sent ten thousand soldiers to drive the troops of the Pope and Spain out of the Valtelline district of the Alps, and thus secured an alliance with the Swiss. We are to note here that fact, which Buckle wields so well, that, though Richelieu was a cardinal of the Roman Church, all these alliances were with Protestant powers against Catholics. Austria and Spain intrigued against him, sowing money in the mountain districts of South France which brought forth those crops of armed men who defended La Rochelle. But he beat them at their own game. He set loose Count Mansfeld, who revived the Thirty Years' War by raising a rebellion in Bohemia; and when one great man, Wallenstein, stood between Austria and ruin, Richelieu sent his monkish diplomatist, Father Joseph, to the German Assembly of Electors, and persuaded them to dismiss Wallenstein and to disgrace him.

But the great Frenchman's masterstroke was his treaty with Gustavus Adolphus. With that keen glance of his he saw and knew Gustavus while yet the world knew him not—while he was battling afar off in the wilds of Poland. Richelieu's plan was formed at once. He brought about a treaty between Gustavus and Poland; then he filled Gustavus' mind with pictures of the wrongs inflicted by Austria on German Protestants, hinted to him probably of a new realm, filled his treasury, and finally hurled against Austria the man who destroyed Tilly, who conquered Wallenstein, who annihilated Austrian supremacy at the battle of Lutzen, who, though in his grave, wrenched Protestant rights from Austria at the treaty of Westphalia, who pierced the Austrian monarchy with the most terrible sorrows it ever saw before the time of Napoleon.

To the main objects of Richelieu's policy already given, might be added two subordinate subjects. The first of these was a healthful extension of French territory. In this Richelieu planned better than the first Napoleon; for while he did much to carry France out to her natural boundaries, he kept her always within them. On the south he added Roussillon, on the east Alsace, on the northeast Artois.

The second subordinate object of his policy sometimes flashed forth brilliantly. He was determined that England should never again interfere on French soil. We have seen him driving the English from La Rochelle and from the Isle of Ré; but he went further. In 1628, on making some proposals to England, he was repulsed with English haughtiness. "They shall know," said the Cardinal, "that they cannot despise me."

Straightway one sees protests and revolts of the Presbyterians of Scotland and Richelieu's agents in the thickest of them. And now what was Richelieu's statesmanship in its sum?

1. In the political progress of France his work has already been sketched as building monarchy and breaking anarchy. Therefore have men said that he swept away old French liberties. What old liberties? Richelieu but tore away the decaying, poisonous husks and rinds which hindered French liberties from their chance of life and growth. Therefore also have men said that Richelieu built up absolutism. The charge is true and welcome. For evidently absolutism was the only force in that age which could destroy the serf-mastering caste. Many a Polish patriot, as he to-day wanders through the Polish villages, groans that absolutism was not built to crush that serf-owning aristocracy which has been the real architect of Poland's ruin. Anyone who reads to much purpose in De Mably, or Guizot, or Henri Martin knows that this part of Richelieu's statesmanship was but a masterful continuation of all great French statesmanship since the twelfth century league of the king and commons, against nobles, and that Richelieu stood in the heirship of all great French statesmen since Suger. That part of Richelieu's work, then, was evidently bedded in the great line of divine purpose running through that age and through all ages.

2. In the internal development of France, Richelieu proved himself a true builder. The founding of the French Academy and of the Jardin des Plantes, the building of the College of Plessis, and the rebuilding of the college of the Sorbonne, are among the monuments of this part-statesmanship. His, also, is much of that praise usually lavished on Louis XIV for the career opened in the seventeenth century to science, literature, and art. He was also a reformer, and his zeal was proved, when in the fiercest of the La Rochelle struggle he found time to institute great reforms not only in the army and navy, but even in the monasteries.

3. On the general progress of Europe, his work must be judged as mainly for good. Austria was the chief barrier to European progress, and that barrier he broke. But a far greater impulse to the general progress of Europe was given by the idea of toleration which he thrust into the methods of European states-

men. He, first of all statesmen in France, saw that in French policy—to use his own words—"A Protestant Frenchman is better than a Catholic Spaniard"; and he, first of all statesmen in Europe, saw that, in European policy, patriotism must outweigh bigotry.

4. His faults in method were many. His underestimate of the sacredness of human life was one; but that was the fault of his age. His frequent workings by intrigue was another; but that also was a vile method accepted by his age. The fair questions, then, are: did he not commit the fewest and smallest wrongs possible in beating back those many and great wrongs? Wrong has often a quick, spasmodic force, but was there not in his arm a steady growing force, which could only be a force of right?

5. His faults in policy crystallized about one; for while he subdued the serf-mastering nobility, he struck no final blow at the serf system itself.

Our running readers of French history need here a word of caution. They follow De Tocqueville, and De Tocqueville follows Biot in speaking of the serf system as abolished in most of France hundreds of years before this. But Biot and De Tocqueville take for granted a knowledge in their readers that the essential vileness of the system, and even many of its most shocking outward features, remained. Richelieu might have crushed the serf system, really, as easily as Louis X and Philip the Long had crushed it nominally. This Richelieu did not.

And the consequences of this great man's fault were terrible. Hardly was he in his grave when the nobles perverted the effort of the Paris Parliament for advance in liberty and took the lead in the fearful revolts and massacres of the Fronde. Then came Richelieu's pupil, Mazarin, who tricked the nobles into order; and Mazarin's pupil, Louis XIV, who bribed them into order. But a nobility borne on high by the labor of a servile class must despise labor; so there came those weary years of indolent gambling and debauchery and "serf-eating" at Versailles.

Then came Louis XV, who was too feeble to maintain even the poor decent restraint imposed by Louis XIV; so the serf-mastering caste became active in a new way, and their leaders in vileness unutterable became at last Fronsac and De Sade.

Then came "the deluge." The spirit of the serf-mastering caste, as left by Richelieu, was a main cause of the miseries which brought on the French Revolution. When the Third Estate brought up their "portfolio of grievances," for one complaint against the exactions of the monarchy there were fifty complaints against the exactions of the nobility.

Then came the failure of the Revolution in its direct purpose; and of this failure the serf-mastering caste was a main cause. For this caste, hardened by ages of domineering over a servile class, despite 4th of August renunciations, would not, could not, accept a position compatible with freedom and order; so earnest men were maddened, and sought to tear out this cancerous mass, with all its burning roots.

But for Richelieu's great fault there is an excuse. His mind was saturated with ideas of the impossibility of inducing freed peasants to work; the impossibility of making them citizens; the impossibility, in short, of making them men. To his view was not unrolled the rich newer world history, to show that a working class is most dangerous when restricted; that oppression is more dangerous to the oppressor than to the oppressed; that if man will hew out paths to liberty, God will hew out paths to prosperity. But Richelieu's fault teaches the world not less than his virtues.

At last on December 3, 1642, the great statesman lay upon his death-bed. The death-hour is a great revealer of motives, and, as with weaker men, so with Richelieu. Light then shot over the secret of his whole life's plan and work. He was told that he must die: he received the words with calmness. As the host, which he believed the veritable body of the Crucified, was brought him, he said: "Behold my Judge before whom I must shortly appear! I pray him to condemn me if I have ever had any other motive than the cause of religion and my country." The confessor asked him if he pardoned his enemies: he answered, "I have none but those of the state."

So passed from earth this strong man. Keen he was in sight, steady in aim, strong in act. A true man, not "non-committal," but wedded to a great policy in the sight of all men; seen by earnest men, of all times, to have marshalled against riot and bigotry and unreason, divine forces and purposes.

GREAT PURITAN EXODUS TO NEW ENGLAND

FOUNDING OF BOSTON

A.D. 1630

JOHN G. PALFREY

Whatever might have been the historic development of New England had it proceeded from the single plantation at Plymouth, it is certain that the growth and character of the new community were vitally affected by the large influx of English Puritans who ten years later followed the Pilgrims to these shores.

Soon after the departure of the Pilgrims from England, in 1620, King James I incorporated a successor to that Plymouth Company under whose patent Plymouth colony was founded. This new company is known as the Council for New England. The territory granted to the council extended from 40° to 48° north latitude, and from the Atlantic to the Pacific. The land was conferred in absolute property, with unlimited powers of legislation and government. Emigrants to New England were placed wholly under the authority of this corporation. The great privileges conferred upon the monopoly caused indignation among James' subjects, but nevertheless the council made numerous grants to settlers in New England.

Meanwhile, dissatisfaction in England increased; in 1625 James was succeeded by his son, Charles I; at Plymouth the Pilgrim colony was struggling for existence; at home the Puritans chafed under the growing despotism of Charles. Out of this unrest came the movement leading to the larger emigration to New England which Palfrey, the New England historian, describes.

THE emigration of the Englishmen who settled at Plymouth had been prompted by religious dissent. In what manner Robinson, who was capable of speculating on political tendencies, or Brewster, whose early position had compelled him to observe them, had augured concerning the prospect of public affairs in their native country, no record tells; while the rustics of the Scrooby congregation, who fled from a government which denied them liberty in their devotions, could have had but little knowledge and no agency in the political sphere. The case was widely different with the founders of the Colony of Massachusetts Bay. That settlement had its rise in a state of things in England which associated religion and politics in an intimate alliance.

Years had passed since the severity of the government had overcome the Separatists, forcing them either to disband their congregations or flee from the kingdom. From the time when Bishop Williams was made keeper of the great seal, four years before the death of King James, the high-commission court again became active, and the condition of Puritans in the Church was day by day more uneasy. While some among them looked for relief to a happy issue of the struggle which had been going on in Parliament, and resigned themselves to await and aid the slow progress of a political and religious reformation in the kingdom, numbers, less confident or less patient, pondered on exile as their best resource, and turned their view to a new home on the Western continent. There was yet a third class, who, through feeble resolution or a lingering hope of better things, deferred the sacrifices which they scarcely flattered themselves they should ultimately escape, and, if they were clergymen, retained their preferments by a reluctant obedience to the canons. The coquetry of Buckingham with the Puritans, inspiring false hopes, was not without effect to excuse indecision and hinder a combined and energetic action.

Among the eminent persons who had reconciled themselves to the course of compromise and postponement was Mr. John White, an important name, which at this point takes its place in New England history. White, who since the second year of King James' reign had been rector of Trinity Church in Dorchester, was a man widely known and greatly esteemed, alike for his professional character and his public spirit. The subject of New England colonization, much canvassed everywhere among the Puritans, who were numerous in the part of the kingdom where he lived, was commended to his notice in a special form. Dorchester, near the British Channel, the principal town of the shire, furnished numbers of those who now made voyages to New England for fishing and trade; and they were often several months upon the coast without opportunity for religious worship and instruction. Mr. White interested himself with the ship-owners to establish a settlement where the mariners might have a home when not at sea, where supplies might be provided for them by farming and hunting, and where they might be brought under religious influences. The result of the conferences was the formation of an unincorporated joint-stock association, under the name of the "Dorchester Adventurers," which collected a capital of three thousand pounds.

The Dorchester company turned its attention to the spot on Cape Ann where now stands the town of Gloucester. The Council for New England, perpetually embarrassed by the oppugnation of the Virginia Company and the reasonable jealousy of Parliament, had recourse to a variety of expedients to realize the benefits vainly expected by its projectors. In carrying out one scheme, that of a division of the common property among the associates, the country about Cape Ann was assigned to Lord Sheffield, better known as a patriot leader under his later title of Earl of Mulgrave. Of him it was purchased for the people of New Plymouth by Edward Winslow, when in England on the business of that colony; and they in turn conveyed to White and his associates such a site as was wanted for their purposes of fishing and planting.

The Dorchester company had probably anticipated this arrangement by despatching a party of fourteen persons to pass the winter. They carried out live stock, and erected a house, with stages to dry fish and vats for the manufacture of salt. Thomas Gardner was overseer of the plantation, and John Tilley had the fishery in charge. Everything went wrong. Mishaps befell the vessels. The price of fish went down. The colonists, "being ill chosen and ill commanded, fell into many disorders and did the company little service." An attempt was made to retrieve affairs by putting the colony under a different direction. The Dorchester partners heard of "some religious and well-affected persons that were lately removed out of New Plymouth, out of dislike of their principles of rigid separation, of which number Mr. Roger Conant was one, a religious, sober, and prudent gentleman."

He was then at Nantasket, with Lyford and Oldham. The partners engaged Conant "to be their governor" at Cape Ann, with "the charge of all their affairs, as well as fishing and planting." With Lyford they agreed that he should "be the minister of the place," while Oldham, "invited to trade for them with the Indians," preferred to remain where he was and conduct such business on his own account. The change was not followed by the profits that had been hoped, and the next year "the adventurers were so far discouraged that they abandoned the further prosecution of this design, and took order for the dissolving of the company on land, and sold away their shipping and other provisions." Another seemed added to the list of frustrated adventurers in New England.

But Mr. White did not despair of its renewal. All along, it is likely, he had regarded it with an interest different from what had yet been avowed. At his instance, when "most part of the land-men returned," "a few of the most honest and industrious resolved to stay behind, and to take charge of the cattle sent over the year before. And not liking their seat at Cape Ann, chosen especially for the supposed commodity of fishing, they transported themselves to Nahumkeike, about four or five leagues distant to the southwest from Cape Ann."

White wrote to Conant, exhorting him "not to desert the business, faithfully promising that if himself with three others, whom he knew to be honest and prudent men, viz., John Woodbury, John Balch, and Peter Palfrey, employed by the adventurers, would stay at Naumkeag, and give timely notice thereof, he would provide a patent for them, and likewise send them whatever they should write for, either men, or provision, or goods wherewith to trade with the Indians." With difficulty Conant prevailed upon his companions to persevere. They "stayed to the hazard of their lives." Woodbury was sent to England for supplies.

"The business came to agitation afresh in London, and being at first approved by some and disliked by others, by argument and disputation it grew to be more vulgar; insomuch that some men, showing good affection to the work, and offering the help of their purses if fit men might be procured to go over, inquiry was made whether any would be willing to engage their persons in the voyage. By this inquiry it fell out that among others they lighted at last on Master Endicott, a man well known to divers persons of good note, who manifested much willingness to accept of the offer as soon as it was tendered, which gave great encouragement to such as were upon the point of resolution to set on this work of erecting a new colony upon the old foundation."

The scheme on foot was no longer one of Dorchester fishermen looking for a profitable exercise of their trade. It had "come to agitation in London," where some men had offered "the help of their purses," and a man of consequence, Humphrey, probably from a county as distant as Lincoln, was already, or very soon after, treasurer of the fund. Matters were ripe for the step of securing a domain for a colony, and the dimensions of the domain show that the colony was not intended to be a small one. A grant of lands extending from the Atlantic to the Western Ocean, and in width from a line of latitude three miles north of the River Merrimac to a line three miles south of the Charles, was obtained from the Council for New England by "Sir Henry Roswell and Sir John Young, knights, and Thomas Southcote, John Humphrey, John Endicott, and Simon Whitcomb, gentlemen," for themselves, "their heirs, and associates." Roswell and Young were gentlemen of Devon, Southcote was probably of the same county, and Whitcomb is believed to have been a London merchant.

Gorges, though not in the counsels of the patentees, supposed himself to understand their object. Having mentioned the angry dissolution by King Charles of his second Parliament, and his imprisonment of some of the patriot leaders, he proceeds to say that these transactions "took all hope of reformation of church government from many not affecting episcopal jurisdiction, nor the usual practice of the Common Prayers of the Church; whereof there were several sorts, though not agreeing among themselves, yet all of like dislike of those particulars. Some of the discreeter sort, to avoid what they found themselves subject unto, made use of their friends to procure from Council for the affairs of New England to settle a colony within their limits; to which it pleased the thrice-honored Lord of Warwick to write to me, then at Plymouth, to condescend that a patent might be granted to such as then sued for it. Whereupon I gave my approbation, so far forth as it might not be prejudicial to my son Robert Gorges' interests, whereof he had a patent under the seal of the Council. Hereupon there was a grant passed as was thought reasonable."

After three months Endicott, one of the six patentees, was despatched, in charge of a small party, to supersede Conant at Naumkeag as local manager. Woodbury had preceded them. They arrived at the close of summer. The persons quartered on the spot, the remains of Conant's company, were disposed to question the claims of the new-comers. But the dispute was amicably composed, and, in commemoration of its adjustment, the place took the name of Salem, the Hebrew name for peaceful. The colony, made up from the two sources, consisted of "not much above fifty or sixty persons," none of them of special importance except Endicott, who was destined to act for nearly forty years a conspicuous part in New England history.

Before the winter, an exploring party either began or made preparations for a settlement at Mishawum, now Charlestown. With another party, Endicott, during Morton's absence in England, visited his diminished company at Merry-Mount, or, as Endicott called it, Mount Dagon, "caused their Maypole to be cut down, and rebuked them for their profaneness, and admonished them to look there should be better walking." The winter proved sickly; an "infection that grew among the passengers at sea, spread also among them ashore, of which many died, some of the scurvy, others of an infectious fever." Endicott sent to Plymouth for medical assistance, and Fuller, the physician of that place, made a visit to Salem.

The New Dorchester Company, like that which had preceded it, and like the company of London Adventurers concerned in that settlement at Plymouth, was but a voluntary partnership, with no corporate powers. The extensive acquaintance of Mr. White with persons disaffected to the rulers in church and state was probably the immediate occasion of advancing the business another step. Materials for a powerful combination existed in different parts of the kingdom, and they were now brought together for united action. The company, having been "much enlarged," a royal charter was solicited and obtained, creating a corporation under the name of the "Governor and Company of the Massachusetts Bay in New England."

This is the instrument under which the colony of Massachusetts continued to conduct its affairs for fifty-five years. The patentees named in it were Roswell and his five associates, with twenty other persons, of whom White was not one. It gave power forever to the freemen of the company to elect annually, from their own number, a governor, deputy-governor, and eighteen assistants, on the last Wednesday of Easter term, and to make laws and ordinances, not repugnant to the laws of England, for their own benefit and the government of persons inhabiting their territory. Four meetings of the company were to be held in a year, and others might be convened in a manner prescribed. Meetings of the governor, deputy-governor, and assistants were to be held once a month or oftener. The governor, deputy-governor, and any two assistants were authorized, but not required, to administer to freemen the oaths of supremacy and allegiance. The company might transport settlers not "restrained by special name." They had authority to admit new associates, and to establish the terms of their admission, and elect and constitute such officers as they should see fit for the ordering and managing of their affairs. They were empowered "to encounter, repulse, repel, and resist by force of arms, as well as by sea as by land, and by all fitting ways and means whatsoever, all such person and persons as should at any time thereafter attempt or enterprise the destruction, invasion, detriment, or annoyance to the said plantation or inhabitants." Nothing was said of religious liberty. The government may have relied upon its power to restrain it, and the emigrants on their distance and obscurity to protect it.

The first step of the new corporation was to organize a government for its colony. It determined to place the local administration in the hands of thirteen counsellors, to retain their offices for one year. Of these, seven besides the governor—in which office Endicott was continued—were to be appointed by the company at home; these eight were to choose three others; and the whole number was to be made up by the addition of such as should be designated by the persons on the spot at the time of Endicott's arrival, described as "old planters."

A proposal had just been accepted from certain "Boston men" to interest themselves in the adventure to the amount of five hundred pounds, being a hundred pounds in addition to what, it appears, they had previously promised, "and to provide able men to send over."

Unfortunately, no letter had been preserved of those sent by Endicott to England at this interesting juncture. There are, however, two letters addressed to him by the company, and one by Cradock, appointed in the charter to be its first governor. With various directions as to the details of his administration, they speak of the "propagation of the Gospel" as "the thing they do profess above all to be their aim in settling this plantation." They enjoin the keeping of "a diligent eye over their own people, and they live unblamable and without reproof." They forbid the planting of tobacco, except under severe restrictions. They order satisfaction to be given to the "old planters" by the offer of incorporation into the company and of a share in the lands. They speak of unsuccessful negotiations with Oldham, who asserted a claim under the patent of Robert Gorges, and give orders for anticipating him in taking possession of Massachusetts Bay. They direct that persons who may prove "not conformable to their government," or otherwise disagreeable, shall not be suffered "to remain within the limits of their grant," but be shipped to England. They prescribe a distribution of the servants among families, with a view to domestic order and Christian instruction and discipline. They enjoin a just settlement with the natives for lands. And they transmit a form of oaths to be taken by the governor and members of the council.

After the organization under the charter, no time was lost in despatching a reënforcement of colonists. Six vessels were prepared, and license was obtained from the lord treasurer for the embarkation of "eighty women and maids, twenty-six children, and three hundred men, with victuals, arms, and tools, and necessary apparel," and with "one hundred forty head of cattle, and forty goats." A committee of the company were careful "to make plentiful provision of godly ministers." Mr. Skelton, Mr. Higginson, and Mr. Bright, members of the Council, with Mr. Smith, another minister, sailed in the first three vessels, which reached Salem about the same time, and were soon followed by the residue of the fleet. Mr. Graves, another of the counsellors, was employed by the associates as an engineer.

Immediately on arriving, he proceeded with "some of the company's servants under his care, and some others," to Mishawum, where he laid out a town. Bright, who was one of his party, returned to England in the following summer, dissatisfied, probably, with the ecclesiastical proceedings which had taken place. Smith went for the present to the fishing-station at Nantasket.

Higginson wrote home: "When we came first to Naumkeag we found about half-score houses, and a fair house newly built for the Governor. We found also abundance of corn planted by them, very good and well-liking. And we brought with us about two hundred passengers and planters more, which, by common consent of the old planters, were all combined together into one body politic, under the same Governor. There are in all of us, both old and new planters, about three hundred, whereof two hundred of them are settled at Naumkeag, now called Salem, and the rest have planted themselves at Masathuset's Bay, beginning to build a town there, which we do call Charleston, or Charlestown. But that which is our greatest comfort and means of defence above all other is, that we have here the true religion and holy ordinances of Almighty God taught among us. Thanks be to God, we have here plenty of preaching and diligent catechizing, with strict and careful exercise and good commendable orders to bring our people into a Christian conversation with whom we have to do withal. And thus we doubt not but God will be with us; and if God be with us, who can be against us?"

Meanwhile, a movement of the utmost importance, probably meditated long before, was hastened by external pressure. The state of public affairs in England in the spring and summer of this year had brought numbers to the decision which had been heretofore approached with sorrowful reluctance, and several persons of character and condition resolved to emigrate at once to the New World. It was necessary to their purpose to secure self-government as far as it could be exercised by British subjects.

Possibly events might permit and require it to be vindicated even beyond that line. At any rate, to be ruled in America by a commercial corporation in England, was a condition in no sort accordant with their aim. At a general court of the company,

Cradock, the Governor, "read certain propositions conceived by himself, viz., that for the advancement of the plantation, the inducing and encouraging persons of worth and quality to transplant themselves and families thither, and for other weighty reasons therein contained (it is expedient) to transfer the government of the plantation to those that shall inhabit there, and not to continue the same in subordination to the company here, as now it is."

The corporation entertained the proposal, and, in view of "the many great and considerable consequences thereupon depending," reserved it for deliberation. Two days before its next meeting, twelve gentlemen, assembled at Cambridge, pledged themselves to each other to embark for New England with their families for a permanent residence, provided an arrangement should be made for the charter and the administration under it to be transferred to that country. Legal advice was obtained in favor of the authority to make the transfer; and on full consideration it was determined, "by the general consent of the company, that the government patent should be settled in New England." The old officers resigned, and their places were filled with persons of whom most or all were expecting to emigrate. John Winthrop was chosen governor, with John Humphrey for deputy-governor, and eighteen others for assistants. Humphrey's departure was delayed, and on the eve of embarkation his place was supplied by Thomas Dudley.

Winthrop, then forty-two years old, was descended from a family of good condition, long seated at Groton, in Suffolk, where he had a property of six or seven hundred pounds a year, the equivalent of at least two thousand pounds at the present day. His father was a lawyer and magistrate. Commanding uncommon respect and confidence from an early age, he had moved in the circles where the highest matters of English policy were discussed, by men who had been associates of Whitgift, Bacon, Essex, and Cecil. Humphrey was "a gentleman of special parts, of learning and activity, and a godly man"; in the home of his father-in-law, Thomas, third earl of Lincoln, the head in that day of the now ducal house of Newcastle, he had been the familiar companion of the patriotic nobles.

Of the assistants, Isaac Johnson, esteemed the richest of the emigrants, was another son-in-law of Lord Lincoln, and a landholder in three counties. Sir Richard Saltonstall of Halifax, in Yorkshire, was rich enough to be a bountiful contributor to the company's operations. Thomas Dudley, with a company of volunteers which he had raised, had served, thirty years before, under Henry IV of France; since which time he had managed the estates of the Earl of Lincoln. He was old enough to have lent a shrill voice to the huzzas at the defeat of the armada, and his military services had indoctrinated him in the lore of civil and religious freedom. Theophilus Eaton, an eminent London merchant, was used to courts and had been minister of Charles I in Denmark. Simon Bradstreet, the son of a Non-conformist minister in Lincolnshire, and a grandson of "a Suffolk gentleman of a fine estate," had studied at Emanuel College, Cambridge. William Vassall was an opulent West-India proprietor. "The principal planters of Massachusetts," says the prejudiced Chalmers, "were English country gentlemen of no inconsiderable fortunes; of enlarged understandings, improved by liberal education; of extensive ambition, concealed under the appearance of religious humility."

But it is not alone from what we know of the position, character, and objects of those few members of the Massachusetts Company who were proposing to emigrate at the early period now under our notice, that we are to estimate the power and the purposes of that important corporation. It had been rapidly brought into the form which it now bore, by the political exigencies of the age. Its members had no less in hand than a wide religious and political reform—whether to be carried out in New England, or in Old England, or in both, it was for circumstances, as they should unfold themselves, to determine. The leading emigrants to Massachusetts were of that brotherhood of men who, by force of social consideration as well as of the intelligence and resolute patriotism, moulded the public opinion and action of England in the first half of the seventeenth century. While the larger part stayed at home to found, as it proved, the short-lived English republic, and to introduce elements into the English Constitution which had to wait another half-century for their secure reception, another part devoted themselves at once to the erection of free institutions in this distant wilderness.

In an important sense the associates of the Massachusetts Company were builders of the British, as well as of the New England, commonwealth. Some ten or twelve of them, including Cradock, the Governor, served in the Long Parliament. Of the four commoners of that Parliament distinguished by Lord Clarendon as first in influence, Vane had been governor of the company, and Hampden, Pym, and Fiennes—all patentees of Connecticut—if not members, were constantly consulted upon its affairs. The latter statement is also true of the Earl of Warwick, the Parliament's admiral, and of those excellent persons, Lord Say and Sele and Lord Brooke, both of whom at one time proposed to emigrate. The company's meetings placed Winthrop and his colleagues in relations with numerous persons destined to act busy parts in the stirring times that were approaching—with Brereton and Hewson, afterward two of the Parliamentary major-generals; with Philip Nye, who helped Sir Henry Vane to "cozen" the Scottish Presbyterian Commissioners in the phraseology of the Solemn League and Covenant; with Samuel Vassall, whose name shares with those of Hampden and Lord Say and Sele the renown of the refusal to pay ship-money, and of courting the suit which might ruin them or emancipate England; with John Venn, who, at the head of six thousand citizens, beset the House of Lords during the trial of Lord Strafford, and whom, with three other Londoners, King Charles, after the battle of Edgehill, excluded from his offer of pardon; with Owen Rowe, the "firebrand of the city"; with Thomas Andrews, the lord mayor, who proclaimed the abolition of royalty.

Sir John Young, named second in the original grant from the Council for New England, as well as in the charter from King Charles, sat in Cromwell's second and third Parliaments. Others of the company, as Vane and Adams, incurred the Protector's displeasure by too uncomplying principles. Six or seven were members of the high court of justice for the King's trial, on which occasion they gave a divided vote. Four were members of the committee of religion, the most important committee of Parliament; and one, the counsellor, John White, was its chairman.

A question had been raised, whether the company had a right, and was legally competent, to convey the charter across the ocean, and execute on a foreign soil the powers conferred by it. Certain it is that no such proceeding is forbidden by the letter of the instrument; and a not disingenuous casuistry might inquire, If the business of the company may be lawfully transacted in a western harbor of Great Britain, why not under the King's flag in a ship at sea or on the opposite shore? It cannot be maintained that such a disposition of a colonial charter would be contrary to the permanent policy of England; for other colonial charters, earlier and later, were granted—Sir William Alexander's, William Penn's, Lord Baltimore's, and those of Rhode Island and Connecticut—to be kept and executed without the realm.

As to the purpose of the grantor, those were not times for such men as the Massachusetts patentees to ask what the King wished or expected, but rather how much of freedom could be maintained against him by the letter of the law or by other righteous means; and no principle of jurisprudence is better settled than that a grant is to be interpreted favorably to the grantees, inasmuch as the grantor, being able to protect himself, is to be presumed to have done so to the extent of his purpose. The eminent Puritan counsellor, John White, the legal adviser of the company in all stages of this important proceeding, instructed them that they could legally use the charter in this manner. Very probably it had been drawn by his own hand, in the form in which it passed the seals, with a care to have it free from any phraseology which might interfere with this disposition of it. Certainly Winthrop and his coadjutors may be pardoned for believing that it was legally subject to the use to which they put it, since such was the opinion of the crown lawyers themselves, when, in the second following generation, the question became important. In the very heat of the persecution which at length broke down the charter, the Chief Justices, Rainsford and North, spoke of it as "making the adventurers a corporation upon the place," and Sawyer, attorney-general in the next reign, expressed the same opinion—"The patent having created the grantees and their assigns a body corporate, they might transfer their charter and act in New England."

He who well weighs the facts which have been presented in connection with the principal emigration to Massachusetts, and other related facts which will offer themselves to notice as we proceed, may find himself conducted to the conclusion that when Winthrop and his associates prepared to convey across the water a charter from the King which, they hoped, would in their beginnings afford them some protection both from himself and through him from the powers of Continental Europe, they had conceived a project no less important than that of laying, on this side of the Atlantic, the foundations of a nation of Puritan Englishmen, foundations to be built upon as future circumstances should decide or allow. It would not perhaps be pressing the point too far to say that in view of the thick clouds that were gathering over their home, they contemplated the possibility that the time was near at hand when all that was best of what they left behind would follow them to these shores; when a renovated England, secure in freedom and pure in religion, would rise in North America; when a transatlantic English empire would fulfil, in its beneficent order, the dreams of English patriots and sages of earlier times.

If such were the aims of the members of the Massachusetts Company, it follows that commercial operations were a merely incidental object of their association. And, in fact, it does not appear that, as a corporation, they ever held for distribution any property except their land; or that they ever intended to make sales of their land in order to a division of the profits among the individual freemen; or that a freeman, by virtue of the franchise, could obtain a parcel of land even for his own occupation; or that any money was ever paid for admission into the company, as would necessarily have been done if any pecuniary benefit was attached to membership. Several freemen of the company—among others the three who were first named in the charter as well as in the patent from the Council for New England—appear to have never so much as attended a meeting. They were men of property and public spirit, who, without intending themselves to leave their homes, gave their influence and their money to encourage such as were disposed to go out and establish religion and freedom in a new country.

The company had no stock, in the sense in which that word is used in speaking of money corporations. What money was needed to procure the charter, to conduct the business under it, and carry out the scheme of colonization was obtained neither by the sale of negotiable securities nor by assessment, but by voluntary contributions from individuals of the company, and possibly from others, in such sums as suited the contributors respectively.

These contributions made up what is called in the records the joint stock, designed to be used in providing vessels and stores for the transportation of settlers. It is true that these contributors, called Adventurers, had more or less expectation of being remunerated for their outlay; and for this purpose two hundred acres of land within the limits of the patent were pledged to them for every fifty pounds subscribed, in addition to a proportional share of the trade which the government of the company was expecting to carry on. But a share of the profits of trade, as of the land, was to be theirs, not because they were freemen, but because they were contributors, which many of the freemen were not, and perhaps others besides freemen were.

When the transfer of the charter and of the government to America had been resolved upon, it was agreed that at the end of seven years a division of the profits of a proposed trade in fish, furs, and other articles should be made among the Adventurers agreeably to these principles; and the management of the business was committed to a board consisting of five persons who expected to emigrate, and five who were to remain in England. But this part of the engagement appears to have been lost sight of; at least never to have been executed. It is likely that the commercial speculation was soon perceived to be unpromising; and the outlay had been distributed in such proportions that the loss was not burdensome in any quarter. The richer partners submitted to it silently, from public spirit; the poorer, as a less evil than that of a further expense and risk of time and money.

From the ship Arbella, lying in the port of Yarmouth, the Governor and several of his companions took leave of their native country by an address, which they entitled "The Humble Request of his Majesty's Loyal Subjects, the Governor and the Company late gone for New England, to the Rest of their Brethren in and of the Church of England." They asked a favorable construction of their enterprise, and good wishes and prayers for its success. With a tenacious affection which the hour of parting made more tender, they said: "We esteem it our honor to call the Church of England, from whence we rise, our dear mother, and cannot part from our native country where she specially resideth, without much sadness of heart, and many tears in our eyes. Wishing our heads and hearts may be as fountains of tears for your everlasting welfare, when we shall be in our poor cottages in the wilderness, overshadowed with the spirit of supplication, through the manifold necessities and tribulations which may not altogether unexpectedly nor, we hope, unprofitably, befall us, and so commending you to the grace of God in Christ, we shall ever rest your assured friends and brethren." The address is said to have been drawn up by Mr. White, of Dorchester.

The incidents of the voyage are minutely related in a journal begun by the Governor on shipboard off the Isle of Wight. Preaching and catechizing, fasting and thanksgiving, were duly observed. A record of the writer's meditations on the great design which occupied his mind while he passed into a new world and a new order of human affairs, would have been a document of the profoundest interest for posterity. But the diary contains nothing of that description. On the voyage Winthrop composed a little treatise, which he called *A Model Christian Charity*. It breathes the noblest spirit of philanthropy. The reader's mind kindles as it enters into the train of thought in which the author referred to "the work we have in hand. It is," he said, "by a mutual consent, through a special overruling Providence, and a more than an ordinary approbation of the churches of Christ, to seek out a place of cohabitation and consortship under a due form of government both civil and ecclesiastical." The forms and institutions under which liberty, civil and religious, is consolidated and assured, were floating vaguely in the musings of that hour.

The Arbella arrived at Salem after a passage of nine weeks, and was joined in a few days by three vessels which had sailed in her company. The assistants, Ludlow and Rossiter, with a party from the west country, had landed at Nantasket a fortnight before, and some of the Leyden people, on their way to Plymouth, had reached Salem a little earlier yet. Seven vessels from Southampton made their voyage three or four weeks later. Seventeen in the whole came before winter, bringing about a thousand passengers.

It is desirable to understand how this population, destined to be the germ of a state, was constituted. Of members of the Massachusetts Company, it cannot be ascertained that so many as twenty had come over. That company, as has been explained, was one formed mainly for the furtherance, not of any private interests, but of a great public object. As a corporation, it had obtained the ownership of a large American territory, on which it designed to place a colony which should be a refuge for civil and religious freedom. By combined counsels, it had arranged the method of ordering a settlement, and the liberality of its members had provided the means of transporting those who should compose it. This done, the greater portion were content to remain and await the course of events at home, while a few of their number embarked to attend to the providing of the asylum which very soon might be needed by them all.

It may be safely concluded that most of the persons who accompanied the emigrant members of the company to New England sympathized with them in their object. It may be inferred from the common expenditures which were soon incurred, that considerable sums of money were brought over. And almost all the settlers may be presumed to have belonged to one or another of the four following classes: (1) Those who paid for their passage and who were accordingly entitled on their arrival to a grant of as much land as if they had subscribed fifty pounds to the "common stock" of the company; (2) those who, for their exercise of some profession, art, or trade, were to receive specified remuneration from the company in money or land; (3) those who paid a portion of their expenses, and after making up the rest by labor at the rate of three shillings a day, were to receive fifty acres of land; (4) indented servants, for whose conveyance their masters were to be remunerated at the rate of fifty acres of land for each. All Englishmen were eligible to the franchise of the Massachusetts Company; but until elected by a vote of the existing freemen no one had any share in the government of the plantation or in the selection of its governors.

The reception of the new-comers was discouraging. More than a quarter part of their predecessors at Salem had died during the previous winter, and many of the survivors were ill or feeble. The faithful Higginson was wasting with a hectic fever, which soon proved fatal. There was a scarcity of all sorts of provisions, and not corn enough for a fortnight's supply after the arrival of the fleet. "The remainder of a hundred eighty servants," who, in the two preceding years, had been conveyed over at heavy cost, were discharged from their indentures, to escape the expense of their maintenance. Sickness soon began to spread, and before the close of autumn had proved fatal to two hundred of this year's emigration. Death aimed at the "shining mark" he is said to love. Lady Arbella Johnson, coming "from a paradise of plenty and pleasure, which she enjoyed in the family of a noble earldom, into a wilderness of wants," survived her arrival only a month; and her husband, singularly esteemed and beloved by the colonists, died of grief a few weeks after. He was a holy man and wise and died in sweet peace."

Giving less than a week to repose and investigations at Salem, Winthrop proceeded with a party in quest of some more attractive place of settlement. He traced the Mystic River a few miles up from its mouth, and, after a three days' exploration, returned to Salem to keep the Sabbath. When ten or eleven vessels had arrived, a day of public thanksgiving was observed in acknowledgment of the divine goodness which had so far prospered the enterprise.

After a sufficient pause for deliberation and conference concerning the forms of organization of the new society, the subject of an ecclesiastical settlement was the first matter to receive attention. On a day solemnized with prayer and fasting, the Reverend Mr. Wilson, after the manner of proceeding in the year before at Salem, entered into a church covenant with Winthrop, Dudley, and Johnson. Two days after, on Sunday, they associated with them three of the assistants, Mr. Nowell, Mr. Sharpe, and Mr. Bradstreet, and two other persons, Mr. Gager and Mr. Colburn. Others were presently added; and the church, so constituted, elected Mr. Wilson to be its teacher, and ordained him to that charge at Mishawum. At the same time Mr. Nowell was chosen to be ruling elder, and Mr. Gager and Mr. Aspinwall to be deacons. From the promptness of these measures, it is natural to infer that they had been the subject of consideration and concert before the landing. But there was some lingering scruple respecting the innovation on accustomed forms; and either for the general satisfaction or to appease some doubters, "the imposition of hands" was accompanied with "this protestation by all, that it was only as a sign of election and confirmation."

In the choice of a capital town, attention was turned to Mishawum, now Charlestown. Here, ten weeks after the landing, the first court of assistants on this side of the water was convened. The assistants present were Saltonstall, Ludlow, Rossiter, Nowell, Sharpe, Pynchon, and Bradstreet. Three others were in the country: Johnson, Endicott, and Coddington. The question first considered was that of provision for the ministers. It was "ordered that houses be built for them with convenient speed at the public charge. Sir Richard Saltonstall undertook to see it done at his plantation (Watertown) for Mr. Phillips, and the Governor at the other plantation for Mr. Wilson." Allowances of thirty pounds a year to each of these gentlemen were to be made at the common charge of the settlements, "those of Mattapan and Salem exempted," as being already provided with a ministry. Provision was also made for Mr. Gager as engineer, and Mr. Penn as beadle. It was ordained "that carpenters, joiners, bricklayers, sawers, and thatchers should not take above two shillings a day, nor any man should give more, under pain of ten shillings to taker and giver"; and "sawers" were restricted as to the price they might take for boards. The use or removal of boats or canoes, without the owner's leave, was prohibited, under penalty of fine and imprisonment. Saltonstall, Johnson, Endicott, and Ludlow were appointed to be justices of the peace, besides the Governor and deputy-governor, who were always to have that trust by virtue of their higher office. And "it was ordered that Morton, of Mount Woolison, should presently be sent for by process." Morton had lately been brought back to Plymouth by Allerton—who incurred much censure on that account—and, repairing to Mount Wollaston, had resumed his old courses.

A recital of the action of the board of assistants at their first meetings on this continent will explain the early exigencies of their administration, and the view entertained by them of their duties and powers. At a second court, held at Charlestown, the following business was transacted. It was agreed "that every third Tuesday there should be a court of assistants held at the

Governor's house." It was "ordered that Thomas Norton, of Mount Wollaston, should presently be set into the bilboes, and after sent prisoner to England by the ship called the Gift, now returning thither; that all his goods should be seized upon to defray the charge of his transportation, payment of his debts, and to give satisfaction to the Indians for a canoe he unjustly took away from them; and that his house should be burned down to the ground, in sight of the Indians, for their satisfaction for many wrongs he had done them from time to time." Mr. Clarke was directed to pay to John Baker the sum of thirty-eight shillings, for cheating him in a sale of cloth. A stipend was granted to Mr. Patrick and Mr. Underhill, as military instructors and officers. The names of Boston, Dorchester, and Watertown were assigned to the places which still bear them. And it was ordered that no plantation should be made within the limits of the patent, without permission from a majority of the Board of Governor and Assistants, and that "a warrant should presently be sent to Agawam (Ipswich) to command those that are planted there forthwith to come away."

At a third court, also held at Charlestown, regulations were enacted against allowing the Indians the use of firearms, and against parting with corn to them, or sending it out of the jurisdiction, without a license. Constables were appointed for Salem and Dorchester. The wages of common laborers were fixed at sixpence a day, and those of mechanics who were employed in building at sixteen pence, in addition to "meat and drink." Order was given for the seizure of "Richard Clough's strong water, for his selling great quantity thereof to several men's servants, which was the occasion of much disorder, drunkenness, and misdemeanor." The execution of a contract between certain parties for the keeping of cattle was defined and enforced. Sir Richard Saltonstall was fined four bushels of malt for absenting himself from the meeting. Thomas Gray, for "divers things objected against him," was ordered "to remove himself out of the limits of this patent before the end of March next." "For the felony committed by him, whereof he was convicted by his own confession," John Gouldburn, as principal, and three other persons, as accessories, were sentenced "to be whipped, and afterward set in the stocks." Servants, "either man or maid," were forbidden to "give, sell, or truck any commodity whatsoever, without license from their master, during the time of their service." An allowance was made to Captains Underhill and Patrick for quarters and rations; and, for their maintenance, a rate of fifty pounds was levied, of which sum Boston and Watertown were assessed eleven pounds each, and Charlestown and Dorchester seven pounds each, Roxbury five pounds, and Salem and Mystic each only three pounds—a sort of indication of the estimated wealth of those settlements respectively.

The public business proceeded at the next two courts after the same manner. A restriction, which it seems had existed under Endicott's administration, on the price of beaver, was removed. A bounty was offered for the killing of wolves, to be paid by the owners of domestic animals in sums proportioned to the amount of their stock. Encouragement was given, by a legal rate of toll, to the setting up of a ferry between Charlestown and Boston. A servant of Sir Richard Saltonstall was sentenced to "be whipped for his misdemeanor toward his master"; and bonds were taken for good behavior in a case of "strong suspicion of incontinency." Sir Richard Saltonstall was fined five pounds for whipping two persons without the presence of another assistant. A man was ordered to be whipped for fowling on the Sabbath-day; another for stealing a loaf of bread; and another for breaking an engagement to pilot a vessel, with the privilege, however of buying off the punishment with forty shillings. The employers of one Knapp, who was indebted to Sir Richard Saltonstall, and of his son, were directed to apply half of their wages to the discharge of the debt. An assessment or sixty pounds was laid on six settlements for the maintenance of Mr. Wilson and Mr. Phillips, of which sum Boston and Watertown were to pay twenty pounds each, and Charlestown half as much; and Roxbury, Mystic, and Winnisimmet were charged with six pounds, three pounds, and one pound respectively.

An epidemic sickness at Charlestown was ascribed to the want of good water. An ample supply of it being found in Boston, a portion of the people removed to that peninsula; and there for the first time after their arrival on this continent, was held one of those quarterly general courts of the Company of Massachusetts Bay, which were prescribed in a provision of the charter.

TRIUMPH AND DEATH OF GUSTAVUS ADOLPHUS AT LUETZEN

A.D. 1632

BENJAMIN CHAPMAN

No actor in the Thirty Years' War left a more brilliant name than Gustavus Adolphus, King of Sweden. His military reputation, which rests on solid achievement, was much enhanced by the victory at Luetzen, although the King early fell on the field. That triumph, which was won largely through the inspiration of his spirit and the shock of its untimely departure, contributed to the remarkable advancement of Sweden which his reign had already inaugurated.

Before the interference of Gustavus in the war, the Catholic party had defeated the Protestants in almost every engagement. The Protestant leaders, Christian IV of Denmark, Count Mansfeld, and Christian of Anhalt, had been no match for Tilly, commanding the force of the Holy League, and Wallenstein, leader of the Imperial army. When Gustavus joined in the conflict, Wallenstein had quitted the service of the Emperor Ferdinand II, and the great Swede's first opponent was Tilly, the imperial generalissimo. Tilly's ruthless sack of Magdeburg, in 1631, brought many hesitating Protestants to the side of Gustavus, and on the field of Leipsic or Breitenfeld, September 7, 1631, he completely overcame his strong enemy. In April following, Tilly, the victor in thirty-six battles, fell in another conflict with Gustavus. The Swedish King continued his campaign in Germany, and November 16, 1632, he met Wallenstein, who again commanded the Imperial forces, and his lieutenant, Count Pappenheim, on the fatal but glorious field of Luetzen. The King had gathered his forces at Erfurt, and there he bade farewell to his Queen, tenderly commending her to the care of the city magistrates.

ON October 30th Gustavus sent Bernhard, Duke of Saxe-Weimar, forward with eleven thousand men to observe Pappenheim. The Duke took the road by Buttstadt to Freiburg, and from thence, after crossing the Saale, to Naumburg, where he arrived just in time to anticipate the enemy.

The next day the King gave the military command at Erfurt to Dupadel, and proceeded himself to Naumburg. Here the joy and confidence which his presence inspired, "as if he had been a god," far from elating him, awakened only in his mind a feeling of humility and a sorrowful presentiment that some disaster to himself would soon convince the Naumburgers of the frailty of the idol in whom they trusted.

On Sunday, November 14th, he learned, by an intercepted letter, that Pappenheim had been sent to Halle, and that the next day the Imperial army was to leave Weissenfels. He would now have attacked Wallentsein at once; but the dissuasions of Kniphausen—it is said—prevailed, and he agreed to defer the hazard of a battle until he should have been reënforced by Duke George of Luneburg and the Elector of Saxony.

Accordingly, having written to the Elector, who lay at Torgau, to meet him at Eilenburg, he was himself marching to Pegau, in that direction, when some gentlemen and peasants of the neighborhood brought him word that Wallensein's troops were still quartered in the villages around Luetzen, and that he was not aware of the King's army being on the march. "Then," exclaimed Gustavus, "I verily believe the Lord has delivered him into my hand," and instantly darted toward his prey.

Luetzen was now in sight; the peasants said it was close at hand. But it proved more distant than this indefinite expression, or the measure of their own eager gaze, had led the Swedes to calculate. Moreover, a small river, the Rippart, that lay between the King and Luetzen, whose narrow bridge could be only passed by one or two at a time, impeded the advance full two hours—a skirmish with Isolani's cavalry, who were quartered at a village near the bridge, may also have occasioned some little loss of time—so that when the Swedish army had reached the fatal field it was nightfall, and too late to begin the battle.

Wallenstein made good use of the delay. On the first intelligence of the King's approach he had written to Pappenheim—the letter is still preserved in the archives of Vienna, stained with Pappenheim's blood—apprising him of the danger, and requiring him to join at daybreak, with every man and gun. During the night and early in the morning, which proved very misty, he mustered his troops, and made his dispositions, deepening the drains by the highroads to form intrenchments for his musketeers.

The King passed the night in his carriage, chiefly in conversation with his generals. Early in the morning he had prayers read to himself by his chaplain, Frabricius. The rest of the army sang Luther's hymn, "Our God is a strong tower"; and Gustavus himself led another hymn—"Jesus Christ our Saviour, he overcame death."

The King mounted his horse without having broken his fast. He wore a plain buff coat, without armor; replying, it is said, to some remark upon this deficiency, that "God was his harness." He addressed a few words of encouragement, first to the Swedes, then to Germans of his army, and to this effect: "My brave and beloved subjects!" he said to the Swedish regiments, "now is the time to prove your discipline and courage, confirmed in many a fight. Yonder is the enemy you have sought so long, not now sheltered by strong ramparts nor posted on inaccessible heights, but ranged in fair and open field. Advance, then, by God's help, not so much to fight as to conquer. Spare not your blood, your lives, for your king, your country, your God; and the present and eternal blessing of the Almighty, and an illustrious name throughout the Christian world, await you. But if, which God forbid, you prove cowards, I swear that not a bone of you shall return to Sweden. The Lord preserve you all!"

To the Germans he said: "My brave allies and fellow-soldiers, I adjure you by your fame, your honor, and your conscience; by the interests temporal and eternal now at stake; by your former exploits, by the remembrance of Tilly and the Breitenfeld—bear yourselves bravely to-day. Let the field before you become illustrious by a similar slaughter. Forward! I will this day not only be your general, but your comrade. I will not only command you, I will lead you on. Add your efforts to mine. Extort from the enemy, by God's help, that victory, of which the chief fruits will be to you and to your children. But if you shrink from the contest, remember that religion, liberty—all will be lost, and that by your remissness."

Having finished his addresses, to which both Swedes and Germans responded by hearty cheers and acclamations, the King cast up his eyes to heaven and said, "O my Lord Jesus! Son of God, bless these our arms, and this day's battle, for thine own glory and holy name's sake." Then, drawing his sword, and waving it over his head, advanced, the foremost of all his army.

The numbers of the two armies at this moment were probably nearly equal. Diodati, indeed, who carried to the Emperor from Wallenstein a verbal report of the battle, which by Ferdinand's order he afterward drew up in writing, stated the Swedish army to have been 25,000 strong, the Imperial 12,000 only. This is to be understood as referring to the beginning of the engagement, before Pappenheim had come up, at which time, on the other hand, Harte and Mauvillon estimate the Imperial force at from 28,000 to 30,000 men, Gfrorer at 25,000—estimates which are as certainly exaggerations as Diodati's diminution of the truth. Gustavus would not only have departed from his avowed maxims and previous practice, he would have run counter to every sound strategical principle, had he attacked without necessity an army numerically so superior. For that the Swedish force amounted in all to not more than 18,000 men there is as much proof almost as it is possible to attain in such a matter.

A rough calculation would make Wallenstein and Pappenheim's whole united force not more than 27,000, unless any reenforcements took place which have not been recorded, or which have escaped my notice. If we estimate Pappenheim's division at 10,000, this will give 17,000 Imperialists on the field before he joined again on the day of the battle. But the *Swedish Intelligencer*, whose information was derived from English officers about the person of Gustavus, conceives that Wallenstein must have had at this time full 20,000, or, as he afterward modifies his opinion, that he must have had 30,000 in all, of whom 10,000 or 12,000 were with Pappenheim.

According to these estimates, then, we may conclude that there were in the Imperial camp at Luetzen, on November 5th, from 15,000 to 18,000, or perhaps even 20,000, men. Such numbers offered to Gustavus, especially under the circumstances, a strong temptation to attack them; and, the Imperial army being so divided, he had a reasonable hope—a hope by which he was justified in forcing the engagement—that he should be able to defeat successively both divisions. Even as it was, Pappenheim's foot not arriving soon enough to support contributed in no small degree to the loss of the battle.

The field, which was intersected by a canal that unites the Saale and the Elster, called the Flossgraben, was almost a level; but of all the accidents afforded by such ground Wallenstein had taken advantage. Luetzen lay to his right a little in front. Between it and three windmills close to his right wing intervened some mud-walled gardens. These he made use of as forts, throwing into them little garrisons, and loopholing the walls. The mill hills he converted into batteries, and the dry ditches by the roadside into breastworks for his musketeers.

The fog having cleared off for a season, at ten o'clock the battle began. The wind and sun were in the King's favor; but Wallenstein had the advantage in weight of artillery and position. Gustavus did not long sustain the cannonade of the enemy before he gave the order to charge toward the highway and dislodge the musketeers who occupied the ditches on the side of it. This being effected, the whole line continued to advance, and the three infantry brigades of the centre took the batteries on the other side of the highroad, but, not being supported in time by their cavalry, who had been impeded by the wayside ditches, lost them again and were compelled to fall back.

When the King knew that the first battery was taken, he uncovered his head and thanked God, but soon after, learning that the centre had been repulsed, he put himself at the head of the Smaland cavalry and charged the Imperial cuirassiers, the "black lads," with whom he had just before told Stalhaske to grapple. Piccolomini hastened to support the cuirassiers; and the Swedes, being overmatched, retreated without perceiving—the fog having again come over—that they had left the King in the midst of the enemy. A pistol-ball now broke his arm; and as the Duke of Lauenburg was supporting him out of the battle, an Imperial cuirassier came behind him and shot him in the back. He then fell from his horse; and, other cuirassiers coming up, one of them completed the work of death.

It is added on the testimony of a young gentleman named Leubelfing, the son of Colonel Leubelfing, of Nuremberg, and page to the Lord Marshal Crailsham, that being near when the King fell, and seeing that his charger, wounded in the neck, had galloped away, he dismounted and offered him his own horse. Gustavus stretched out his hands to accept the offer; and the page attempted to lift him from the ground, but was unable. In the mean time some cuirassiers, attracted to the spot, demanded who the wounded man was. Leubelfing evaded the question or refused to answer; but the King himself exclaimed, "I am the King of Sweden," when he received four gunshot wounds and two stabs, which quickly released him from the agony of his broken arm, the bone of which had pierced the flesh and protruded. The Imperialist soldiers about the King, each anxious to possess some trophy, had stripped the body to the shirt, and were about to carry it off when a body of Swedish cavalry, charging toward the spot, dispersed them.

His death was immediately communicated, by one of the few who were about his person when he fell, to the Swedish generals. His charger, galloping loose and bloody about the field, announced to many more that some disaster had befallen him. The whole extent of the calamity, however, was not generally known; but a burning desire ran through the ranks to rescue him, if living; to avenge him, if dead. The noble Bernhard of Saxe-Weimar sustained and animated the enthusiasm. Having whispered to Kniphausen that Gustavus was dead, he asked him what was to be done? Kniphausen answered that his troops were in good order, and that retreat was practicable; to which the fiery Duke answered that it was not a question of retreat, but of vengeance in victory. This said, he assumed the command, and, upon Stenbock's lieutenant-colonel hesitating to advance when he ordered him, passed his sword through his body, and led on to the attack three other regiments, after a few words which gave fresh fuel to their ardor. Again the lost ground is won, the lost batteries are recovered. Wallenstein's ammunition explodes, and seven of his guns are captured.

Stalhanske rallies his Finlanders, drives back the Imperial cuirassiers, and bears away the King's body—easily distinguished from the rest of the slain by its heroic stature. But many still are the vicissitudes of that memorable day. Pappenheim brings fresh masses and fresh courage into the field. He is slain; content to die, since Gustavus, the foe of the Emperor and of his faith, breathes no longer; but Piccolomini and Tershy have inherited his spirit. The Swedes are beaten back; several standards and royal banners are won by the Imperialists. Count

Brahé is mortally wounded; and of his division—the flower of all the army, the brave veterans "who have been so long accustomed to conquer that they knew not how to yield"—there remains but an inconsiderable fraction.

During all these vicissitudes the cool intrepidity of Kniphausen had kept the second line of the centre unbroken; and when, between three and four o'clock, the fog cleared off, and Duke Bernhard, who had expected a very different appearance, saw it standing firm and in good order, he raised his voice once more to renew the assault. This charge again changed the aspect of the battle; but the mist again spreading, again the Swedes are baffled when within a grasp of victory. The fifth and decisive charge was made just before sunset, when the arrival of Pappenheim's foot encouraged the Imperialists to make a final and desperate struggle. Kniphausen's fresh troops were now brought into action. The sharp ring of the musketry, the shouts of those full of life and hope, stifled once more the groans of the wounded comrades, in whom life was expiring and hope was dead. Both sides fought bravely, admirably; and, had strength and courage alone determined this last agony, doubtful indeed would have been its issue. But the Swedish cannon now again opened their flaming mouths upon the right flank and front of the Imperialists; and the effect was terrible: rank upon rank and file upon file fell beneath that crushing fire; so that when darkness thickened around the still contending armies, taking advantage of its cover, and leaving behind him the guns which had not been already captured, Wallenstein gave the signal to retreat, and drew off from the field.

Thus ended this day of mingled glory and sadness, the mists and confusion of which have in a great measure obscured its history. The numbers engaged, the order of battle on the side of the Imperialists, the number of the slain, the period of Pappenheim's arrival, what part of his forces were actually engaged; above all, the circumstances of the King's death, are perplexed amid the contrariety of contemporary narrations, representing partly the imperfection of human testimony and partly the different interests, jealousies, and suspicions of the times.

Among the last may be mentioned the imputation cast upon the Duke Francis Albert of Lauenburg, of having, according to previous compact with the Imperialists, murdered the King on the field of battle. This he is said to have effected as he was leading him away wounded, by placing a pistol behind him, and shooting him in the back. The Duke, who was now about thirty-two years of age, had served during the Mantuan war in the Imperial army, but, from some impression that he had been neglected, joined Gustavus two or three weeks before the battle of Luetzen, as a volunteer. After the King had fallen, supposing that all was lost, he ran away to Weissenfels, and did not appear again among the Swedish ranks until next morning, when the cool reception he received from the generals induced him probably to leave and go to Dresden, where he obtained from his relation, the Elector of Saxony, the rank of field-marshal under Arnim. Wallenstein courted his friendship by restoring to him without ransom some of his attendants captured at Luetzen. The Duke was not ungrateful, and took a zealous part in the negotiations between Wallenstein and the Elector of Saxony, and Duke Bernhard of Saxe-Weimar in January and February, 1634. On the night of Wallenstein's assassination he was arrested by Gordon and sent to Vienna, where he remained a year in imprisonment, but, at the expiration of that time, by embracing the Roman Catholic faith, obtained at once his freedom and a command in the Imperial army in Silesia. In the battle of Sweidnitz, May 30, 1642, he was wounded and taken prisoner. Torstenson rescued him with difficulty from the vengeance of the Swedish soldiers; and the next day he died of his wounds.

The story that he had murdered the King had at one time taken such a hold upon the Swedes that no historian of that nation could venture to treat it as a fable. But a full examination of the facts by Forster shows upon how slight a foundation the charge has rested. The motive of personal animosity arising out of a blow given by the King to the Duke is destroyed by the fact that the quarrel in which the insult is supposed to have been given was not with Duke Francis, but with his brother. The corroboration of his guilt, that he wore the device of Wallenstein's officers in the field, a green scarf, is annihilated by the answer that Wallenstein's officers did not wear green scarfs, but crimson. And the only direct evidence of his crime falls to pieces against counter-evidence of still greater weight. Even the Swedes themselves, if they still retain the convictions of their forefathers, have grown tolerant of opposite convictions; and Geijer has not scrupled to intimate, with tolerable plainness, that he considers the charge against the Duke of Saxe Lauenburg unproved.

Gustavus' body was brought on a powder-wagon to the hamlet of Meuchen, where it was placed for the night in the church, before the altar. The next day it was carried to the schoolmaster's house, until he, being joiner of the village also, constructed the simple shell in which it was conveyed to Weissenfels. There the body was embalmed by the King's apothecary, Caspar, who counted in it nine wounds. The heart, which was uncommonly large, was preserved by the Queen in a golden casket. A trooper, who had been wounded at the King's side, who remained at Meuchen until his wound was healed, assisted by some peasants, rolled a large stone toward the spot where he fell. They were unable, however, to bring the stone, now called the "Swede's Stone," to the exact spot, from which it stands some thirty or forty paces distant.

The death of Gustavus Adolphus cast a gloom over the whole of Europe. Even foes could lament the fall of so noble an enemy. To his subjects, to his allies, to the bondmen who looked to him for redress and deliverance, his loss was a heartrending sorrow. Grave and aged senators wrung their hands and sobbed aloud when intelligence reached Stockholm. In the unfortunate Frederick of Bohemia it produced, as we have seen, a depression that contributed probably to this death.

Nor was the grief shown by the many merely political or selfish, excited because the public or individual hopes centred in the King seemed to have perished with him. A heartfelt loyalty, a strong personal admiration and attachment, intermingled with other sources of regret and dignified the sorrow.

It would have been strange had it been otherwise. There were in Gustavus most of the advantages and amenities of person and character which make a popular king, a man admired and beloved. In his latter years, indeed, he no longer possessed the graceful form that had belonged to him when he was an ardent and favored suitor of Ebba Brahé; but the slight inclination to corpulency that grew with him as he advanced toward middle age detracted probably little, if at all, from the commanding dignity of his person. His countenance to the last retained its captivating sweetness and expressive variety. It was a countenance of which the most accomplished pencil could give in one effort only an inadequate idea, and which Vandyke—to whose portrait of the King none of the engravings which I have seen, probably, do justice—has represented only in repose.

But in the varying play of Gustavus' features men could read his kindness of heart, his large powers of sympathy, his quick intelligence, his noble, chivalrous nature. And these were infinitely attractive. There, too—it must not be concealed—they could often discern the flash of anger, to be followed quickly by the rough speech which gave pain and offence where a little self-control and consideration might have spared a pang and prevented a quarrel.

This propensity to anger diminished in some degree both the popularity and merit of Gustavus; yet he rarely permitted his anger to rage beyond a harsh expression, and with generous instinct he knew how to open the door of reconciliation, not only by frankly confessing his irritability, and by conferring fresh favors, but also by demanding fresh services from those noble natures which in his heat and rashness he had injured or pained.

In the field he shared the dangers of his soldiers with a courage liable, doubtless, to the charge of temerity, but to which, no less than to his participation in their hardships, his sympathy with their feelings, and his great military talents, he owed, under God, his success and renown. That his military fame was well founded, that no series of accidents could have produced success, at once so splendid and so uniform, we must have believed, though all professional authorities had been silent; but the special merit of no other commander has been more generally acknowledged by those of his own craft. His most celebrated living rival and the greatest conqueror of modern times have both set their seals to it. Wallenstein on two separate occasions pronounced him the greatest captain of his age; and among the eight best generals whom, in his judgment, the world had ever seen, Napoleon gave a place to Gustavus Adolphus.

RECANTATION OF GALILEO

A.D. 1633

SIR OLIVER LODGE

From Socrates to Galileo, as from the Church's early martyrs to its latest victims, runs the same story of conflict between the free human spirit and the repressive environment of custom acting through personal will or through constituted power.

When in 1633 Galileo, standing before the Inquisition at Rome, denied his own great work and swore that earth stood still, science staggered under the heavy blow. Galileo was being punished, not directly for the great astronomical discoveries he had made with his telescope, but for asserting that they proved, or that he believed in, the Copernican system. This declared that the earth moved, while the churchmen had interpreted the Bible to mean that it did not.

Thus science, threatened in the person of its greatest leader, terrified by his sufferings, no longer dared proclaim the thing it saw. Descartes and many another thinker, though throbbing with the eagerness of the new dawning light, hushed their voices, hid their views. They were philosophers, not martyrs. What this newly roused vigor of thought might have accomplished except for the repressive hand of the Church we cannot tell. As it was, the supremacy of intellect passed away from Catholic Italy, turned from the South to the North, from Galileo to Newton and Leibnitz. The forced recantation of the great astronomer thus stands out as one of the events which have changed the course of destiny.

IN 1615 Pope Paul V wrote requesting Galileo to come to Rome to explain his views. He went, was well received, made a special friend of Cardinal Barberino—an accomplished man in high position, who became, in fact, the next Pope. Galileo showed cardinals and others his telescope, and to as many as would look through it he showed Jupiter's satellites and his other discoveries. He had a most successful visit. He talked, he harangued, he held forth in the midst of fifteen or twenty disputants at once, confounding his opponents and putting them to shame.

His method was to let the opposite arguments be stated as

fully and completely as possible, himself aiding, and often adducing, the most forcible and plausible arguments against his own views; and then, all having been well stated, he would proceed to utterly undermine and demolish the whole fabric, and bring out the truth in such a way as to convince all honest minds. It was this habit that made him such a formidable antagonist. He never shrank from meeting an opposing argument, never sought to ignore it or cloak it in a cloud of words. Every hostile argument he seemed to delight in, as a foe to be crushed, and the better and stronger they sounded the more he liked them. He knew many of them well, he invented a number more, and, had he chosen, could have out-argued the stoutest Aristotelian on his own grounds. Thus did he lead his adversaries on, almost like Socrates, only to ultimately overwhelm them in a more hopeless rout. All this in Rome, too, in the heart of the Catholic world. Had he been worldly-wise, he would certainly have kept silent and unobtrusive till he had leave to go away again. But he felt like an apostle of the new doctrines, whose mission it was to proclaim them even in this centre of the world and of the Church.

Well, he had an audience with the Pope—a chat an hour long—and the two parted good friends, mutually pleased with each other.

He writes that he is all right now, and might return home when he liked. But the question began to be agitated whether the whole system of Copernicus ought not to be condemned as impious and heretical. This view was persistently urged upon the Pope and college of cardinals, and it was soon to be decided upon.

Had Galileo been unfaithful to the Church he could have left them to stultify themselves in any way they thought proper, and himself had gone; but he felt supremely interested in the result, and he stayed. He writes:

"So far as concerns the clearing of my own character, I might return home immediately; but although this new question regards me no more than all those who for the last eighty years have supported those opinions both in public and private, yet, as perhaps I may be of some assistance in that part of the discussion which depends on the knowledge of truths ascertained by means of the sciences which I profess, I, as a zealous and Catholic Christian, neither can nor ought to withhold that assistance which my knowledge affords, and this business keeps me sufficiently employed."

It is possible that his stay was the worst thing for the cause he had at heart. Anyhow, the result was that the system was condemned, and both the book of Copernicus and the epitome of it by Kepler were placed on the forbidden list,[1] and Galileo himself was formally ordered never to teach or to believe the motion of the earth.

He quitted Rome in disgust, which before long broke out in satire. The only way in which he could safely speak of these views now was as if they were hypothetical and uncertain, and so we find him writing to the Archduke Leopold, with a presentation copy of his book on the tides, the following:

"This theory occurred to me when in Rome while the theologians were debating on the prohibition of Copernicus' book, and of the opinion maintained in it of the motion of the earth, which I at that time believed: until it pleased those gentlemen to suspend the book, and declare the opinion false and repugnant to the Holy Scriptures. Now, as I know how well it becomes me to obey and believe the decisions of my superiors, which proceed out of more knowledge than the weakness of my intellect can attain to, this theory which I send you, which is founded on the motion of the earth, I now look upon as a fiction and a dream, and beg your highness to receive it as such. But as poets often learn to prize the creations of their fancy, so in like manner do I set some value on this absurdity of mine. It is true that when I sketched this little work I did hope that Copernicus would not, after eighty years, be convicted of error; and I had intended to develop and amplify it further, but a voice from heaven suddenly awakened me, and at once annihilated all my confused and entangled fancies."

This sarcasm, if it had been in print, would probably have been dangerous. It was safe in a private letter, but it shows us his real feelings. However, he was left comparatively quiet for a time. He was getting an old man now, and passed the time studiously enough, partly at his house in Florence, partly at his villa in Arcetri, a mile or so out of the town.

[1] They remained there till 1835, when they were dropped.

Here was a convent, and in it his two daughters were nuns. One of them, who passed under the name of Sister Maria Celeste, seems to have been a woman of considerable capacity—certainly she was of a most affectionate disposition—and loved and honored her father in the most dutiful way.

This was a quiet period of his life, spoiled only by occasional fits of illness and severe rheumatic pains, to which the old man was always liable. Many little circumstances are known of this peaceful time. For instance, the convent clock won't go, and Galileo mends it for them. He is always doing little things for them, and sending presents to the lady superior and his two daughters.

He was occupied now with problems in hydrostatics and on other matters unconnected with astronomy: a large piece of work which I must pass over. Most interesting and acute it is, however.

In 1623, when the old Pope died, there was elected to the papal throne, as Urban VIII, Cardinal Barberino, a man of very considerable enlightenment, and a personal friend of Galileo's, so that both he and his daughters rejoice greatly, and hope that things will come all right, and the forbidding edict be withdrawn.

The year after this election he manages to make another journey to Rome to compliment his friend on his elevation to the pontifical chair. He had many talks with Urban, and made himself very agreeable.

Encouraged, doubtless, by marks of approbation, and reposing too much confidence in the individual good-will of the Pope, without heeding the crowd of half-declared enemies who were seeking to undermine his reputation, he set about, after his return to Florence, his greatest literary and most popular work, *Dialogues on the Ptolemaic and Copernican Systems*. This purports to be a series of four conversations between three characters: Salviati, a Copernican philosopher; Sagredo, a wit and scholar, not specially learned, but keen and critical, and who lightens the talk with chaff; Simplicio, an Aristotelian philosopher, who propounds the stock absurdities which served instead of arguments to the majority of men.

The Aristotelians were furious, and represented to the Pope

that he himself was the character intended by Simplicio, the philosopher whose opinions get alternately refuted and ridiculed by the other two, till he is reduced to an abject state of impotence.

The infirm old man was instantly summoned to Rome. His friends pleaded his age—he was now seventy—his ill-health, the time of year, the state of the roads, the quarantine existing on account of the plague. It was all of no avail; to Rome he must go, and on February 14th he arrived.

His daughter at Arcetri was in despair; and anxiety and fastings and penances self-inflicted on his account dangerously reduced her health.

At Rome he was not imprisoned, but he was told to keep indoors and show himself as little as possible. He was allowed, however, to stay at the house of the Tuscan ambassador instead of in jail.

By April he was removed to the chambers of the Inquisition and examined several times. Here, however, the anxiety was too much, and his health began to give way seriously; so, before long, he was allowed to return to the ambassador's house; and, after application had been made, was allowed to drive in the public garden in a half-closed carriage. Thus in every way the Inquisition dealt with him as leniently as they could. He was now their prisoner, and they might have cast him into their dungeons, as many another had been cast. By whatever they were influenced—perhaps the Pope's old friendship, perhaps his advanced age and infirmities—he was not so cruelly used.

Still, they had their rules; he *must* be made to recant and abjure his heresy; and, if necessary, torture must be applied. This he knew well enough, and his daughter knew it, and her distress may be imagined. Moreover, it is not as if they had really been heretics, as if they hated or despised the Church of Rome. On the contrary, they loved and honored the Church. They were sincere and devout worshippers, and only on a few scientific matters did Galileo presume to differ from his ecclesiastical superiors: his disagreement with them occasioned him real sorrow; and his dearest hope was that they could be brought to his way of thinking and embrace the truth.

This condition of things could not go on. From February to

June the suspense lasted. On June 20th he was summoned again, and told he would be wanted all next day for a rigorous examination. Early in the morning of the 21st he repaired thither, and the doors were shut. Out of those chambers of horror he did not reappear till the 24th. What went on all those three days no one knows. He himself was bound to secrecy. No outsider was present. The records of the Inquisition are jealously guarded. That he was technically tortured is certain; that he actually underwent the torment of the rack is doubtful. Much learning has been expended upon the question, especially in Germany. Several eminent scholars have held the fact of actual torture to be indisputable—geometrically certain, one says—and they confirm it by the hernia from which he afterward suffered, this being a well-known and frequent consequence.

Other equally learned commentators, however, deny that the last stage was reached. For there are five stages all laid down in the rules of the Inquisition, and steadily adhered to in a rigorous examination, at each stage an opportunity being given for recantation, every utterance, groan, or sigh being strictly recorded. The recantation so given has to be confirmed a day or two later, under pain of a precisely similar ordeal.

The five stages are: (1) The official threat in the court; (2) the taking to the door of the torture-chamber and renewing the official threat; (3) the taking inside and showing the instruments; (4) undressing and binding upon the rack; (5) *territio realis*. Through how many of these ghastly acts Galileo passed I do not know. I hope and believe not the last.

There are those who lament that he did not hold out, and accept the crown of martyrdom thus offered to him. Had he done so we know his fate—a few years' languishing in the dungeons, and then the flames. Whatever he ought to have done, he did not hold out—he gave way. At one stage or another of the dread ordeal he said: "I am in your hands. I will say whatever you wish." Then was he removed to a cell while his special form of perjury was drawn up.

The next day, clothed as a penitent, the venerable old man was taken to the convent of Minerva, where the cardinals and prelates were assembled for the purpose of passing judgment upon him.

The judgment sentences him: (1) To the abjuration, (2) to formal imprisonment for life, (3) to recite the seven penitential psalms every week.

Ten cardinals were present; but, to their honor, be it said, three refused to sign; and this blasphemous record of intolerance and bigoted folly goes down the ages with the names of seven cardinals immortalized upon it. This having been read, he next had to read word for word the abjuration which had been drawn up for him, and then sign it.

THE ABJURATION OF GALILEO

"I, Galileo Galilei, son of the late Vincenzo Galilei, of Florence, aged seventy years, being brought personally to judgment, and kneeling before your Most Eminent and Most Reverend Lords Cardinals, General Inquisitors of the universal Christian republic against heretical depravity, having before my eyes the Holy Gospels, which I touch with my own hands, swear that I have always believed, and now believe, and with the help of God will in future believe, every article which the Holy Catholic and Apostolic Church of Rome holds, teaches, and preaches. But because I have been enjoined by this Holy Office altogether to abandon the false opinion which maintains that the sun is the centre and immovable, and forbidden to hold, defend, or teach the said false doctrine in any manner, and after it hath been signified to me that the said doctrine is repugnant with the Holy Scripture, I have written and printed a book, in which I treat of the same doctrine now condemned, and adduce reasons with great force in support of the same, without giving any solution, and therefore have been judged grievously suspected of heresy; that is to say, that I held and believed that the sun is the centre of the universe and is immovable, and that the earth is not the centre and is movable; willing, therefore, to remove from the minds of your Eminences, and of every Catholic Christian, this vehement suspicion rightfully entertained toward me, with a sincere heart and unfeigned faith, I abjure, curse, and detest the said errors and heresies, and generally every other error and sect contrary to Holy Church; and I swear that I will never more in future say or assert anything verbally, or in writing, which may give rise to a similar suspicion of me; but if I shall know any heretic, or anyone suspected of heresy, that I will denounce him to this Holy Office, or to the Inquisitor or Ordinary of the place where I may be; I swear, moreover, and promise, that I will fulfil and observe fully, all the penances which have been or shall be laid on me by this Holy Office. But if it shall happen that I violate any of my said promises, oaths, and protestations (which God avert!), I subject myself to all the pains and punishments which have been decreed and promulgated by the sacred canons, and other general and particular constitutions, against delinquents of this description. So may God help me, and his Holy Gospels which I touch with my own hands. I, the above-named Galileo Galilei, have abjured, sworn, promised, and bound myself as above, and in witness thereof with my own hand have subscribed this present writing of my abjuration, which I have recited word for word. At Rome, in the Convent of Minerva, June 22, 1633. I, Galileo Galilei, have abjured as above with my own hand."

Those who believe the story about his muttering to a friend, as he rose from his knees, "*E pur si muove*" ("And yet it does move"), do not realize the scene.

There was no friend in the place. It would have been fatally dangerous to mutter anything before such an assemblage. He was by this time an utterly broken and disgraced old man; wishful, of all things, to get away and hide himself and his miseries from the public gaze; probably with his senses deadened and stupefied by the mental sufferings he had undergone, and no longer able to think or care about anything—except perhaps his daughter—certainly not about any motion of this wretched earth.

Far and wide the news of the recantation spread. Copies of the abjuration were immediately sent to all universities, with instructions to the professors to read it publicly. At Florence, his home, it was read out in the cathedral church, all his friends and adherents being specially summoned to hear it.

For a short time more he was imprisoned in Rome, but at length was permitted to depart, nevermore of his own will to return.

EDUCATIONAL REFORM OF COMENIUS

A.D. 1638

S. S. LAURIE

John Amos Comenius (1592–1671) is now generally recognized as the founder of modern education. Just what his work has been is best left to Mr. Laurie, the leading authority upon his life. What the schools were before his time is almost too dreary a picture to attempt to draw. Everything was hopelessly haphazard, almost hopelessly uninteresting. Only in the schools of the Jesuits was anything approaching skill employed to stimulate the learner. If a child did not advance, the teacher held himself no way responsible. The lad was adjudged a dullard and left to remain in his stupidity with the rest of the blockhead world.

The chief work of Comenius, the *Didactica Magna*, was probably finished about 1638, and was shown in manuscript to many persons at that time. Its ideas as to education were widely accepted, and its influence and that of its author spread rapidly over much of Europe. The publication of his works was delayed until 1657.

IN the history of education it is important to recognize the existence of the two parallel streams of intellectual and spiritual regeneration. The leaders of both, like the leaders of all great social changes, at once bethought themselves of the schools. Their hope was in the young, and hence the reform of education early engaged their attention.

The improvements made in the grammar-schools under the influence of Melanchthon and Sturm, and in England of Colet and Ascham, did not endure, save in a very limited sense. Pure classical literature was now read—a great gain certainly, but this was all. There was no tradition of method, as was the case in the Jesuit order. During the latter half of the sixteenth century, the complaints made of the state of the schools, the waste of time, the barbarous and intricate grammar rules, the cruel discipline, were loud and long, and proceeded from men of the highest intellectual standing. To unity in the Reformed churches they looked, but looked in vain, for a settlement of opinion, and to the school they looked as the sole hope of the future. The school, as it actually existed, might have well filled them with despair.

Even in the universities Aristotelian physics and metaphysics, and with them the scholastic philosophy, still held their own. The reforms initiated mainly by Melanchthon had not, indeed, contemplated the overthrow of Aristotelianism. He and the other humanists merely desired to substitute Aristotle himself in the original for the Latin translation from the Arabic, necessarily misleading, and the Greek and Latin classics for barbarous epitomes. These very reforms, however, perpetuated the reign of Aristotle, when the spirit that actuated the Reformers was dead, and there had been a relapse into the old scholasticism. The Jesuit reaction, also, which recovered France and South Germany for the papal see, was powerful enough to preserve a footing for the metaphysical theology of St. Thomas Aquinas and the schoolmen. In England, Milton was of opinion that the youth of the universities were, even so late as his time, still presented with an "asinine feast of sow-thistles." These retrogressions in school and university serve to show how exceedingly difficult it is to contrive any system of education, middle or upper, which will work itself when the contrivers pass from the scene. Hence the importance, it seems to us, of having in every university, as part of the philosophical faculty, a department for the exposition of this very question of education—surely a very important subject in itself as an academic study, and in its practical relations transcending perhaps all others. How are the best traditions of educational theory and practice to be preserved and handed down if those who are to instruct the youth of the country are to be sent forth to their work from our universities with minds absolutely vacant as to the principles and history of their profession—if they have never been taught to ask themselves the question, "What am I going to do?" "Why?" and "How?" This subject is one worthy of consideration both by the universities and the state. It was the want of method that led to the decline of schools after the Reformation period; it was the study of method which gave the Jesuits the superiority that on many parts of the Continent they still retain.[1]

[1] Mr. Laurie's work was written in 1881. Considerable changes have since been made along the lines which he suggests.

In 1605 there appeared a book which was destined to place educational method on a scientific foundation, although its mission is not yet, it is true, accomplished. This was Francis Bacon's *Advancement of Learning*, which was followed some years later by the *Organum*. For some time the thoughts of men had been turning to the study of nature. Bacon represented this movement, and gave it the necessary impulse by his masterly survey of the domain of human knowledge, his pregnant suggestions, and his formulation of scientific method. Bacon was not aware of his relations to the science and art of education; he praises the Jesuit schools, not knowing that he was subverting their very foundations. We know inductively: that was the sum of Bacon's teaching. In the sphere of outer nature, the scholastic saying, "*Nihil est in intellectu quod non prius fuerit in sensu*," was accepted, but with this addition, that the impressions on our senses were not themselves to be trusted. The mode of verifying sense-impressions, and the grounds of valid and necessary inference, had to be investigated and applied. It is manifest that if we can tell how it is we know, it follows that the method of intellectual instruction is scientifically settled.

But Bacon not only represented the urgent longing for a coordination of the sciences and for a new method, he also represented the weariness of words, phrases, and vain subtleties which had been gradually growing in strength since the time of Montaigne, Ludovicus Vives, and Erasmus. The poets, also, had been placing nature before the minds of men in a new aspect. The humanists, as we have said, while unquestionably improving the aims and procedure of education, had been powerless to prevent the tendency to fall once more under the dominion of words, and to revert to mere form. The realism of human life and thought, which constituted their *raison d'être*, had been unable to sustain itself as a principle of action, because there was no school of method. It was the study of the realities of sense that was finally to place education on a scientific basis, and make reaction, as to method at least, impossible.

The thought of any age determines the education of the age which is to succeed it. Education follows; it does not lead. The school and the church alike march in the wake of science, philosophy, and political ideas. We see this illustrated in every epoch of human history, and in none so conspicuously as in the changes which occurred in the philosophy and education of ancient Rome during the lifetime of the elder Cato, and in modern times during the revival of letters and the subsequent rise of the Baconian induction. It is impossible, indeed, for any great movement of thought to find acceptance without its telling to some extent on every department of the body politic. Its influence on the ideas entertained as to the education of the rising generation must be, above all, distinct and emphatic. Every philosophical writer on political science has recognized this, and has felt the vast significance of the educational system of a country both as an effect—the consequence of a revolution in thought—and as a cause, a moving force of incalculable power in the future life of a commonwealth. Thus it was that the humanistic movement which preceded and accompanied the Reformation of religion shook to its centre the mediæval school system of Europe; and that subsequently the silent rise of the inductive spirit subverted its foundations.

Bacon, though not himself a realist in the modern and abused sense of that term, was the father of realism. It was this side of his teaching which was greedily seized upon, and even exaggerated. Educational zeal now ran in this channel. The conviction of the churches of the time, that one can make men what one pleases—by fair means or foul—was shared by the innovators. By education, rightly conceived and rightly applied, the enthusiasts dreamed that they could manufacture men, and, in truth, the Jesuits had shown that a good deal could be done in this direction. The new enthusiasts failed to see that the genius of Protestantism is the genius of freedom, and that man refuses to be manufactured except on suicidal terms. He must first sacrifice that which is his distinctive title to manhood—his individuality and will. That the prophets of educational realism should have failed to see this is not to be laid at their door as a fault; it merely shows that they belonged to their own time, and not to ours. They failed then, as some fail now, to understand man and his education, because they break with the past. The record of the past is with them merely a record of blunders. The modern humanist more wisely accepts it as the storehouse of the thoughts and life of human reason. In the life of man each individual of the race best finds his own true life. This is modern humanism—the realism of thought.

Yet it is to the sense-realists of the earlier half of the seventeenth century that we owe the scientific foundations of educational method, and the only indication of the true line of answer to the complaints of the time. In their hands sense-realism became allied with Protestant theology, and pure humanism disappeared. They were represented first by Wolfgang von Ratich, a native of Holstein, born in 1571. Ratich was a man of considerable learning. The distractions of Europe, and the want of harmony, especially among the churches of the Reformation, led him to consider how a remedy might be found for many existing evils. He thought that the remedy was to be found in an improved school system—improved in respect both of the substance and method of teaching. In 1612, accordingly, he laid before the Diet of the German empire at Frankfort a memorial, in which he promised, "with the help of God, to give instruction for the service and welfare of all Christendom."

The torch that fell from Ratich's hand was seized, ere it touched the ground, by John Amos Comenius, who became the head, and still continues the head, of the sense-realistic school. His works have a present and practical, and not merely a historical and speculative, significance.

Not only had the general question of education engaged many minds for a century and more before Comenius arose, but the apparently subsidiary, yet all-important, question of method, in special relation to the teaching of the Latin tongue, had occupied the thoughts and pens of many of the leading scholars of Europe. The whole field of what we now call secondary instruction was occupied with the one subject of Latin; Greek, and occasionally Hebrew, having been admitted only in the beginning of the sixteenth century, and then only to a subordinate place. This of necessity. Latin was the one key to universal learning. To give to boys the possession of this key was all that teachers aimed at until their pupils were old enough to study rhetoric and logic. Of these writers on the teaching of Latin, the most eminent were Sturm, Erasmus, Melanchthon, Lubinus, Vossius, Sanctius (the author of the *Minerva*), Ritter, Helvicus, Bodinus, Valentinus Andreæ, and, among Frenchmen, Cœcilius Frey. Nor were

Ascham and Mulcaster in England the least significant of the critics of method. Comenius was acquainted with almost all previous writers on education, except probably Ascham and Mulcaster, to whom he never alludes. He read everything that he could hear of with a view to find a method, and he does not appear ever to have been desirous to supersede the work of others. If he had found what he wanted, he would, we believe, have promulgated it, and advocated it as a loyal pupil. That he owed much to the previous writers is certain; but the prime characteristic of his work on Latin was his own. Especially does he introduce a new epoch in education, by constructing a general methodology which should go beyond mere Latin, and be equally applicable to all subjects of instruction.

Before bringing his thoughts into definite shape, he wrote to all the distinguished men to whom he could obtain access. He addressed Ratich, among others, but received no answer; many of his letters also were returned, because the persons addressed could not be found. Valentinus Andreæ wrote to him in encouraging terms, saying that he gladly passed on the torch to him. His mind became now much agitated by the importance of the question and by the excitement of discovery. He saw his whole scheme assuming shape under his pen, and was filled, like other zealous men, before and since, with the highest hopes of the benefits which he would confer on the whole human race by his discoveries. He resolved to call his treatise *Didactica Magna*, or *Omnes omnia docendi Artificium*. He found a consolation for his misfortunes in the work of invention, and even saw the hand of Providence in the coincidence of the overthrow of schools, through persecutions and wars, and those ideas of a new method which had been vouchsafed to him, and which he was elaborating. Everything might now be begun anew, and untrammelled by the errors and prejudices of the past.

Some scruples as to a theologian and pastor being so entirely preoccupied with educational questions he had, however, to overcome. "Suffer, I pray, Christian friends, that I speak confidentially with you for a moment. Those who know me intimately know that I am a man of moderate ability and of almost no learning, but one who, bewailing the evils of his time, is eager to remedy them, if this in any be granted me to do, either by my own discoveries or by those of another—none of which things can come save from a gracious God. If, then, anything be here found well done, it is not mine, but his, who from the mouths of babes and sucklings hath perfected praise, and who, that he may in verity show himself faithful, true, and gracious, gives to those who ask, opens to those who knock, and offers to those who seek. Christ my Lord knows that my heart is so simple that it matters not to me whether I teach or be taught, act the part of teacher of teachers or disciple of disciples. What the Lord has given me I send forth for the common good." His deepest conviction was that the sole hope of healing the dissensions of both church and state lay in the proper education of youth.

When he had completed his *Great Didactic*, he did not publish it, for he was still hoping to be restored to his native Moravia, where he proposed to execute all his philanthropic schemes; indeed, the treatise was first written in his native Slav or Czech tongue. In 1632 there was convened a synod of the Moravian Brethren at Lissa, at which Comenius, now forty years of age, was elected to succeed his father-in-law, Cyrillus, as bishop of the scattered brethren—a position which enabled him to be of great service, by means of correspondence, to the members of the community, who were dispersed in various parts of Europe. Throughout the whole of his long life he continued this fatherly charge, and seemed never quite to abandon the hope of being restored, along with his fellow-exiles, to his native land—a hope doomed to disappointment. In his capacity of pastor-bishop he wrote several treatises, such as a *History of the Persecutions of the Brotherhood*, an account of the Moravian Church discipline and order, and polemical tracts against a contemporary Socinian.

Meanwhile his great didactic treatise, which had been written in his native Czech tongue, was yet unpublished. He was, it would appear, stimulated to the publication of it by an invitation he received in 1638, from the authorities in Sweden, to visit their country and undertake the reformation of their schools. He replied that he was unwilling to undertake a task at once so onerous and so invidious, but that he would gladly give the benefit of his advice to anyone of their own nation whom they might select for the duty. These communications led him to resume his labor on the *Great Didactic*, and to translate it into Latin, in which form it finally appeared.

Humanism, which had practically failed in the school, had, apart from this fact, no attractions for Comenius, and still less had the worldly wisdom of Montaigne. He was a leading Protestant theologian—a pastor and bishop of a small but earnest and devoted sect—and it was as such that he wrote on education. The best results of humanism could, after all, be only culture, and this not necessarily accompanied by moral earnestness or personal piety: on the contrary, probably dissociated from these, and leaning rather to scepticism and intellectual self-indulgence.

At the same time it must be noted that he never fairly faced the humanistic question; he rather gave it the cold shoulder from the first. His whole nature pointed in another direction. When he has to speak of the great instruments of humanistic education—ancient classical writers—he exhibits great distrust of them, and, if he does not banish them from the school altogether, it is simply because the higher instruction in the Latin and Greek tongues is seen to be impossible without them. Even in the universities, as his pansophic scheme shows, he would have Plato and Aristotle taught chiefly by means of analyses and epitomes. It might be urged in opposition to this view of the antihumanism of Comenius, that he contemplated the acquisition of a good style in Latin in the higher stages of instruction: true, but in so far as he hid so, it was merely with a practical aim—the more effective, and, if need be, oratorical, enforcement of moral and religious truth. The beauties and subtleties of artistic expression had little charm for him, nor did he set much store by the graces. The most conspicuous illustration of the absence of all idea of art in Comenius is to be found in his school drama. The unprofitable dreariness of that production would make a reader sick were he not relieved by a feeling of its absurdity.

The educational spirit of the Reformers, the conviction that all—even the humblest—must be taught to know God, and Jesus Christ whom he has sent, was inherited by Comenius in its completeness. In this way, and in this way only, could the ills of Europe be remedied and the progress of humanity assured.

While, therefore, he sums up the educational aim under the threefold heads of Knowledge, Virtue, and Piety or Godliness, he in truth has mainly in view the last two. Knowledge is of value only in so far as it forms the only sound basis, in the eyes of a Protestant theologian, of virtue and godliness. We have to train for a hereafter.

In virtue and godliness Comenius did not propose to teach anything save what the Reformed religion taught. His characteristic merits in this department of instruction were:

1. Morality and godliness were to be taught from the first. Parents and teachers were to begin to train at the beginning of the child's conscious life.

2. Parents and teachers were to give milk to babes, and reserve the stronger meat for the adolescent and adult mind. They were to be content to proceed gradually, step by step.

3. The method of procedure was not only to be adapted to the growing mind, but the mode of enforcement was to be mild, and the manner of it kind and patient.

Had Comenius done nothing more than put forth and press home these truths he would have deserved our gratitude as an educationalist.

But he did more than this. He related virtue and godliness to knowledge. By knowledge Comenius meant knowledge of nature and of man's relation to nature. It is this important characteristic of Comenius' educational system that reveals the direct influence of Bacon and his school. To the great Verulam he pays reverence for what he owed him, but he owed him even more than he knew.

In this field of knowledge, the leading characteristic of the educational system of Comenius is his realism. We have pointed out, in contradiction of the assumptions of the modern sensationalist school, that the humanists were in truth realists, and it may be safely said that there can be no question among competent judges as to the realism which ought to characterize all rational and sound instruction. The question rather is as to the field in which the real is to be sought—in the mind of man, or in external nature. As the former may be called humanistic-realism, so the latter may be called sense- or naturalistic-realism. Of the latter, Comenius is the true founder, although his indebtedness to Ratich was great. Mere acquisition of the ordered facts of nature, and man's relation to them, was with him the great aim—if not the sole aim—of all purely intellectual instruction. And here there necessarily entered the governing idea, encyclopædism or pansophism. Let all the sciences, he said, be taught in their elements in all schools, and more fully at each successive stage of the pupil's progress. It is by knowledge that we are what we are, and the necessary conclusion from this must be, let all things be taught to all.

It is at this point that many will part company with Comenius. The mind stored with facts, even if these be ordered facts, will not necessarily be much raised in the scale of humanity as an intelligence. The natural powers may be simply overweighted by the process, and the natural channels of spontaneous reason choked. In education, while our main business is to promote the growth of moral purpose and of a strong sense of duty, we have to support these by the discipline of intelligence, and by training to power and work rather than by information. On the other hand, only those who are ignorant of the history and the recognized results of education will wholly abjure realism in the Comenian sense; but it has to be assigned is own place, and nothing more than this, in the education of a human being. The sum of the matter seems to be this, that while a due place in all education is to be assigned to sense-realistic studies, especially in the earlier years of family and school life, the humanistic agencies must always remain the most potent in the making of a man.

Comenius and his followers again confound knowledge with wisdom. He affirms that "all authors are to be banished from school except those that give a knowledge of useful things." Wisdom is certainly not to be opposed to knowledge, but it depends more on a man's power of discrimination, combination, and imagination than on the extent of his mental store of facts. Were it not so, our whole secondary education, and all the purely disciplinal part of our university instruction would be very far astray. If the ancient tongues are to be learned simply with a view to the sum of knowledge they contain, it would be absurd to waste the time of our youth over them. It would be better to impose on our universities the duty of furnishing guaranteed translations for the use of the public. We shall not, however, involve ourselves in controversy here, as our object is merely to point out, generally, the strong and weak points of our author.

Next in importance to pansophy or encyclopædism, and closely connected with it, is the principle that a knowledge of words and of things should go hand in hand. Words are to be learned through things. Properly interpreted, and under due limitations, this principle will, we presume, be now generally accepted. We say, under due limitations, because it is manifest that the converse preposition, that "things are learned through words," is easily capable of proof, and is indeed, in our opinion, the stronghold of humanistic teaching in its earlier or school stages.

It is in the department of method, however, that we recognize the chief contribution of Comenius to education. The mere attempt to systematize was a great advance. In seeking, however, for foundations on which to erect a coherent system, he had had to content himself with first principles which were vague and unscientific.

Modern psychology was in its infancy, and Comenius had little more than the generalizations of Plato and Aristotle, and those not strictly investigated by him, for his guide. In training to virtue, moral truth and the various moralities were assumed as if they emerged full-blown in the consciousness of man. In training to godliness, again, Christian dogma was ready to his hand. In the department of knowledge, that is to say, knowledge of the outer world, Comenius rested his method on the scholastic maxim, "*Nihil est in intellectu quod non prius fuerit in sensu.*" This maxim he enriched with the Baconian induction, comprehended by him, however, only in a general way. It was chiefly, however, the imagined harmony of physical and mental process that yielded his method. He believed that the process of the growth of external things had a close resemblance to the growth of the mind. Had he lived in these days he would doubtless have endeavored to work out the details of his method on a purely psychological basis; but in the then state of psychology he had to find another thread through the labyrinth. The mode of demonstration which he adopted was thus, as he himself called it, the syncretic or analogical. Whatever may be said of the harmony that exists between the growth of nature and of mind, there can be no doubt that the observation of the former is capable of suggesting, if it does not furnish, many of the rules of educational method.

From the simple to the complex, from the particular to the general, the concrete before the abstract, and all, step by step, and even by insensible degrees—these were among his leading principles of method. But the most important of all his principles was derived from the scholastic maxim quoted above. As all is from sense, let the thing to be known be itself presented to the senses, and let every sense be engaged in the perception of it. When it is impossible, from the nature of the case, to present the object itself, place a vivid picture of it before the pupil. The mere enumeration of these few principles, even if we drop out of view all his other contributions to method and school-management, will satisfy any man familiar with all the more recent treatises on education, that Comenius, even after giving his precursors their due, is to be regarded as the true founder of modern method, and that he anticipates Pestalozzi and all of the same school.

When we come to consider Comenius' method as applied specially to language, we recognize its general truth, and the teachers of Europe and America will now be prepared to pay it the homage of theoretical approval at least. To admire, however, his own attempt at working out his linguistic method is impossible, unless we first accept his encyclopædism. The very faults with which he charged the school practices of the time are simply repeated by himself in a new form. The boy's mind is overloaded with a mass of words—the name and qualities of everything in heaven, on the earth, and under the earth. It was impossible that all these things, or even pictures of them, could be presented to sense, and hence his books must have inflicted a heavy burden on the merely verbal memory of boys. We want children to grow into knowledge, not to swallow numberless facts made up into boluses. Again, the amount that was to be acquired within a given time was beyond the youthful capacity. Any teacher will satisfy himself of this who will simply count the words and sentences in the *Janua* and *Orbis* of Comenius, and then try to distribute these over the schooltime allowed them. Like all reformers, Comenius was oversanguine. I do not overlook the fact that command over the Latin tongue as a vehicle of expression was necessary to those who meant to devote themselves to professions and to learning, and that Comenius had his justification for introducing a mass of vocables now wholly useless to the student of Latin. But even for his own time, Comenius, under the influence of his encyclopædic passion, overdid his task. His real merits in language-teaching lie in the introduction of the principle of graduated reading-books, in the simplification of Latin grammar, in his founding instruction in foreign tongues on the vernacular, and in his insisting on method in instruction. But these were great merits, too soon forgotten by the dull race of schoolmasters, if, indeed, they were ever fully recognized by them till quite recent times.

Finally, Comenius' views as to the inner organization of a school were original, and have proved themselves in all essential respects correct.

The same may be said of his scheme for the organization of a state system—a scheme which is substantially, *mutatis mutandis*, at this moment embodied in the highly developed system of Germany.

When we consider, then, that Comenius first formally and fully developed educational method, that he introduced important reforms into the teaching of languages, that he introduced into schools the study of nature, that he advocated with intelligence, and not on purely sentimental grounds, a milder discipline, we are justified in assigning to him a high, if not the highest, place among modern educational writers. The voluminousness of his treatises, their prolixity, their repetitions, and their defects of styles have all operated to prevent men studying him. The substance of what he has written has been, I believe, faithfully given by me, but it has not been possible to transfer to these pages the fervor, the glow, and the pious aspirations of the good old bishop.

FIRST WRITTEN FREE CONSTITUTION IN THE WORLD

EARLIEST UNION AMONG AMERICAN COLONIES

A.D. 1639-1643

G. H. HOLLISTER JOHN MARSHALL

That a colonizing people should, almost at the moment of their arrival in a new home, proceed to enact the fundamental law of a civil state is a remarkable fact in history. The manner in which this was done in Connecticut, and the character of the constitution there made in 1639, six years after the first English settlement, render it a memorable event in the development of American government.

As the Connecticut Constitution was not only the first instrument of its kind, but also formed, in many respects, a pattern for others which became the organic laws of American States, so the first union of colonies, in 1643, is important not alone as being the first, but also as foreshadowing the later confederation and the final union of the States themselves.

This model of an American union, following so closely upon the earliest creation of an American civil constitution, is concisely described by the great Chief Justice Marshall.

G. H. HOLLISTER

WE read, in treatises upon elementary law, of a time antecedent to all law, when men theoretically are said to have met together and surrendered a part of their rights for a more secure enjoyment of the remainder. Hence, we are told, human governments date their origin. This dream of the enthusiast as applied to ages past, in Connecticut for the first time and upon the American soil became a recorded verity.

Here at last we are permitted to look on and see the foundations of a political structure laid. We can count the workmen, and we have become familiar with the features of the master-builders. We see that they are most of them men of a new type. Bold men they are, who have cut loose from old associations, old prejudices, old forms; men who will take the opinions of no man unless he can back them up with strong reasons; clear-sighted, sinewy men, in whom the intellect and the moral nature predominate over the more delicate traits that mark an advanced stage of social life. Such men as these will not, however, in their zeal to cast off old dominions, be solicitous to free themselves and their posterity from all restraint; for no people are less given up to the sway of unbridled passions. Indeed, they have made it a main part of their business in life to subdue their passions. Laws, therefore, they must and will have, and laws that, whatever else they lack, will not want the merit of being fresh and original.

As it has been, and still is, a much debated question, what kind of men they were—some having overpraised and others rashly blamed them—let us, without bigotry, try if we cannot look at them through a medium that shall render them to us in all their essential characteristics as they were. That medium is afforded us by the written constitution that they made of their own free will for their own government. This is said to give the best portrait of any people; though in a nation that has been long maturing, the compromise between the past and present, written upon almost every page of its history, cannot have failed in some degree to make the likeness dim. Yet, of such a people as we are describing, who may be said to have no past, who live not so much in the present as in the future, and who forge as with one stroke the constitution that is to be a basis of their laws—are we not provided with a mirror that reflects every lineament with the true disposition of light and shade? If it is a stern, it is yet a truthful, mirror. It flatters neither those who made it nor those blear-eyed maskers, who, forgetful of their own distorted visages, look in askance, and are able to see nothing to admire in the sober, bright-eyed faces of their fathers who gaze down upon them from the olden time.

The preamble of this constitution begins by reciting the fact that its authors are, "under Almighty God, inhabitants and residents of Windsor, Hartford, and Wethersfield, upon the river of Connecticut." It also states that, in consonance with the word of God, in order to maintain the peace and union of such a people, it is necessary that "there should be an orderly and decent government established," that shall "dispose of the affairs of *the people* at all seasons." "We do therefore," say they, "associate and conjoin ourselves to be as one public state or commonwealth." They add, further, that the first object aimed at by them is to preserve the liberty and the purity of the gospel and the discipline of their own churches; and, in the second place, to govern their *civil affairs* by such rules as their written constitution and the laws enacted under its authority shall prescribe. To provide for these two objects—the liberty of the Gospel, as they understood it, and the regulation of their own civil affairs, they sought to embody in the form of distinct decrees, substantially the following provisions:

1. That there shall be every year two general assemblies or courts, one on the second Thursday of April, the other on the second Thursday of September; that the one held in April shall be called the court of election, wherein shall be annually chosen the magistrates—one of whom shall be the governor—and other public officers, who are to administer justice according to the laws here established; where there are no laws provided to do it in accordance with the laws of God; and that these rulers shall be elected by all the freemen within the limits of the commonwealth, who have been admitted inhabitants of the towns where they severally live, and who have taken the oath of fidelity to the new state; and that they shall all meet at one place to hold this election.

2. It is provided that after the voters have all met and are ready to proceed to an election, the first officer to be chosen shall be a governor, and after him a body of magistrates and other officers. Every voter is to bring in, to those who are appointed to receive it, a piece of paper with the name of him whom he would have for governor written upon it, and he that has the greatest number of papers with his name written upon them was to be governor for that year. The other magistrates were elected in the following manner. The names of all the candidates were first given to the secretary for the time being, and written down by him, in the order in which they were given; the secretary was then to read the list over aloud and severally nominate each person whose name was so written down, in its order, in a distinct voice, so that all the citizen voters could hear it. As

each name was read, they were to vote by ballot, either for or against it, as they liked; those who voted in favor of the nominee did it by writing his name upon the ballot—those who voted against him simply gave in a blank ballot; and those only were elected whose names were written upon a majority of all the paper ballots handed in under each nomination. These papers were to be received and counted by sworn officers appointed by the court for that purpose. Six magistrates, besides the governor, were to be elected in this way. If they failed to elect so many by a majority vote, then the requisite number was to be filled up by taking the names of those who had received the highest number of votes.

3. The men thus to be nominated and balloted for were to be propounded at some general court held before the court of election, the deputies of each town having the privilege of nominating any two whom they chose. Other nominations might be made by the court.

4. No person could be chosen governor oftener than once in two years. It was requisite that this officer should be a member of an approved congregation, and that he should be taken from the magistrates of the commonwealth. But no qualification was required in a candidate for the magistracy, except that he should be chosen from the freemen. Both governor and magistrates were required to take a solemn oath of office.

5. To this court of election the several towns were to send their deputies, and after the elections were over the court was to proceed, as at other courts, to make laws or do whatever was necessary to further the interests of the commonwealth.

6. These two regular courts were to be convened by the governor himself, or by his secretary, by sending out a warrant to the constables of every town, a month at least before the day of session. In times of danger or public exigency the governor and a majority of the magistrates might order the secretary to summon a court, with fourteen days' notice, or even less, if the case required it, taking care to state their reasons for so doing to the deputies when they met. If, on the other hand, the governor should neglect to call the regular courts, or, with the major part of the magistrates, should fail to convene such special ones as were needed, then the freemen, or a major part of them, were

required to petition them to do it. If this did not serve, then the freemen, or a majority of them, were clothed with the power to order the constables to summon the court, after which they might meet, choose a moderator, and do any act that it was lawful for the regular courts to do.

7. On receiving the warrants for these general courts the constables of each town were to give immediate notice to the freemen, either at a public gathering or by going from house to house, that at a given place and time they should meet to elect deputies to the general court, about to convene, and "to agitate the affairs of the commonwealth." These deputies were to be chosen by vote of the electors of the town who had taken the oath of fidelity; and no man not a freeman was eligible to the office of deputy. The deputies were to be chosen by a major vote of all the freemen present, who were to make their choice by written paper ballots—each voter giving in as many papers as there were deputies to be chosen, with a single name written on each paper. The names of the deputies when chosen were indorsed by the constables, on the back of their respective warrants, and returned into court.

8. The three towns of the commonwealth were each to have the privilege of sending four deputies to the general court. If other towns were afterward added to the jurisdiction, the number of their deputies was to be fixed by the court. The deputies represented the towns, and could bind them by their votes in all legislative matters.

9. The deputies had power to meet after they were chosen and before the session of the general court, to consult for the public good, and to examine whether those who had been returned as members of their own body were legally elected. If they found any who were not so elected, they might seclude them from their assembly, and return their names to the court, with their reasons for so doing. The court, on finding these reasons valid, could issue orders for a new election, and impose a fine upon such men as had falsely thrust themselves upon the towns as candidates.

10. Every regular general court was to consist of the governor and at least four other magistrates, with the major part of the deputies chosen from the several towns. But if any court hap-

pened to be called by the freemen, through the default of the governor and magistrates, that court was to consist of a majority of the freemen present, or their deputies, and a *moderator*, chosen by them. In the general court was lodged the "*supreme power of the commonwealth.*" In this court the governor or moderator had power to command liberty of speech, to silence all disorders, and to put all questions that were to be made the subject of legislative action, but not to vote himself unless the court was equally divided, when he was to give the casting vote. But he could not adjourn or dissolve the court without the major vote of the members. Taxes also were to be ordered by the court; and when they had agreed upon the sum to be raised, a committee was to be appointed of an equal number of men from each town to decide what part of that sum each town should pay.

This first constitution of the New World was simple in its terms, comprehensive in its policy, methodical in its arrangement, beautiful in its adaptation of parts to a whole, of means to an end. Compare it with any of the constitutions of the Old World then existing. I say nothing of those libels upon human nature, the so-called constitutions of the Continent of Europe —compare it reverently, as children speak of a father's roof, with that venerated structure, the British Constitution. How complex is the architecture of the latter! here exhibiting the clumsy work of the Saxon, there the more graceful touch of later conquerors; the whole colossal pile, magnificent with turrets and towers, and decorated with armorial devices and inscriptions, written in a language not only dead, but never native to the island; all eloquent, indeed, with the spirit of ages past, yet haunted with the cry of suffering humanity and the clanking of chains that come up from its subterranean dungeons.

Mark, too, the rifts and seams in its gray walls—traces of convulsion and revolution. Proud as it is, its very splendor shows the marks of a barbarous age. Its tapestry speaks a language dissonant to the ears of freemen. It tells of exclusive privileges, of divine rights, not in the people, but in the king, of primogeniture, of conformities, of prescriptions, of serfs and lords, of attainder that dries up like a leprosy the fountains of inheritable blood; and, lastly, it discourses of the rights of British subjects, in eloquent language, but sometimes with qualifications that startle the ears of men who have tasted the sweets of a more enlarged liberty. Such was the spirit of the British Constitution, and code of the seventeenth century. I do not blame it that it was not better; perhaps it could not then have been improved without risk. Improvement in an old state is the work of time. But I have a right to speak with pride of the more advanced freedom of our own.

The Constitution of Connecticut sets out with the practical recognition of the doctrine that all ultimate power is lodged with the people. The body of the people is the body politic. From the people flow the fountains of law and justice. The governor and the other magistrates, the deputies themselves, are but a kind of committee, with delegated powers to act for the free planters. Elected from their number, they must spend their short official term in the discharge of the trust, and then descend to their old level of citizen voters. Here are to be no interminable parliaments. The majority of the general court can adjourn it at will. Nor is there to be an indefinite prorogation of the Legislature at the will of a single man. Let the governor and the magistrates look to it. If they do not call a general court, the planters will take the matter into their own hands and meet in a body to take care of their neglected interests.

One of the most striking features in this new and at the same time strange document is that it will tolerate no rotten-borough system. Every deputy who goes to the Legislature is to go from his own town, and is to be a free planter of that town. In this way he will know what is the will of his constituents and what their wants are.

This paper has another remarkable trait. There is to be no taxation without representation in Connecticut. The towns, too, are recognized as independent municipalities. They are the primary centres of power older than the constitution—the makers and builders of the State. They have given up to the State a part of their corporate powers, as they received them from the free planters, that they may have a safer guarantee for the keeping of the rest. Whatever they have not given up they hold in absolute right.

How strange, too, that in defining so carefully and astutely the limits of the government, these constitution-makers should have forgotten the King. One would but suppose that those who indited this paper were even aware of the existence of titled majesty beyond what belonged to the King of kings. They mention no supreme power save that of the commonwealth, which speaks and acts through the general court.

Such was the Constitution of Connecticut. I have said it was the oldest of the American constitutions. More than this, I might say, it is the mother of them all. It has been modified in different States to suit the circumstances of the people and the size of their respective territories; but the representative system peculiar to the American republics was first unfolded by Ludlow—who probably drafted the Constitution of Connecticut—and by Hooker, Haynes, Wolcott, Steele, Sherman, Stone, and the other far-sighted men of the colony, who must have advised and counselled to do what they and all the people in the three towns met together in a mass to sanction and adopt as their own. Let me not be understood to say that I consider the framers of this paper perfect legislators or in all respects free from bigotry and intolerance. How could they throw off in a moment the shackles of custom and old opinion? They saw more than two centuries beyond their own era. England herself at this day has only approximated, without reaching, the elevated table-land of constitutional freedom, whose pure air was breathed by the earliest planters of Connecticut. Under this constitution they passed, it is true, some quaint laws, that sometimes provoke a smile, and, in those who are unmindful of the age in which they lived, sometimes a sneer.

I shall speak of these laws in order, I hope with honesty and not too much partiality. It may be proper to say here, however, that for one law that has been passed in Connecticut of a bigoted or intolerant character, a diligent explorer into the English court records or statute-books for evidences of bigotry and revolting cruelty could find twenty in England. "Kings have been dethroned," says Bancroft, the eloquent American historian, "recalled, dethroned again, and so many constitutions framed or formed, stifled or subverted, that memory may despair of a complete catalogue; but the people of Connecticut have found no reason to deviate essentially from the government as established by their fathers. History has ever celebrated the commanders of armies on which victory has been entailed, the heroes who have won laurels in scenes of carnage and rapine. Has it no place for the founders of states, the wise legislators who struck the rock in the wilderness, and the waters of liberty gushed forth in copious and perennial fountains?"

JOHN MARSHALL

About this period many evidences were given of a general combination of the neighboring Indians against the settlements of New England; and apprehensions were also entertained of hostility from the Dutch of Manhadoes. A sense of impending danger suggested the policy of forming a confederacy of the sister-colonies for their mutual defence. And so confirmed had the habit of self-government become since the attention of England was absorbed in her domestic dissensions that it was not thought necessary to consult the parent state on this important measure. After mature deliberation articles of confederation were digested; and in May, 1643, they were conclusively adopted.

By them "The United Colonies of New England"—Massachusetts, Plymouth, Connecticut, and New Haven—entered into a firm and perpetual league, offensive and defensive.

Each colony retained a distinct and separate jurisdiction; no two colonies could join in one jurisdiction without the consent of the whole; and no other colony could be received into the confederacy without the like consent.

The charge of all wars was to be borne by the colonies respectively, in proportion to the male inhabitants of each between sixteen and sixty years of age.

On notice of an invasion given by three magistrates of any colony, the confederates were immediately to furnish their respective quotas. These were fixed at one hundred from Massachusetts, and forty-five from each of the other parties to the agreement. If a larger armament should be found necessary, commissioners were to meet and ascertain the number of men to be required.

Two commissioners from each government, being church members, were to meet annually on the first Monday in September. Six possessed the power of binding the whole. Any measure approved by a majority of less than six was to be referred to the general court of each colony, and the consent of all was necessary to its adoption.

They were to choose annually a president from their own body, and had power to frame laws or rules of a civil nature and of general concern. Of this description were rules which respected their conduct toward the Indians, and measures to be taken with fugitives from one colony to another.

No colony was permitted, without the general consent, to engage in war, but in sudden and inevitable cases.

If, on any extraordinary meeting of the commissioners, their whole number should not assemble, any four who should meet were empowered to determine on a war, and to call for the respective quotas of the several colonies, but not less than six could determine on the justice of the war or settle the expenses or levy the money for its support.

If any colony should be charged with breaking an article of the agreement, or with doing an injury to another colony, the complaint was to be submitted to the consideration and determination of the commissioners of such colonies as should be disinterested.

This union, the result of good-sense and of a judicious consideration of the real interests of the colonies, remained in force until their charters were dissolved. Rhode Island, at the instance of Massachusetts, was excluded; and her commissioners were not admitted into the congress of deputies, which formed the confederation.

ABOLITION OF THE COURT OF STAR-CHAMBER

POPULAR REVOLT AGAINST CHARLES I

A.D. 1641

HENRY HALLAM — LORD MACAULAY

Before the accession of Charles I, in 1625, the separation between the Church of England and the Puritans, which had been slowly widening for half a century, had become so serious as to be a menace to the peaceful stability of the kingdom. Charles began his reign with repressive measures against the Puritan influences. His use of the Star-chamber and similar tribunals is an important subject of study in connection with the preliminary steps on both sides which led at last to the great civil war.

From the first, Charles aimed at despotic power, which he was wont to seek in "dark and crooked ways." The House of Commons stood against him on the popular side. He dissolved his first Parliament and levied taxes by his own will; dissolved another Parliament, and did the same, adding other acts of usurpation and oppression. His third Parliament showed increased opposition to his methods, and accordingly he decided to change them. The Parliament passed (1628) the Petition of Right, the second English Magna Charta, and Charles ratified it. By this act the King was bound to raise no more moneys without consent of Parliament, not to imprison anyone contrary to law, not to billet the military in private houses, and to subject none to martial law. From 1629 to 1640 Charles governed without a parliament, replenishing his exchequer by various extraordinary means.

In the following accounts of the previous workings of the Star-chamber, Charles' star-chamber methods, his illegal procedures, nis violations of the Petition of Rights, and of the consequent changes in the relations of his person and government to the people, a very significant period of transition in English history is summarized by the ablest hands.

HENRY HALLAM

THE levies of tonnage and poundage without authority of Parliament; the exaction of monopolies; the extension of the forests; the arbitrary restraints of proclamations; above all, the general exaction of ship-money, form the principal articles of charge against the government of Charles, so far as relates to its inroads on the subject's property. These were maintained by a vigilant and unsparing exercise of jurisdiction in the Court of Star-chamber. It was the great weapon of executive power under Elizabeth and James; nor can we reproach the present reign with innovation in this respect, though in no former period had the proceedings of this court been accompanied with so much violence and tyranny. But this will require some fuller explication.

I hardly need remind the reader that the jurisdiction of the ancient Concilium Regis Ordinarium, or Court of Star-chamber, continued to be exercised, more or less frequently, notwithstanding the various statutes enacted to repress it; and that it neither was supported by the act erecting a new court in the 3d of Henry VII nor originated at that time. The records show the Star-chamber to have taken cognizance both of civil suits and of offences throughout the time of the Tudors. But precedents of usurped power cannot establish a legal authority in defiance of the acknowledged law. It appears that the lawyers did not admit any jurisdiction in the council, except so far as the statute of Henry VII was supposed to have given it. "The famous Plowden put his hand to a demurrer to a bill," says Hudson, "because the matter was not within the statute; and, although it was then overruled, yet Mr. Sergeant Richardson, thirty years after, fell again upon the same rock, and was sharply rebuked for it." The chancellor, who was the standing president of the Court of Star-chamber, would always find pretences to elude the existing statutes, and justify the usurpation of this tribunal.

The civil jurisdiction claimed and exerted by the Star-chamber was only in particular cases, as disputes between alien merchants and Englishmen, questions of prize or unlawful detention of ships, and, in general, such as now belong to the court of admiralty; some testamentary matters, in order to prevent appeals to Rome, which might have been brought from the ecclesiastical courts; suits between corporations, "of which," says Hudson, "I dare undertake to show above a hundred in the reigns of Henry VII and Henry VIII, or sometimes between men of great power and interest, which could not be tried with fairness by the common law"; for the corruption of sheriffs and juries furnished an apology for the irregular, but necessary, interference of a controlling authority. The ancient remedy, by means of attaint, which renders a jury responsible for an unjust verdict, was almost gone into disuse, and, depending on the integrity of a second jury, not always easy to be obtained; so that in many parts of the kingdom, and especially in Wales, it was impossible to find a jury who would return a verdict against a man of good family, either in a civil or criminal proceeding.

The statutes, however, restraining the council's jurisdiction, and the strong prepossession of the people as to the sacredness of freehold rights, made the Star-chamber cautious of determining questions of inheritance, which they commonly remitted to the judges; and from the early part of Elizabeth's reign they took a direct cognizance of any civil suits less frequently than before, partly, I suppose, from the increased business of the court of chancery and the admiralty court, which took away much wherein they had been wont to meddle, partly from their own occupation as a court of criminal judicature, which became more conspicuous as the other went into disuse. This criminal jurisdiction is that which rendered the Star-chamber so potent and so odious an auxiliary of a despotic administration.

The offences principally cognizable in this court were forgery, perjury, riot, maintenance, fraud, libel, and conspiracy. But, besides these, every misdemeanor came within the proper scope of its inquiry; those especially of public importance, and for which the law, as then understood, had provided no sufficient punishment; for the judges interpreted the law in early times with too great narrowness and timidity, defects which, on the one hand, raised up the overruling authority of the court of chancery as the necessary means of redress to the civil suitor who found the gates of justice barred against him by technical pedantry, and on the other, brought this usurpation and tyranny of the Star-chamber upon the kingdom by an absurd scrupulosity about punishing manifest offences against the public good.

Thus corruption, breach of trust and malfeasance in public affairs, attempts to commit felony, seem to have been reckoned not indictable at common law, and came, in consequence, under the cognizance of the Star-chamber. In other cases its jurisdiction was merely concurrent; but the greater certainty of conviction and the greater severity of punishment rendered it incomparably more formidable than the ordinary benches of justice. The law of libel grew up in this unwholesome atmosphere, and was moulded by the plastic hands of successive judges and attorneys-general. Prosecutions of this kind, according to Hudson, began to be more frequent from the last years of Elizabeth, when Coke was attorney-general; and it is easy to conjecture what kind of interpretation they received. To hear a libel sung or read, says that writer, and to laugh at it and make merriment with it, have ever been held a publication in law. The gross error that it is not a libel if it be true, has long since, he adds, been exploded out of this court.

Among the exertions of authority practised in the Star-chamber which no positive law could be brought to warrant he enumerates "punishments of breach of proclamations before they have the strength of an act of Parliament; which this court hath stretched as far as ever any act of Parliament did. As in the 41st of Elizabeth, builders of houses in London were sentenced, and their houses ordered to be pulled down, and the materials to be distributed to the benefit of the parish where the building was; which disposition of the goods soundeth as a great extremity, and beyond the warrant of our laws; and yet, surely, very necessary, if anything would deter men from that horrible mischief of increasing that head which is swollen to a great hugeness already."

The mode of process was sometimes of a summary nature; the accused person being privately examined, and his examination read in court, if he was thought to have confessed sufficient to deserve sentence, it was immediately awarded without any formal trial or written process. But the more regular course was by information filed at the suit of the attorney-general or, in certain cases, of a private relator. The party was brought before the court by writ of subpœna, and, having given bond, with sureties not to depart without leave, was to put in his answer upon oath, as well to the matters contained in the information as to special interrogatories. Witnesses were examined upon interrogatories, and their depositions read in court. The course of proceeding, on the whole, seems to have nearly resembled that of the chancery.

It was held competent for the court to adjudge any punishment short of death. Fine and imprisonment were of course the most usual. The pillory, whipping, branding, and cutting off the ears grew into use by degrees. In the reigns of Henry VII and Henry VIII, we are told by Hudson, the fines were not so ruinous as they have been since, which he ascribes to the number of bishops who sat in the court, and inclined to mercy, "and I can well remember," says he, "that the most reverend Archbishop Whitgift did ever constantly maintain the liberty of the free charter, that men ought to be fined, *salvo contenemento*. But they have been of late imposed according to the nature of the offence, and not the estate of the person. The slavish punishment of whipping," he proceeds to observe, "was not introduced till a great man of the common law, and otherwise a worthy justice, forgot his place of session, and brought it in this place too much in use." It would be difficult to find precedents for the aggravated cruelties inflicted on Leighton, Lilburne, and others; but instances of cutting off the ears may be found under Elizabeth.

The reproach, therefore, of arbitrary and illegal jurisdiction does not wholly fall on the government of Charles. They found themselves in possession of this almost unlimited authority. But doubtless, as far as the history of proceedings in the Star-chamber are recorded, they seem much more numerous and violent in the present reign than in the two preceding. Rushworth has preserved a copious selection of cases determined before this tribunal. They consist principally of misdemeanors, rather of an aggravated nature, such as disturbances of the public peace, assaults accompanied with a good deal of violence, conspiracies, and libels. The necessity, however, for such a paramount court to restrain the excesses of powerful men no longer existed, since it can hardly be doubted that the common administration of the law was sufficient to give redress in the time of Charles I, though we certainly do find several instances of violence and outrage by men of a superior station in life, which speak unfavorably for the state of manners in the kingdom.

But the object of drawing so large a number of criminal cases into the Star-chamber seems to have been twofold: first, to inure men's minds to an authority more immediately connected with the crown than the ordinary courts of law and less tied down to any rules of pleading or evidence; secondly, to eke out a scanty revenue by penalties and forfeitures. Absolutely regardless of the provision of the Great Charter, that no man shall be amerced even to the full extent of his means, the counsellors of the Star-chamber inflicted such fines as no court of justice, even in the present reduced value of money, would think of imposing. Little objection, indeed, seems to lie, in a free country, and with a well-regulated administration of justice, against the imposition of weighty pecuniary penalties, due consideration being had of the offence and the criminal. But, adjudged by such a tribunal as the Star-chamber, where those who inflicted the punishment reaped the gain, and sat, like famished birds of prey, with keen eyes and bended talons, eager to supply for a moment by some wretch's ruin, the craving emptiness of the exchequer, this scheme of enormous penalties became more dangerous and subversive of justice, though not more odious, than corporal punishment.

A gentleman of the name of Allington was fined twelve thousand pounds for marrying his niece. One, who had sent a challenge to the Earl of Northumberland, was fined five thousand pounds; another for saying the Earl of Suffolk was a base lord, four thousand pounds to him, and a like sum to the King. Sir David Forbes, for opprobrious words against Lord Wentworth, incurred five thousand pounds to the King and three thousand pounds to the party. On some soap-boilers, who had not complied with the requisitions of the newly incorporated company, mulcts were imposed of one thousand five hundred pounds and one thousand pounds. One man was fined and set in the pillory for engrossing corn, though he only kept what grew on his own land, asking more in a season of dearth than the overseers of the poor thought proper to give. Some arbitrary regulations with respect to prices may be excused by a well-intentioned though mistaken policy. The charges of inns and taverns were fixed by the judges; but even in those a corrupt motive was sometimes blended. The company of vintners, or victuallers, having refused to pay a demand of the lord-treasurer, one penny a quart for all wine drunk in their houses, the Star-chamber, without information filed or defence made, interdicted them from selling or dressing victuals till they submitted to pay forty shillings for each tun of wine to the King.

It is evident that the strong interest of the court in these fines must not only have had a tendency to aggravate the punishment, but to induce sentences of condemnation on inadequate proof. From all that remains of proceedings in the Star-chamber, they seem to have been very frequently as iniquitous as they were severe. In many celebrated instances, the accused party suffered less on the score of any imputed offence than for having provoked the malice of a powerful adversary, or for notorious dissatisfaction with the existing government. Thus Williams, Bishop of Lincoln, once lord-keeper the favorite of King James, the possessor for a season of the power that was turned against him, experienced the rancorous and ungrateful malignity of Laud, who, having been brought forward by Williams into the favor of the court, not only supplanted by his intrigues, and incensed the King's mind against his benefactor, but harassed his retirement by repeated persecutions. It will sufficiently illustrate the spirit of these times to mention that the sole offence imputed to the Bishop of Lincoln in the last information against him in the Star-chamber was that he had received certain letters from one Osbaldiston, master of Westminster school, wherein some contemptuous nickname was used to denote Laud.

It did not appear that Williams had ever divulged these letters; but it was held that the concealment of a libellous letter was a high misdemeanor. Williams was therefore adjudged to pay five thousand pounds to the King and three thousand to the Archbishop, to be imprisoned during pleasure, and to make a submission; Osbaldiston to pay a still heavier fine, to be deprived of all his benefices, to be imprisoned and make submission, and, moreover, to stand in the pillory before his school in Dean's yard, with his ears nailed to it. This man had the good fortune to conceal himself; but the Bishop of Lincoln, refusing to make the required apology, lay about three years in the Tower, till released at the beginning of the Long Parliament.

It might detain me too long to dwell particularly on the punishments inflicted by the Court of Star-chamber in this reign. Such historians as have not written in order to palliate the tyranny of Charles, and especially Rushworth, will furnish abundant details, with all those circumstances that portray the barbarous and tyrannical spirit of those who composed that tribunal. Two or three instances are so celebrated that I cannot pass them over. Leighton, a Scots divine, having published an angry libel against the hierarchy, was sentenced to be publicly whipped at Westminster and set in the pillory, to have one side of his nose slit, one ear cut off, and one side of his cheek branded with a hot iron; to have the whole of this repeated the next week at Cheapside, and to suffer perpetual imprisonment in the Fleet. Lilburne, for dispersing pamphlets against the bishops, was whipped from the Fleet prison to Westminster, there set in the pillory, and treated afterward with great cruelty. Prynne, a lawyer of uncommon erudition and a zealous Puritan, had printed a bulky volume, called *Histriomastix*, full of invectives against the theatre, which he sustained by a profusion of learning. In the course of this he adverted to the appearance of courtesans on the Roman stage, and, by a satirical reference in his index, seemed to range all female actors in the class. The Queen, unfortunately, six weeks after the publication of Prynne's book, had performed a part in a mask at court. This passage was accordingly dragged to light by the malice of Peter Heylin, a chaplain of Laud, on whom the Archbishop devolved the burden of reading this heavy volume in order to detect its offences.

Heylin, a bigoted enemy of everything Puritanical, and not scrupulous as to veracity, may be suspected of having aggravated, if not misrepresented, the tendency of a book much more tiresome than seditious. Prynne, however, was already obnoxious, and the Star-chamber adjudged him to stand twice in the pillory, to be branded in the forehead, to lose both his ears, to pay a fine of five thousand pounds, and to suffer perpetual imprisonment. The dogged Puritan employed the leisure of a jail in writing a fresh libel against the hierarchy. For this, with two other delinquents of the same class, Burton a divine, and Bastwick a physician, he stood again at the bar of that terrible tribunal. Their demeanor was what the court deemed intolerably contumacious, arising, in fact, from the despair of men who knew that no humiliation would procure them mercy. Prynne lost the remainder of his ears in the pillory; and the punishment was inflicted on them all with extreme and designed cruelty, which they endured, as martyrs always endure suffering, so heroically as to excite a deep impression of sympathy and resentment in the assembled multitude. They were sentenced to perpetual confinement in distant prisons. But their departure from London and their reception on the road were marked by signal expressions of popular regard; and their friends resorting to them even in Launceston, Chester, and Carnarvon castles, whither they were sent, an order of council was made to transport them to the isles of the Channel.

It was the very first act of the Long Parliament to restore these victims of tyranny to their families. Punishments by mutilation, though not quite unknown to the English law, had been of rare occurrence; and thus inflicted on men whose station appeared to render the ignominy of whipping and branding more intolerable, they produced much the same effect as the still greater cruelties of Mary's reign, in exciting a detestation of that ecclesiastical dominion which protected itself by means so atrocious.

THOMAS BABINGTON MACAULAY

Now commenced a new era. Many English kings had occasionally committed unconstitutional acts; but none had ever systematically attempted to make himself a despot, and to reduce the Parliament to a nullity. Such was the end which Charles distinctly proposed to himself. From March, 1629, to April, 1640, the Houses were not convoked. Never in our history had there been an interval of eleven years between Parliament and Parliament. Only once had there been an interval of even half that length. This fact alone is sufficient to refute those who represent Charles as having merely trodden in the footsteps of the Plantagenets and Tudors.

It is proved, by the testimony of the King's most strenuous supporters, that, during this part of his reign, the provisions of the Petition of Right were violated by him, not occasionally, but constantly, and on system; that a large part of the revenue was raised without any legal authority; and that persons obnoxious to the government languished for years in prison, without being ever called upon to plead before any tribunal.

For these things history must hold the King himself chiefly responsible. From the time of his third Parliament he was his own prime minister. Several persons, however, whose temper and talents were suited to his purposes, were at the head of different departments of the administration.

Thomas Wentworth, successively created Lord Wentworth and Earl of Strafford, a man of great abilities, eloquence, and courage, but of a cruel and imperious nature, was the counsellor most trusted in political and military affairs. He had been one of the most distinguished members of the opposition, and felt toward those whom he had deserted that peculiar malignity which has, in all ages, been characteristic of apostates. He perfectly understood the feelings, the resources, and the policy of the party to which he had lately belonged, and had formed a vast and deeply meditated scheme which very nearly confounded even the able tactics of the statesmen by whom the House of Commons had been directed. To this scheme, in his confidential correspondence, he gave the expressive name of Thorough.

His object was to do in England all, and more than all, that Richelieu was doing in France: to make Charles a monarch as absolute as any on the Continent; to put the estates and the personal liberty of the whole people at the disposal of the crown; to deprive the courts of law of all independent authority, even in ordinary questions of civil right between man and man; and to punish with merciless rigor all who murmured at the acts of the government, or who applied, even in the most decent and regular manner, to any tribunal for relief against those acts.

This was his end; and he distinctly saw in what manner alone this end could be attained. There was, in truth, about all his notions a clearness, a coherence, a precision, which, if he had not been pursuing an object pernicious to his country and to his kind, would have justly entitled him to high admiration. He saw that there was one instrument, and only one, by which his vast and daring projects could be carried into execution. That instrument was a standing army. To the forming of such an army, therefore, he directed all the energy of his strong mind. In Ireland, where he was viceroy, he actually succeeded in establishing a military despotism, not only over the aboriginal population, but also over the English colonists, and was able to boast that, in that island, the King was as absolute as any prince in the whole world could be.

The ecclesiastical administration was, in the mean time, principally directed by William Laud, Archbishop of Canterbury. Of all the prelates of the Anglican Church, Laud had departed furthest from the principles of the Reformation and had drawn nearest to Rome. His theology was more remote than even that of the Dutch Arminians from the theology of the Calvinists. His passion for ceremonies, his reverence for holidays, vigils, and sacred places, his ill-concealed dislike of the marriage of ecclesiastics, the ardent and not altogether disinterested zeal with which he asserted the claims of the clergy to the reverence of the laity, would have made him an object of aversion to the Puritans, even if he had used only legal and gentle means for the attainment of his ends. But his understanding was narrow; and his commerce with the world had been small. He was by nature rash, irritable, quick to feel for his own dignity, slow to sympathize with the sufferings of others, and prone to the error, common in superstitious men, of mistaking his own peevish and malignant moods for emotions of pious zeal.

Under his direction every corner of the realm was subjected to a constant and minute inspection. Every little congregation of Separatists was tracked out and broken up. Even the devotions of private families could not escape the vigilance of his spies. Such fear did his rigor inspire that the deadly hatred of the Church, which festered in innumerable bosoms, was generally disguised under an outward show of conformity. On the very eve of troubles, fatal to himself and to his order, the bishops of several extensive dioceses were able to report to him that not a single dissenter was to be found within their jurisdiction.

The tribunals afforded no protection to the subject against the civil and ecclesiastical tyranny of that period. The judges of the common law, holding their situations during the pleasure of the King, were scandalously obsequious. Yet, obsequious as they were, they were less ready and less efficient instruments of arbitrary power than a class of courts the memory of which is still, after the lapse of more than two centuries, held in deep abhorrence by the nation. Foremost among these courts in power and in infamy were the Star-chamber and the High Commission, the former a political, the latter a religious, inquisition. Neither was a part of the old constitution of England. The Star-chamber had been remodelled, and the High Commission created, by the Tudors.

The power which these boards had possessed before the accession of Charles had been extensive and formidable, but had been small indeed when compared with that which they now usurped. Guided chiefly by the violent spirit of the primate, and freed from the control of Parliament, they displayed a rapacity, a violence, a malignant energy, which had been unknown to any former age. The government was able through their instrumentality, to fine, imprison, pillory, and mutilate without restraint. A separate council which sat at York, under the presidency of Wentworth, was armed, in defiance of law, by a pure act of prerogative, with almost boundless power over the northern counties. All these tribunals insulted and defied the authority of Westminster hall, and daily committed excesses which the most distinguished royalists have warmly condemned. We are informed by Clarendon that there was hardly a man of note in the realm who had not personal experience of the harshness and greediness of the Star-chamber, that the High Commission had so conducted itself that it had scarce a friend left in the kingdom, and that the tyranny of the Council of York had made the Great Charter a dead letter on the north of the Trent.

The government of England was now, in all points but one, as despotic as that of France. But that one point was all-important. There was still no standing army. There was therefore no security that the whole fabric of tyranny might not be subverted in a single day; and if taxes were imposed by the royal authority for the support of an army, it was probable that there would be an immediate and irresistible explosion. This was the difficulty which more than any other perplexed Wentworth. The Lord Keeper Finch, in concert with other lawyers who were employed by the government, recommended an expedient which was eagerly adopted. The ancient princes of England, as they called on the inhabitants of the counties near Scotland to arm and array themselves for the defence of the border, had sometimes called on the maritime counties to furnish ships for the defence of the coast. In the room of ships, money had sometimes been accepted. This old practice it was now determined, after a long interval, not only to revive, but to extend. Former princes had raised ship-money only in time of war: it was now exacted in a time of profound peace. Former princes, even in the most perilous wars, had raised ship-money only along the coasts: it was now exacted from the inland shires. Former princes had raised ship-money only for the maritime defence of the country: it was now exacted, by the admission of the royalists themselves, with the object, not of maintaining a navy, but of furnishing the King with supplies which might be increased at his discretion to any amount, and expended at his discretion for any purpose.

The whole nation was alarmed and incensed. John Hampden, an opulent and well-born gentleman of Buckinghamshire, highly considered in his own neighborhood, but as yet little known to the kingdom generally, had the courage to step forward, to confront the whole power of the government, and take on himself the cost and the risk of disputing the prerogative to which the King laid claim. The case was argued before the judges in the exchequer chamber. So strong were the arguments against the pretensions of the crown that, dependent and servile as the judges were, the majority against Hampden was the smallest possible. Still there was a majority. The interpreters of the law had pronounced that one great and productive tax might be imposed by the royal authority. Wentworth justly observed that it was impossible to vindicate their judgment except by reasons directly leading to a conclusion which they had not ventured to draw. If money might legally be raised without the consent of Parliament for the support of a fleet, it was not easy to deny that money might, without consent of Parliament, be legally raised for the support of an army.

The decision of the judges increased the irritation of the people. A century earlier, irritation less serious would have produced a general rising. But discontent did not now so readily, as in an earlier age, take the form of rebellion. The nation had been long steadily advancing in wealth and in civilization. Since the great northern earls took up arms against Elizabeth seventy years had elapsed; and during those seventy years there had been no civil war. Never, during the whole existence of the English nation, had so long a period passed without intestine hostilities. Men had become accustomed to the pursuits of peaceful industry, and, exasperated as they were, hesitated long before they drew the sword.

This was the conjuncture at which the liberties of the nation were in the greatest peril. The opponents of the government began to despair of the destiny of their country; and many looked to the American wilderness as the only asylum in which they could enjoy civil and spiritual freedom. There a few resolute Puritans, who, in the cause of their religion, feared neither the rage of the ocean nor the hardships of uncivilized life, neither the fangs of savage beasts nor the tomahawks of more savage men, had built, amid the primeval forests, villages which are now great and opulent cities, but which have, through every change, retained some trace of the character derived from their founders. The government regarded these infant colonies with aversion, and attempted violently to stop the stream of emigration, but could not prevent the population of New England from being largely recruited by stout-hearted and God-fearing men from every part of the old England. And now Wentworth exulted in the near prospect of Thorough. A few years might probably suffice for the execution of his great design. If strict economy were observed, if all collision with foreign powers were carefully avoided, the debts of the crown would be cleared off: there would be funds available for the support of a large military force; and that force would soon break the refractory spirit of the nation.

At this crisis an act of insane bigotry suddenly changed the whole face of public affairs. Had the King been wise, he would have pursued a cautious and soothing policy toward Scotland till he was master in the South. For Scotland was of all his kingdoms that in which there was the greatest risk that a spark might produce a flame, and that a flame might become a conflagration. The government had long wished to extend the Anglican system over the whole island, and had already, with this view, made several changes highly distasteful to every Presbyterian.

One innovation, however, the most hazardous of all, because it was directly cognizable by the senses of the common people, had not yet been attempted. The public worship of God was still conducted in the manner acceptable to the nation. Now, however, Charles and Laud determined to force on the Scots the English liturgy, or rather a liturgy which, wherever it differed from that of England, differed, in the judgment of all rigid Protestants, for the worse.

To this step, taken in the mere wantonness of tyranny, and in criminal ignorance or more criminal contempt of public feeling, England owes her freedom. The first performance of the foreign ceremonies produced a riot. The riot rapidly became a revolution. Ambition, patriotism, fanaticism, were mingled in one headlong torrent. The whole nation was in arms. The power of England was, indeed, as appeared some years later, sufficient to coerce Scotland; but a large part of the English people sympathized with the religious feelings of the insurgents, and many Englishmen who had no scruple about antiphonies and genuflexions, altars and surplices, saw with pleasure the progress of a rebellion which seemed likely to confound the arbitrary projects of the court and to make the calling of a parliament necessary.

For the senseless freak which had produced these effects Wentworth is not responsible. It had, in fact, thrown all his plans into confusion. To counsel submission, however, was not in his nature. An attempt was made to put down the insurrection by the sword; but the King's military means and military talents were unequal to the task. To impose fresh taxes on England in defiance of law would, at this conjuncture, have been madness. No resource was left but a Parliament; and in the spring of 1640 a parliament was convoked.

The nation had been put into good humor by the prospect of seeing constitutional government restored and grievances redressed. The new House of Commons was more temperate and more respectful to the throne than any which had sat since the death of Elizabeth. The moderation of this assembly has been highly extolled by the most distinguished royalists, and seems to have caused no small vexation and disappointment to the chiefs of the opposition; but it was the uniform practice of Charles—a practice equally impolitic and ungenerous—to refuse all compliances with the desires of his people, till those desires were expressed in a menacing tone. As soon as the Commons showed a disposition to take into consideration the grievances under which the country had suffered during eleven years, the King dissolved the Parliament with every mark of displeasure.

Between the dissolution of this short-lived assembly and the meeting of that ever-memorable body known by the name of the Long Parliament, intervened a few months, during which the yoke was pressed down more severely than ever on the nation, while the spirit of the nation rose up more angrily than ever against the yoke. Members of the House of Commons were questioned by the privy council touching their parliamentary conduct, and thrown into prison for refusing to reply. Ship-money was levied with increased rigor. The lord mayor and the sheriffs of London were threatened with imprisonment for remissness in collecting the payments. Soldiers were enlisted by force. Money for their support was exacted from their counties. Torture, which had always been illegal, and which had recently been declared illegal even by the servile judges of that age, was inflicted for the last time in England in the month of May, 1640.

Everything now depended on the event of the King's military operations against the Scots. Among his troops there was little of that feeling which separates professional soldiers from the mass of a nation and attaches them to their leaders. His army, composed for the most part of recruits, who regretted the plough from which they had been violently taken, and who were imbued with the religious and political sentiments then prevalent throughout the country, was more formidable to himself than to the enemy. The Scots, encouraged by the heads of the English opposition, and feebly resisted by the English forces, marched across the Tweed and the Tyne, and encamped on the borders of Yorkshire. And now the murmurs of discontent swelled into an uproar by which all spirits save one were overawed. But the voice of Strafford was still for Thorough; and he even, in this extremity, showed a nature so cruel and despotic that his own pikemen were ready to tear him in pieces.

There was yet one last expedient which, as the King flattered himself, might save him from the misery of facing another House of Commons. To the House of Lords he was less averse.

The bishops were devoted to him; and though the temporal peers were generally dissatisfied with his administration, they were, as a class, so deeply interested in the maintenance of order and in the stability of ancient institutions that they were not likely to call for extensive reforms. Departing from the uninterrupted practice of centuries, he called a great council consisting of lords alone. But the lords were too prudent to assume the unconstitutional functions with which he wished to invest them. Without money, without credit, without authority even in his own camp, he yielded to the pressure of necessity.

In November, 1640, met that renowned Parliament which, in spite of many errors and disasters, is justly entitled to the reverence and gratitude of all who, in any part of the world, enjoy the blessings of constitutional government.

During the year which followed, no very important division of opinion appeared in the Houses. The civil and ecclesiastical administration had, through a period of nearly twelve years, been so oppressive and so unconstitutional that even those classes of which the inclinations are generally on the side of order and authority were eager to promote popular reforms and to bring the instruments of tyranny to justice. It was enacted that no interval of more than three years should ever elapse between Parliament and Parliament, and that, if writs under the great seal were not issued at the proper time, the returning officers should, without such writs, call the constituent bodies together for the choice of representatives. The Star-chamber, the High Commission, the Council of York were swept away. Men who, after suffering cruel mutilations, had been confined in remote dungeons regained their liberty. On the chief ministers of the crown the vengeance of the nation was unsparingly wreaked. The lord keeper, the primate, the lord lieutenant were impeached. Finch saved himself by flight. Laud was flung into the Tower. Strafford was put to death, beheaded by act of attainder. On the day on which this act passed, the King gave his assent to a law by which he bound himself not to adjourn, prorogue, or dissolve the existing Parliament without its own consent.

FOUNDING OF MONTREAL

A.D. 1642

ALFRED SANDHAM

The history of Montreal dates back to October, 1535, when Jacques Cartier first landed on the island. An Indian village, called Hochelaga, existed here at this time. Its outline was circular; and it was encompassed by three rows of palisades, or rather picket fences, one within the other, well secured and put together. A single entrance was left in this rude fortification, but guarded with pikes and stakes, and every precaution taken against siege or attack. Cartier named the place Mount Royal, from the elevation that rose in rear of the site, a little way back from the river St. Lawrence. It first began to be settled by Europeans in 1542, and exactly one century afterward the spot destined for the city was, with due solemnities, consecrated at the era of Maissoneuve and named Ville Marie, a designation which it retained for a long period. In 1760 it was taken by the English. Since then it has taken great leaps in the way of progress until to-day it is the chief commercial city in Canada and the largest city in the Dominion. Montreal has the further advantage, in its natural situation, of being at the head of ocean navigation. Its population to-day, including suburbs, is in the neighborhood of 350,000.

ON the death of Champlain (on December 25, 1635), M. de Montmagny was appointed governor of New France; but so little attention was paid to the wants of the colony that its prosperity was much retarded, the fur trade alone being conducted with any spirit. But great vigor was manifested in religious matters and several institutions were erected. In 1630 the Hôtel Dieu, at Quebec, was founded by three nuns sent out by the Duchesse d'Aiguillon, and Madame de la Peltrie brought out from France at her own charge another body of nuns, who established the Ursuline convent. The peopling and fortifying of the island of Montreal, with the view of repressing the incursions of the Iroquois and the conversion of the Indians, had occupied the entire attention of the first missionaries, and in 1640 the whole of this domain was ceded to a company for that purpose.

Jerome le Royer de la Dauversière, a collector of taxes at La Flêche, in Anjou, and a young priest of Paris, Jean Jacques Olier by name, having met each other, formed the idea of establishing at Montreal three religious communities: one of priests to convert the Indians, one of nuns to nurse the sick, and one of nuns to teach the children of the Indians and of the colonists. It was an easy matter to talk over these plans; but, in order to carry them out, they must first raise some money. For this purpose Olier laid the matter before some of his wealthy penitents, while Dauversière succeeded in securing the Baron de Fanchamp, a devout Christian and a wealthy man, who, considering the enterprise as one calculated to further his spiritual interests, was eager to take part in it. Shortly afterward three others were secured, and the six together formed the germ of the "Société de Notre Dame de Montréal." Among them they raised seventy-five thousand livres.

Previous to this the island of Montreal had been granted to M. de Lauson, a former president of the Company of One Hundred Associates, and his son possessed the exclusive monopoly of the fisheries on the St. Lawrence. After much persuasion Dauversière and Fanchamp succeeded in securing from him a transfer of his title to them; and to make the matter more secure they obtained, in addition, a grant of the island from its former owners, the Hundred Associates. That company, however, reserved the western extremity of the island for themselves, as a site for a fort and stores. The younger Lauzon also gave Dauversière and his company the right of fishery within two leagues of the shores of the island, which favor they were to acknowledge by a yearly donation of ten pounds of fish. These grants were afterward confirmed by the King, and thus Dauversière and his companions became "Lords of the Isle of Montreal."

They now proceeded to mature their plan, which was to send out forty men to take possession of Montreal, intrench themselves, and raise crops, after which they would build houses for the priests and convents for the nuns. It was necessary, however, that some competent person should be secured who should take command of the expedition and act as governor of the newly acquired isle. To fill this important position it was desirable that to the qualities of the statesman should be added the courage of the soldier. One in whom these were combined was found in the person of Paul de Chomedey, Sieur de Maisonneuve, a devout Christian, an able statesman, and a valiant soldier. Maisonneuve at once accepted the position, while many wealthy ladies contributed toward defraying the expense of the undertaking and also became members of the "Association of Montreal." In February, 1641, the Associates, with Olier at their head, assembled in the Church of Notre Dame at Paris, and before the altar of the Virgin "solemnly consecrated Montreal to the Holy Family" and to be called "Ville-Marie de Montréal."

Maisonneuve with his party, forty-five in number, reached Quebec too late to ascend the river. On their arrival at that place they were received with jealousy and distrust. The agents of the Company of One Hundred Associates looked on them with suspicion, and Montmagny, the Governor, feared a rival in Maisonnenve. Every opposition was thrown in their way, and Montmaguy tried to persuade Maisonneuve to exchange the island of Montreal for that of Orleans. But Maisonneuve was not to be deceived, and he expressed his determination to found a colony at Montreal, "even if every tree on the island was an Iroquois."

During the winter Maisonneuve employed his men in various labors for the future benefit of the colony, but principally in building a boat in which to ascend the river. While staying at Quebec the party gained an unexpected addition to their numbers in the person of Madame de la Peltrie, who joined them, and took with her all the furniture she had lent the Ursulines.

On May 8, 1642, Maisonneuve embarked from St. Michael, and on the 17th his little flotilla, a pinnace, a flat-bottomed craft moved by sails, and two row-boats, approached Montreal, and all on board raised in unison a hymn of praise. Montmagny was there to deliver the island, on behalf of the Company of One Hundred Associates; while here, too, was Father Vimont, superior of the missions. On the following day they glided along the green and solitary shores, now thronged with the life of a busy city, and landed on the spot which Champlain, thirty-one years before, had chosen as the fit site of a settlement. It was a tongue or triangle of land, formed by the junction of a rivulet with the

St. Lawrence. This rivulet was bordered by a meadow, and beyond rose the forest with its vanguard of scattered trees. Early spring flowers were blooming in the young grass, and the birds flitted among the boughs.

Maisonneuve sprang ashore and fell on his knees. His followers imitated his example; and all joined their voices in songs of thanksgiving. Tents, baggage, arms, and stores were landed. Here were the ladies with their servants; Montmagny, no willing spectator; and Maisonneuve, a warlike figure, erect and tall, his men clustering around him—soldiers, sailors, artisans, and laborers—all alike soldiers at need. They kneeled in reverent silence as the host was raised aloft; and when the rite was over the priest turned and addressed them: "You are a grain of mustard-seed that shall rise and grow until its branches overshadow the land. You are few, but your work is the work of God. His smile is on you, and your children shall fill the land." Then they pitched their tents, lighted their fires, stationed their guards, and lay down to rest. Such was the birthnight of Montreal. The following morning they proceeded to form their encampment, the first tree being felled by Maisonneuve. They worked with such energy that by the evening they erected a strong palisade, and had covered their altar with a roof formed of bark. It was some time after their arrival before their enemies, the Indians, were made aware of it, and they improved the time by building some substantial houses and in strengthening their fortifications.

The activity and zeal of Maisonneuve induced him to make a voyage to France to obtain assistance for his settlement. Though his difficulties were great, he yet was enabled to induce one hundred men to join his little establishment on the island. Notwithstanding this addition to his force, the progress of the colony was greatly retarded by the frequent attacks of the Indians. These enemies soon became a cause of great trouble to the colonists, and it was dangerous to pass beyond the palisades, as the Indians would hide for days, waiting to assail any unfortunate straggler. Although Maisonneuve was brave as man could be, he knew that his company was no match for the wily enemy, owing to their ignorance of the mode of Indian warfare; therefore he kept his men as near the fort as possible. They, however, failed to appreciate his care of them, and imputed it to cowardice. This led him to determine that such a feeling should not exist if he could possibly remove it. He therefore ordered his men to prepare to attack the Indians, at the same time signifying his intention to lead them himself. He sallied forth at the head of thirty men, leaving D'Aillebout with the remainder to hold the fort. After they had waded through the snow for some distance they were attacked by the Iroquois, who killed three of his men and wounded several others. Maisonneuve and his party held their ground until their ammunition began to fail, and then he gave orders to retreat, he himself remaining till the last. The men struggled on for some time facing the enemy, but finally they broke their ranks and retreated in great disorder toward the fort. Maisonneuve, with a pistol in each hand, held the Iroquois in check for some time. They might have killed him, but they wished to take him prisoner. Their chief, desiring this honor, rushed forward, but just as he was about to grasp him Maisonneuve fired and he fell dead. The Indians, fearing that the body of their chief would fall into the hands of the French, rushed forward to secure it, and Maisonneuve passed safely into the fort. From that day his men never dared to impute cowardice to him.

In 1644 the island of Montreal was made over to the Sulpicians of Paris, and was destined for the support of that religious order. In 1658 Viscount d'Argenson was appointed governor of Canada, but the day he landed the Iroquois murdered some Algonquin Indians under the very guns of Quebec. The Indians seemed determined to exterminate the French. In addition to keeping Quebec in a state little short of actual siege, they massacred a large number of the settlers at Montreal. D'Argenson having resigned, the Baron d'Avagnon was appointed governor (1661), and on his arrival visited the several settlements throughout the country. He was surprised to find them in such a deplorable condition, and made such representation to the King, as to the neglect of the Company of One Hundred Associates, that M. de Monts, the King's commissioner, was ordered to visit Canada and report on its condition. At the same time four hundred more troops were added to the colonial garrison. The arrival of these troops gave life and confidence to the colonists and relieved Montreal from its dangers. The representations made by M. de Monts, as well as those of the Bishop of Quebec, determined Louis XIV to demand their charter from the Company of One Hundred Associates and to place the colony in immediate connection with the crown. As the profits of the fur trade had been much diminished by the hostility of the Iroquois, the company readily surrendered its privileges. As soon as the transfer was completed, D'Avagnon was recalled and M. de Mesy was appointed governor for three years. Canada was thus changed into a royal government, and a council of state was nominated to cooperate with the Governor in the administration of affairs. This council consisted of the Governor, the Bishop of Quebec, and the intendant, together with four others to be named by them, one of whom was to act as attorney-general.

PRESBYTERIANISM ESTABLISHED

MEETING OF THE WESTMINSTER ASSEMBLY

A.D. 1643

DAVID MASSON

Official recognition of Presbyterianism in Great Britain marked a distinct departure in ecclesiastical affairs. The Westminster Assembly, whose confession and catechisms, while not accepted in England, became, and still remain, the doctrinal standards of the Scotch and American Presbyterian churches, was one of the most important religious convocations ever held. The Presbyterian form of church government has been adopted by various sects, whose representatives are found in many parts of the world.

The great object of the Westminster Assembly was to dictate, dogmatically, articles of faith and a form of worship that should be compulsory. It was mainly owing to the influence of Oliver Cromwell, who stood for toleration and independence, within limits, that the assembly did not have its way.

Masson, the great authority on this subject, gives in the following pages a clear and comprehensive account of the religious situation in Great Britain at the time, of the composition of the assembly, and of its labors during the five years and more of its continuance.

AT the time of the meeting of the Westminster Assembly there was a tradition in the Puritan mind of England of two varieties of opinions as to the form of church government or discipline that should be substituted for episcopacy.

In the first place there was a tradition of the system of views known as Presbyterianism. From the beginning of Elizabeth's reign, if not earlier, there had been Nonconformists who held that some form of the consistorial model which Calvin had set up in Geneva, and which Knox enlarged for Scotland, was the best for England, too. Thus Fuller, who dates the use of the term "Puritans," as a nickname for the English Nonconformists generally, from the year 1564, and who goes on to say that within a few years after that date the chief of those to whom that term was first applied were either dead or very aged, adds: "Behold, another generation of active and zealous Nonconformists succeeded them: of these Coleman, Button, Halingham, and Benson (whose Christian names I cannot recover) were the chief; inveighing against the established church discipline, accounting everything from Rome that was not from Geneva, endeavoring in all things to conform the government of the English Church to the Presbyterian Reformation."

Actually, in 1572, Fuller proceeds to tell us, a presbytery, the first in England, was set up at Wandsworth in Surrey; *i.e.*, in that year a certain number of ministers of the Church of England organized themselves privately, without reference to bishops or other authorities, into a kind of presbyterial consistory, or classical court, for the management of the church business of their neighborhood. The heads of this Presbyterian movement, which gradually extended itself to London, were Mr. Field, lecturer at Wandsworth, Mr. Smith of Mitcham, Mr. Crane of Roehampton, Messrs. Wilcox, Standen, Jackson, Bonham, Saintloe, Travers, Charke, Barber, Gardiner, Crook, and Egerton; with whom were associated a good many laymen. A summary of their views on the subject of church government was drawn out in Latin, under the title *Disciplina Ecclesiæ sacra ex Dei Verbo descripta*, and, though it had to be printed at Geneva, became so well known that, according to Fuller, "*Secundum usum Wandsworth* was as much honored by some as *secundum usum Sarum* by others."

The English Presbyterianism thus asserting itself and spreading found its ablest and most energetic leader in the famous Thomas Cartwright (1535–1603). No less by practical ingenuity than by the pen, he labored for presbytery; and under his direction Presbyterianism attained such dimensions that between 1580 and 1590 there were no fewer than five hundred beneficed clergymen of the Church of England, most of them Cambridge men, all pledged to general agreement in a revised form of the Wandsworth Directory of Discipline, all in private intercommunication among themselves, and all meeting occasionally, or at appointed times, in local conferences, or even in provincial and general synods. In addition to London, the parts of the country thus most leavened with Presbyterianism were the shires of

Warwick, Northampton, Rutland, Leicester, Cambridge, and Essex.

Of course such an anomaly, of a Presbyterian organization of ministers existing within the body of the prelatic system established by law, and to the detriment or disintegration of that system, could not be tolerated; and, when Whitgift had procured sufficient information to enable him to seize and prosecute the chiefs, it was, in fact, stamped out. But the recollection of Cartwright and of Presbyterian principles remained in the English mind through the reigns of James and Charles, and characterized the main mass of the more effective and respectable Puritanism of those reigns. In other words, most of those Puritans, whether ministers or of the laity, who still continued members of the Church, only protesting against some of its rules and ceremonies, conjoined with this nonconformity in points of worship a dissatisfaction with the prelatic constitution of the Church, and a willingness to see the order of bishops removed, and the government of the Church remodelled on the Presbyterian system of parochial courts, classical or district meetings, provincial synods, and national assemblies.

During the supremacy of Laud, indeed, when any such wholesale revolution seemed hopeless, it is possible that English Puritanism within the Church had abandoned in some degree its dreamings over the Presbyterian theory, and had sunk, through exhaustion, into mere sighings after a relaxation of the established episcopacy. But the success of the Presbyterian revolt of the Scots in 1638, and their continued triumph in the two following years, had worked wonders. All the remains of native Presbyterian tradition in England had been kindled afresh, and new masses of English Puritan feeling, till then acquiescent in episcopacy, had been whirled into a passion for presbytery and nothing else. When the Long Parliament, at its first meeting (November, 1640), addressed itself to the question of a reform of the English Church, the force that beat against its doors most strongly from the outside world of English opinion consisted no longer of mere sighings after a limitation of episcopacy, but of a formed determination of myriads to have done with episcopacy root and branch, and to see a church government substituted somewhat after the Scottish pattern.

Two years more of discussion in and out of Parliament had vastly enlarged the dimensions of this revived and newly created English Presbyterianism. The passion for presbytery among the English laity had pervaded all the counties; and scores and hundreds of parish ministers who had kept as long as they could within the limits of mere Low-church Anglicanism, and had stood out, in their private reasonings, for the lawfulness and expediency of an order of officers in the Church superior to that of simple presbyters, if less lordly than the bishops, had been swept out of their scruples, and had joined themselves, even heartily, to the Presbyterian current. Thus, when the Westminster Assembly met (July, 1643), to consider, among other things, what form of church government the Parliament should be advised to establish in England in lieu of the episcopacy which it had been resolved to abolish, the injunction almost universally laid upon them by already formed opinion among the parliamentarians of England, whether laity or clergy out of the assembly, seemed to be that they should recommend conformity with Scottish presbytery. All the citizenship, all the respectability of London, for example, was resolutely Presbyterian, and of the one hundred twenty parish ministers of the city, surrounding the assembly, only three, so far as could be ascertained, were not of strict Presbyterian principles.

Nevertheless, amid all this apparent prevalence of Presbyterianism, there was a stubborn tradition in England of another set of antiprelatic views, long stigmatized by the nickname of Brownism, but known latterly as Independency or Congregationalism.

Independents and Presbyterians are quite agreed in maintaining that the terms "bishop" or overseer, and "presbyter" or elder, were synonymous in the pure or primitive Church, and applied indifferently to the same persons, and that prelacy and all its developments were subsequent corruptions. The peculiar tenet of independency, distinguishing it from Presbyterianism, consists in something else. It consists in the belief that the only organization recognized in the primitive Church was that of the voluntary association of believers into local congregations, each choosing its own office-bearers and managing its own affairs, independently of neighboring congregations, though willing occasionally to hold friendly conferences with such neighboring congregations, and to profit by the collective advice. Gradually, it is asserted, this right or habit of occasional friendly conference between neighboring congregations had been mismanaged and abused, until the true independency of each voluntary society of Christians was forgotten, and authority came to be vested in synods or councils of the office-bearers of the churches of a district or province.

This usurpation of power by synods or councils, it is said, was as much a corruption of the primitive-church discipline as was prelacy itself, or the usurpation of power by eminent individual presbyters, assuming the name of "bishops" in a new sense. Nay, the one usurpation had prepared the way for the other; and, especially after the establishment of Christianity in the Roman Empire by the civil power, the two usurpations had gone on together, until the church became a vast political machinery of councils, smaller or larger, regulated by a hierarchy of bishops, archbishops, and patriarchs, all pointing to the popedom. The error of the Presbyterians, it is maintained, lies in their not perceiving this natural and historical connection of the two usurpations, and so retaining the synodical tyranny while they would throw off the prelatic.

Not having recovered the true original idea of an *ecclesia* as consisting simply of a society of individual Christians meeting together periodically and united by a voluntary compact, while the great invisible church of a nation or of the world consists of the whole multitude of such mutually independent societies harmoniously moved by the unseen Spirit present in all, Presbyterians, it is said, substitute the more mechanical image of a visible collective church for each community or nation, try to perfect that image by devices borrowed from civil polity, and find the perfection they seek in a system of national assemblies, provincial synods, and district courts of presbyters, superintending and controlling individual congregations. Independency, on the other hand, would purify the aggregate Church to the utmost, by throwing off the synodical tyranny as well as the prelatic, and restoring the complete power of discipline to each particular church or society of Christians formed in any one place.

So, I believe, though with varieties of expression, English In-